FIRE BREATHING

CHRISTIANS

FIRE BREATHING

CHRISTIANS

THE COMMON BELIEVER'S CALL TO
REFORMATION, REVIVAL, AND
REVOLUTION

FIRE BREATHING CHRISTIANS
4th Edition, Revised (Cover/Format B)

Published by:
R3VOLUTION PRESS
Chapel Hill, TN

Jacket and interior designs by Scott Alan Buss

All Bible verses, unless otherwise noted, are taken from the *English Standard Version* (Copyright © 2001 and used by permission of Crossway Bibles, a division of Good News Publishers).

Also quoted:
The New King James Version
Copyright © 1979,1980,1982. Used by permission ofThomas Nelson, Inc. All rights reserved.

The New Living Translation
Copyright © 1996, 2004. Used by permission of Tyndale House Publishers, Inc. All rights reserved.

R3VOLUTION PRESS Books are available at special discounts for bulk purchases. R3VOLUTION PRESS also publishes books in electronic formats. For more information, please visit www.R3VOLUTIONPRESS.com or www.FireBreathingChristians.com.

ISBN 13 Digit: 978-0-9838122-4-1
Printed in the United States of America

For Gram and Kristi—
the two women God used most in my life to demonstrate
His sovereign grace, incomparable love,
and perfect plan for creation.

SLAVE

MATTHEW 25:21

CONTENTS

INTRO TO *FIRE*

THE POWER AND PURPOSE OF THE COMMON BELIEVER

"FIRE...God of Abraham, the God of Isaac, the God of Jacob, and not of the philosophers and savants. Certitude. Feeling. Joy. Peace."

BLAISE PASCAL

I can remember holding my wife's hand when she died. Even now I can vividly recall the moment before and the moment after, but it was the difference between the two that struck me with a force I'd not anticipated. It was in that instant following her ascent to paradise that I realized fully for the first time the fact of death—the permanent passing of a good and beautiful thing from this flawed and fallen world. The moment before, Kristi was there. Her spirit and mind were with me. The potential for every good and miraculous thing that might be realized through them was there with me. Then, in a breath, they were gone.

From a secular perspective, this was pure tragedy. Twenty-five-year-olds aren't supposed to be diagnosed with cancer and twenty-nine-year-olds aren't supposed to die. From my own weak and flawed perspective, this was a time of great loss and pain—the quintessential example of "a time to mourn." From God's perspective, this was a demonstration of matchless love and flawless timing, all according to the perfect plan He had ordained since before the dawn of creation.

It was in the midst of these competing claims to truth that I was blessed with clarity. The God who had so lovingly sustained and encouraged me through a four-year saga of hope and sorrow had then graciously provided the precious prize of certainty. Just as I'd discovered a deeper meaning of death, so too I had been presented with the gift of peace through a divinely inspired clarity. For the first time, I came to personally realize that God's plan was not merely perfect in a broad, general sense, but it was flawless perfection for each and every one of us on an individual level—even for me.

It was a simple concept, really, yet one of impossible weight, all of which seemed to relentlessly press on my mind. I was simultaneously numb from the profound turn that life had just taken with Kristi's passing and awestruck at what I was beginning to see clearly for the first time. It was at once a wonderful and frightening experience; one that left me feeling both desperately small and boundlessly hopeful. As I struggled with these apparent contradictions, I developed into a confused American thirty-something-year-old Christian man. And that was a good thing.

In the following weeks and months, I prayed, studied and sought the thoughts of others who had been exposed to this convicting and invigorating clarity. This search led me to many wonderful and inspirational stories, including that of a man named Blaise Pascal.

God-Given Fire

Therefore let us be grateful for receiving a kingdom that cannot be shaken, and thus let us offer to God acceptable worship, with reverence and awe, for our God is a consuming fire.

HEBREWS 12:28–29

Blaise Pascal (June 19, 1623–August 19, 1662) was a child prodigy who became a prominent mathematician, physicist, and philosopher. By the age of nineteen, he invented what many consider to be the first computer (it was a calculating device that he crafted to help his father, who was a tax collector). What I found most intriguing about his biography was its "Night of Fire" episode.

In the late 1640s, Pascal came into contact and subsequently wrestled with Jansenism, a branch of Catholicism that emphasized the fall of man through sin and the necessity of divine grace. Pascal struggled with and contemplated this philosophy well into the 1650s; though during that time, he embraced neither its views nor the God claimed as their author.

Then, on November 23, 1654, not long after a brush with death at the Neuilly-sur-Seine Bridge, he was overwhelmed by an intense vision. Between the hours of 10:30 and 12:30 at night, Blaise Pascal experienced what has come to be known as his "Night of Fire." He recorded the experience immediately in a note, which began: *"Fire. God of Abraham, the God of Isaac, the God of Jacob, not of the philosophers and savants..."* and concluded by quoting Psalm 119:16: *"I will not forget thy word. Amen."* He then sewed the written note into his coat and always transferred it when he changed clothes. The presence of the note was discovered accidentally by a servant after Pascal's death...that is, if you believe in accidents.

I no longer believe in accidents, and that's the point. Well, one of them, anyway.

After reading Pascal's story for the first time, I couldn't help but be overwhelmed and, I must admit, even a bit suspicious. The sheer power of it all was quite impressive, no doubt, but almost too fantastic to be true. Yet there it was, and as I pondered this dramatic episode further, my mind was propelled from one biblical account to another. The fire of which Pascal so passionately wrote inspired my recollection of John the Baptist's announcing Jesus' coming to "baptize with the Holy Spirit and fire" as well as images of Pentecost as recorded in the book of Acts:

> *When the day of Pentecost arrived, they were all together in one place. And suddenly there came from heaven a sound like a mighty rushing wind, and it filled the entire house where they were sitting. And divided tongues as of fire appeared to them and rested on each one of them.*
>
> ACTS 2:1–3

These accounts painted the once suspicious Night of Fire in a very different light. They seemed to me to proclaim that Blaise Pascal's experience, while utterly fantastic and awe-inspiring in so many beautiful ways, was nonetheless quite possible—indeed, in a very real sense *likely*—in the life of a believer. The more I studied, the more I became convinced that Spirit *and* fire are not merely possible, they are to be *expected*. They are to be *assumed* in the life of a Christian.

Just the thought of such a thing as this is worthy of pause, I think, and pause I did. My frazzled mind grappled at length with what was, for me, a wonderful and intimidating new truth: Christ has come to baptize with the Holy Spirit and fire. And even better, He doesn't seem to be selective with this Spirit and fire. He gives them to *every* believer.

This magnificent power might come over you in an intense vision on a November night, or it may make itself known as you hold the hand of a loved one who is passing from this life and into the next. It may lay its claim upon you while you struggle and cry out from the deepest place of despair or while you happily sit and read under a shade tree on the perfect, sunny day. Whenever or wherever it may have come to you, I cannot know or say, though I can be certain of two things:

Every Christian has been baptized with the Holy Spirit and fire.

Every Christian has been blessed in this manner for a great, God-centered and God-glorifying purpose.

The first aim of *Fire Breathing Christians* is to identify the God-given fire in every Spirit-filled believer so that they might actively and enthusiastically fan its flame. From one Common Believer to another, my initial goal is to impress upon every Christian man, woman, boy, and girl who may read these words that they have both an amazing power and a unique, individual purpose, regardless of their place, position, title, or role in this fallen world. There is nothing in your past—no failing or flaw—that alters this truth in the least. *Every Christian* has been called to otherwise impossible heights and equipped to attain them.

So it is that you and I have been brought together today for a great purpose. (And you thought this whole "pick up a book and have a look" thing was quite random, didn't you?)

While we could hardly have imagined, much less properly planned such a meeting as this, we can now know that it has been both imagined and planned by the same Master who inspired matchless "certitude, feeling joy and peace" in one particular man on the night of November 23, 1654.

The God who claims and empowers great leaders and theologians is no less interested and takes no less joy in any other father, mother, daughter, or son. He seeks to lift them all to the same impossible height. As I am selfishly fond of pointing out, He takes great pleasure in using the weakest vessels to accomplish the most magnificent tasks. And His fire is not solely reserved for child prodigies or prominent philosophers.

This truth serves our purpose very well, as the change that America so desperately needs cannot be imposed from a pulpit. It will not be a product of seminary training. It will not come via decree or proclamation from the high places of man. It will come from the front lines, the grass roots, and the trenches. It is the Christian shopkeeper, landscaper, plumber, and homemaker *in* the pew who holds the keys to victory. They will make or break our cause.

It is the fire from above burning within these people that can heal a dying culture and restore a once-great nation. But this fire knows only one source and one goal—the one and only true God of biblical Christianity. Insofar as He, and He alone, is our center in all things, it will hold and we will accomplish otherwise impossible tasks.

To this end, every Common Believer has been called to this battle and equipped for victory.

The Common Believer

While this is certainly not a book of high theology, there are going to be some critical terms and concepts that must be defined as we go along. With that in mind, *Fire Breathing Christians* will make regular reference to the Common Believer. With this term, I aim simply to address every genuine Christian convert and adherent to biblical truth, regardless of position, place, role or title.

The commonality expressed in this title is threefold:

1. Common in status as adopted sons and daughters of God the Father.
2. Common in submission to God the Son as Savior and Lord.
3. Common in submission to biblical truth as authoritative in all things.

This category covers theologians, fieldworkers, philosophers, housewives, political leaders, policemen, fishermen, fathers, daughters, sons, and students. It includes all biblically defined Christians without any compulsion to exalt one above another or rank them in any order of perceived significance. These are the people that must be equipped so that they might successfully engage the culture.

We simply cannot continue to surrender most battles, cede most battlefields, and then hope to somehow win the war raging about that culture. We cannot wait for a good and godly leader to emerge or for somebody else—*anybody else*—to "do something." We cannot wait for God to miraculously do what He has called and equipped *us* to do. You and I—each and every Common Believer—must take it upon ourselves to engage the enemy on every front. The arts…business…politics…these are the fields of battle that we are called *and equipped* to conquer.

Fire Breathing Christians is one Common Believer's attempt to guide his brothers and sisters toward the Word of God so that they might be equipped to win the war we are all called to wage. In this, we will examine many spheres of life and areas of conflict between Christianity and its opposition throughout contemporary American society. We will see where we are, how we got here, and what we must do to restore our nation's biblical foundation, one individual submission to Christ at a time.

Our preparation will begin with a detailed examination of the culture war as it currently stands on a variety of fronts; a survey of the battlefield, so to speak. As the self-helpers like to say, the first step to a solution is admitting that there is a problem, and when it comes to the state of American culture, we clearly have one of those. Many of them, actually, but each of these problems shares one root cause: Ours is a nation in open rebellion against truth and its author. The God of Christianity is hated here. This is the reality with which we must contend. This is our great challenge.

But we must never forget that within every great challenge lies great opportunity, and never more so than with this conflict in these last days. Our God has placed us in this particular place at this specific time to meet this unique challenge. He has equipped us for combat and called us to victory. These most comforting truths must not be forgotten as we take a first hard look at the field of battle.

Post-Christian America

American Christendom is in a free-falling state of collapse. Having conformed to the world she was commissioned to transform, the church has accommodated, embraced, and exalted an astounding variety of heretical concepts that would have been unimaginable to believers of just a generation past. Homosexual priests have claimed many a pulpit, the biblical definitions of family and gender roles have been largely abandoned, business and politics have come to be regarded as "separate matters", church discipline is virtually non-existent, and Christ-less education has become the accepted norm. At the root of it all is an open tolerance of the biblical illiteracy that has come to permeate the church and define the average contemporary American Christian life.

As the church has surrendered to the lethargic, lazy spirit of this age, her enemies have advanced on all fronts. From within, liberal progressives win convert after convert through their zealous evangelical efforts. From without, an American culture at war with the faith that brought it into being batters, pounds, and assaults every biblical truth from every conceivable angle in a suicidal quest to remove from sight and memory every vestige of a once-cherished God.

Is this cause for despair? Should biblically submissive American Christians abandon all hope and concede that the culture—and perhaps even the church itself—has been lost to the enemy?

Absolutely not!

However brazenly the church may have spurned her Lord, we may be eternally thankful that in His matchless grace He has chosen not to return the favor. Far from abandoning us, He has called us to His side in these last days so that we might be empowered to stand and fight.

He has long been about the business of preparing us for this day and preparing this day for us. Throughout the age of American decomposition, He has allowed warnings to sound through the words of many good men and women.

Two such men published books in the early nineties, with each approaching the ongoing culture war from a unique perspective. Robert Bork's *The Tempting of America—The Political Seduction of the Law*, written in the aftermath of his defeated nomination to the Supreme Court, was a brilliant and sobering account of a national judicial system that had lost its way. His detailed and compelling chronicle of America's continued flight from her founding constitutional principles served both as a frightening diagnosis and a prophetic warning. Was Judge Bork's warning heeded?

In the era of Barack Hussein Obama and Sonia Sotomayor, the answer is as obvious as it is unsettling. The "original understanding" of the Constitution so skillfully defined and defended in *The Tempting of America* continues to find itself openly undermined by the forces of progressive liberalism. In the wake of this ongoing assault on the constitutional foundation of the nation, we find ourselves moving ever closer to a state of overtly anti-Christian judicial tyranny.

In the classic work of apologetics, *Christianity in Crisis*, Hank Hanegraaff applied the illuminating light of scriptural truth to the church from within, focusing on the burgeoning movement of heretical philosophies that had come to permeate Christendom at every level and on a massive scale. Christians, the book maintained, had come to embrace and emulate a wide variety of cultic systems of thought in some form or fashion, and the cost to the church had been catastrophic. Hanegraaff predicted that if this trend continued, the church would find her already questionable influence further compromised, ultimately to the point of becoming a non-factor in the culture.

> To avert this crisis, we must shift from perceiving God as a means to an end to recognizing that He *is* the end. We must shift from a theology based on *temporary* perspectives to one based on *eternal* perspectives.
>
> And while change must come, it clearly will not come easily. Those who are feeding this cancer occupy some of the most powerful platforms within Christianity. They control vast resources and stand to lose multiplied millions of dollars if they are exposed.

The stakes are so high that those who are plunging Christianity into crisis seem willing to do and say virtually anything to silence opposition and rally support.[1]

Was Hanegraaff's warning heeded? Has Christendom embraced God as its ultimate end (or even as its ultimate beginning), submitting to His will wherever it may lead? Or is He still largely viewed as a tool to be used in the exercise of *our* will and pursuit of *our* desires all on *our* schedule?

Put another way, have you ever heard of Joel Osteen?

In the era of American Christ-less Christianity, the answer is clear and horrifying. The church has been utterly compromised, giving herself over to a Mr. Potato Jesus brand of religion that encourages adherents to add or remove any accessory from their customizable little pseudo-god in pursuit of personal acceptance and corporate relevance. The church has come to openly embrace virtually every counter-Christian concept in some form or fashion. As a result, the term "Christian" itself has lost most of its definitive power. It has become little more than a synonym for "good person." That is, if you still believe in "good." The results of this have been predictably devastating to the church, and where the church has been so effectively crippled by her enemies, the culture at large has suffered incalculable loss.

Biblical Christianity finds itself under siege from without and actively undermined from within. A nation once consecrated to the God of Abraham, Isaac, and Jacob has fallen into a state of complete rebellion.

Terms of Engagement

In *Mere Christianity*, C.S. Lewis described the path of the Common Believer as follows:

> The Christian way is different: harder, and easier. Christ says, 'Give me All. I don't want so much of your time and so much of your money and so much of your work: I want You. I have not come to torment your natural self, but to kill it. No half-measures are any good. I don't want to cut off a branch here and a branch there, I want to have the whole tree down. I don't want to drill the tooth, or crown it, or stop it, but to have it out. Hand over the whole natural self, all the desires which you think innocent as well as the ones you think wicked—the whole outfit. I will give you a new self instead. In fact, I will give you Myself: my own will shall become yours.'[2]

This is a fine initial description of the core truth that will serve as our guide. Christ wants *all* of you and He wants *all* of me. You and I are called to fully submit every area of life to Him. Our notions of politics, the arts, education, and economics are all to be subjected completely to His will if we are to have any hope of peace, prosperity, and victory in the culture war that has ravaged the America that God has given us. It is from this perspective that *Fire Breathing Christians* seeks to empower each and every Common Believer. It is from this launching point that we will examine the spirit of relativism that has consumed the culture and the spirit of compromise that has corrupted the church.

We will see—many times in our adversaries' own words—crystal clear expressions of rebellion against and contempt for the God of Christianity. We will witness the enemy boldly proclaim, exalt, and advocate opposition to virtually every clearly pronounced truth of Scripture. We will then examine these actions and the motivations behind them in light of biblical truth. In this, we will gain a crucial understanding of not only *what* the enemies of Christianity are doing, but *why* they are compelled to do so.

This understanding is vital. After all, if we do not know what our adversaries are doing and why, any attempt to effectively engage them on the cultural battlefield will prove futile. Only when we have this knowledge in hand are we properly equipped to achieve victory. Only then can we finally liberate American culture from the secular forces of relativism and humanism that have come to dominate and enslave her. With our enemies identified, their strategies understood and the battlefield surveyed, we will then fix our minds on the God-given blueprint for victory.

As we consider the many challenges before us and begin down the path towards cultural engagement, we are well served to consciously cling to three essential aspects of the Holy Spirit as evidenced in the life of the obedient Common Believer:

1. A humble spirit—We must never forget that every slave of the enemy is only acting according to their fallen nature. We were once just as they are now. We must always earnestly pray for their regeneration by God's sovereign hand and treat them accordingly: with love, patience, and respect whenever possible. Our boldness must always be "in the Lord," and not of ourselves.

2. A servant's spirit—We must always aspire to actively, consciously submit to the will of God the Holy Spirit, who dwells within us. We must serve Him *completely* and in all areas of life.

3. A martyr's spirit—We must be willing to pay any price for the sake of advancing the Kingdom of Christ. Any means any.

While our God has baptized us with Spirit and fire, we must never imagine for a moment that one will ever contradict the other. The passion and power given every Common Believer is essential to success, but we must remain vigilant against our inclination to pervert or distort these treasures for the purpose of self-exaltation or excessive criticism of another.

Through Christ and our complete submission to His will in all things, there is no obstacle, challenge, or opponent that we cannot conquer. Through a process of thoughtful, prayerful preparation followed by obedient execution of His perfect plan for battle, we can finally engage the culture, achieve victory, and restore our fallen nation.

Fire Breathing Christians is aimed at guiding the Common Believer through this process. In doing so, it is my hope that readers will come to realize what may at first seem to be an unexpected benefit from such a book as this: everyday application.

Lest there be any confusion, the aim here is not to promote the everyday application of *Fire Breathing Christians*. At least not as an end. No, the goal here is to encourage and guide every Common Believer toward everyday study and application of the revealed truth of Holy Scripture. If *Fire Breathing Christians* is to be rightly applied, the first step in that application will always be to seek, find, and submit to truth as revealed in the Bible. That is where God-given hope and power lie in their undiluted, unmatched, and eternally relevant form. This is where our fire is fed.

While much of what is covered in these pages deals with large scale and lofty sounding bits of high drama and grand strategy, as we pass each milepost along our journey, we will see with great clarity that each problem under consideration and its biblically prescribed solution has direct application to our lives on a very personal level. We will pause at each of these markers to observe and learn how it is that we are to apply these specific scriptural principles to our everyday lives on an individual level, and as we do so we will grow.

When properly understood, this book should challenge and inspire positive change not only at an institutional or organized political level, but in the morning commute and at the kitchen table. It should shape not only our view of "how the world should be," but how our families, friendships, and personal relationships should be. This is not a top-down message. The Bible-based, culture-transforming change advocated here is one that must begin at the roots before it can progress to the treetop.

The great challenges facing our country cannot be met on a national level if they are not first overcome in each of our hearts and homes. It is in the everyday life of the Common Believer that this culture war will be won or lost, so our growth is essential. It is essential to our peace, our happiness, and our ultimate victory.

In concluding this introduction to what *Fire Breathing Christians* is, I am compelled to take at least a moment to clarify what it is *not*.

Though one of the central themes presented here is the empowerment and unique purpose of each and every Common Believer, this is in no way intended to minimize the significance or importance of good, God-fearing leadership. Church history is replete with examples of wonderful men and women who have faithfully served Christ and led His people through the careful use of biblically sound instruction, made possible only through long years of study and personal submission. I do not in even the slightest sense aim to exalt any Common Believer, myself included, above the need for such divinely provided leadership and guidance.

This is also not a work that seeks to denigrate theology, doctrine, or dogma as trivial or unimportant to the Common Believer. Quite the contrary! Theology, doctrine, and dogma are *essential* to the Christian life, as they literally define it. The approach taken here will be to address pertinent doctrinal matters as we go along without stopping to dwell at length or dive to the furthest depths with regard to any single one of them. I wholeheartedly encourage the pursuit of such depth and will commend the inspired, inquisitive Christian to seek out other works to aid them with their ongoing growth. Biblically-rooted, Christ-centered knowledge is the greatest thing that a human mind can experience, so its unending pursuit should be the most natural sort of desire for every Common Believer.

With the principles of everyday application firmly grasped in one hand and commitment to biblically sound intellectual pursuit in the other, we are well equipped to begin our journey on an individual level so that we might eventually realize transformation on a national scale.

The Secular Inquisition

You and I live in a post-Christian America that is rapidly transitioning into an anti-Christian state. This shift can still be reversed, but only for a little while longer and only if Common Believers embrace their responsibility to engage the culture. It is my prayer and hope that our God will make use of these words to encourage and empower you to that end.

The Fire Breathing Christian has become both an endangered species and the most feared of creatures from the liberal humanist perspective now dominating the scene. I am convinced that by removing Spirit- and fire-filled believers from that endangered list we can both help every anti-Christian leftist in the nation realize their darkest fears and return America to her God-glorifying foundation. Put another way, we can accomplish great things and have a whole lotta fun in the process.

We will begin our preparation for battle by considering one believer's stand and the subsequent hate movement mobilized for her destruction. In this example we will find a great deal of valuable information concerning the nature and strategies of our opposition as well as a clear and powerful warning to every Common Believer who would dare take to the field of battle: You *will* be hated.

American culture is at war with God, His Word, and His people. The active suppression and silence of all Christian thought is a primary goal of the forces currently guiding secular civilization. We now live in an age of Secular Inquisition and must prepare accordingly.

So I invite you now, one Common Believer to another, that we might begin this most important journey together in the name of the one true God, who is a consuming fire.

Surveying the Field of Battle

1

Welcome to the Secular Inquisition

Fear and Loathing of the Common Believer

I baptize you with water for repentance, but he who is coming after me is mightier than I, whose sandals I am not worthy to carry. He will baptize you with the Holy Spirit and fire.

JOHN THE BAPTIST IN MATTHEW 3:11

And you will be hated by all for my name's sake. But the one who endures to the end will be saved.

JESUS IN MARK 13:13

"Even apart from its political implications, the rollout of the Sarah Palin vice presidential candidacy may be regarded decades from now as a nationally shared Rorschach test of enormous cultural significance." This was Jeffrey Bell's observation as recorded in *The Weekly Standard* just seventeen days after Alaska Governor

Sarah Palin was selected to become Senator John McCain's running mate in the 2008 presidential campaign. He went on to describe what was rapidly becoming a perfect storm of political paranoia:

From the instant of Palin's designation on Friday, August 29, the American left went into a collective mass seizure from which it shows no sign of emerging. The left blogosphere and elite media have, for the moment, joined forces and become indistinguishable from each other, and from the supermarket tabloids, in their desire to find and use anything that will criminalize and/or humiliate Palin and her family...

In her acceptance speech last Wednesday night, anyone could see the poise and skill that undoubtedly attracted McCain's attention months ago, when few others were even aware that he was looking. But it was precisely the venom of the left's assault that heightened the drama and made it a riveting television event. Palin benefited from her ability to project full awareness of the volume and relentlessness of the attacks without showing a scintilla of resentment or self-pity.

This is a rare talent, one shared by Franklin D. Roosevelt and Ronald Reagan. For this quality to have even a chance to develop there must be something real to serve as an emotional backdrop: disproportionate, crazy-seeming rage by one's political enemies. Roosevelt was on his party's national ticket five times and Reagan sought the presidency four times. Each became governor of what at the time was the nation's most populous state. It took Roosevelt and Reagan decades of national prominence and pitched ideological combat to achieve the gift of enemies like these. Yet the American left awarded Sarah Palin this gift seemingly within a microsecond of her appearance on the national stage in Dayton, Ohio. Why?[5]

The Assassination of Sarah Palin

For the American left, reasons for fear and loathing of Sarah Palin are legion; almost too numerous to list. But we'll try anyway:

She is a woman (which would normally be a plus). She is a fiscal conservative (which offsets much of the aforementioned bonus for womanhood). She is a social conservative (this more than finishes off any remaining "female benefit"). She comes from humble roots and embraces a Judeo-Christian ethic. She is a generally happy wife and mother of five. Making matters worse on the last point, the youngest of her children, Trig, was prenatally diagnosed with Down syndrome. The problem for the secular left wasn't the diagnosis itself; it was that Mrs. Palin had subsequently allowed her son to live.

For this crime she could not be forgiven.

Little Trig became something of an unintended lightning rod as a result. The sweet little boy born to a loving, honorable Christian mother presented to the American left a clear and present threat to the very heart of its liberal orthodoxy…by simply *living*.

With their foundations shaken and insecurities exposed, "progressive" women lashed out, leading the charge in a wild attempt to eviscerate Sarah Palin. Their seething hatred was proudly and forcefully displayed at every opportunity.

South Carolina Democrat Party chairwoman Carol Fowler pronounced that John McCain had chosen a running mate "whose primary qualification seems to be that she hasn't had an abortion." The *Washington Post*'s Wendy Doniger observed that Palin's "greatest hypocrisy is in her pretense that she is a woman." "Comedian" Margaret Cho joined the crowd of merry, blissfully content feminists by chiming in with:

"They shouldn't have the right to call themselves Christian, for they have no Christ-like attributes. I am a feminist and a Christian, and when I see Sarah Palin, I see neither. And it's official: She is evil."

Through this parade of insult and vilification, our nation was exposed to the full force and character of secular liberal womanhood. And it wasn't pretty. Then again, secular feminism rarely is or wants to be.

Eight months after Sarah Palin's acceptance speech at the Republican Party National Convention in Minneapolis-St. Paul, Minnesota, Americans were given another revealing glimpse into the philosophy shaping their nation's culture.

This moment came when a young woman from the American West committed the unpardonable sin of politically incorrect public speech. This violation of the new American speech code inspired the unrestrained wrath of vigilant thought police across the nation. The whole episode began on April 19th of 2009, when the following question echoed through the Theatre for the Performing Arts in Planet Hollywood Resort and Casino in Las Vegas, Nevada:

"Vermont recently became the first state to legalize same-sex marriage. Do you think every state should follow suit? Why or why not?"

This was the question asked of Carrie Prejean, representing the state of California in the Miss USA pageant. The question was asked by openly gay pageant judge Perez Hilton as a part of the Miss USA selection process.

Miss Prejean answered Hilton's politically and religiously motivated question as follows:

"I think it's great that Americans are able to choose one or the other. We live in a land that you can choose same-sex marriage or opposite marriage. And, you know what? In my country and in my family, I think that—I believe that—a marriage should be between a man and a woman. No offense to anybody out there, but that's how I was raised and that's how I think that it should be: Between a man and a woman. Thank you."

While for many of us it may be difficult to imagine a more respectful, defensive, kind and even sheepish defense of the *actual* institution of marriage than that which Miss Prejean offered, the simple fact that she affirmed a personal belief, *when asked*, that marriage was to be "between a man and a woman," was enough for impartial, unbiased, politically, and religiously neutral judge Perez Hilton to come completely unglued.

As a result of honestly answering the question put to her in an excruciatingly polite manner consistent with the well-reasoned and time-tested beliefs of the overwhelming majority of American citizens since the founding of the nation, Carrie Prejean was denied the Miss USA crown and Perez Hilton went into full blown offended drama queen mode.

Hilton immediately recorded a video blog for release on YouTube, which included the following fabulous commentary:

"Hello...okay...so...Miss USA literally just finished and I *have* to make a video blog. Everybody's gonna be talking about it! I was *the* YouTube moment of the show—the pageant—when I asked Miss California her question, and when she gave *the...worst...answer...in pageant history!* She got *booed!* I think that was the first time in Miss USA *e-ver* that a contestant has been booed. Now, lemme explain to you: She lost, not because she doesn't believe in gay marriage. Miss California lost because she's a *dumb b----,* okay? This is how a person with half a brain answers the question I posed to her, which is: 'Vermont recently legalized same-sex marriages. Do you think other states should follow suit? Why or why not?' Well, if *I* was Miss California, with *half a brain,* I would have said, *'hmm…*Perez, that's a *great question!* That's a very *hot topic* in our country right now, and *I* think that that is a question that each state should decide for themselves, because that's how *our* forefathers designed our government, you know. The states rule themselves, and then there's certain laws which are federal.' She could have said *something* along those lines, but *she didn't!* She gave an *awful, awful* answer, which alienated *so* many people, and Miss California—Miss USA—she doesn't alienate, she *unites!* She *inspires!* I am *so* disappointed in Miss California representing my country, not because she doesn't believe in gay marriage, but because she doesn't *inspire* and she doesn't *unite!* And that is what a Miss California and a Miss USA *should.* And I could *not believe* when she became first runner up! If *that girl* would have won *Miss* USA—California—I would have *gone up* on stage—*I shit you not*—I would have gone up on stage, *snatched* that tiara off her head and run out the door. And then I probably would have been arrested, but you know what? *So be it! Ooooh!* Thank *goodness* Miss South Carolina won—or North Carolina—whichever one won, because she deserved it *so much more!* Okay…I need a cocktail now."

In a subsequent appearance on NBC's *Today Show,* the lovely and gracious Mr. Hilton went on to further elaborate on his open-minded, inclusive philosophy of kindness and tolerance: "I personally would have appreciated it, had she left her *politics* and her religion *out*, because Miss USA represents *all* Americans. I think I gave her the easy way out. She could have answered that question so many different ways. She could have said, 'Well, I wanna leave my *politics* out of the question and I think that it's important for the states to make those decisions for themselves, and I think that would have been a better answer than the one that she gave, because the answer she gave alienated *myself*, millions of gays and lesbians, their friends, their family, their coworkers, and their supporters. And Miss USA is not a person that's alienating. *Miss USA is not a person that's politically incorrect!* Miss USA is someone who represents me, who represents all America and is *inclusive*."

After pausing for a moment of intermission to digest those bits of brilliance and purge any thoughts of Perez Hilton *as* Miss California from our temporarily scarred psyches, we are well served to consider a question of our own: Throughout this incident and the firestorm of controversy that followed, Carrie Prejean's position was painted as suspiciously defensive in most Statist media presentations, while the Perez Hilton position was generally treated as normative and therefore worthy of *less* scrutiny or criticism than Miss Prejean's. Why is this so?

The answer to this question as well as many related issues swirling about the perpetual conspiracy to assassinate Sarah Palin are found in the very nature and identity of the counter-Christian culture in which we live. In an America teetering on the brink of a shift from post-Christian to anti-Christian state, the Secular Inquisition has begun.

Welcome to the Secular Inquisition

If the world hates you, know that it has hated me before it hated you.

JESUS IN JOHN 15:18

All animals are equal, but some animals are more equal than others.

GEORGE ORWELL, *ANIMAL FARM*

While Carrie Prejean's tepid, defensive, limp-wristed (and she didn't even get points for *that*), ever-so polite response to Perez Hilton's question did indeed cost her the title of Miss USA, it also managed to reap a wealth of useful information. However flamboyant a representative of contemporary American leftism Mr. Hilton may be, his views are largely representative of the hyper-relativistic brand of secular humanism that currently dictates the course and rate of decline for our culture. Sadly, Hilton's *is* the favored position, at least from the perspective of the secular forces driving our nation. This makes the Prejean/Hilton exchange worthy of further consideration.

I'd like to begin this examination by offering a list of post-Christian American truths made plain through Perez Hilton's response to Carrie Prejean:

1. Biblically submissive Christians cannot represent America. "All of America" includes ridiculous living caricatures of homosexuality; it does *not* include Bible believing Christians.

2. Biblically submissive Christians *can be excluded* in the name of inclusiveness. Put another way, alienating Christians is perfectly acceptable for the simple reason that they are perceived to alienate others.

3. Political expression is reserved *exclusively* for those expressing politically correct views.

4. Religious expressions, if they must be made at all, are allowed only insofar as they conform completely to anti-Christian standards, thus rendering the Christian silent.

5. Political and religious questions, when asked of a Christian by an anti-Christian, cannot be answered honestly or accurately, as the Christian response must universally conform to anti-Christian standards and is therefore impossible. In this light, anti-Christians really do not ask Christians questions at all—they merely use a question format to *inform* the Christian of truth from an anti-Christian perspective. It's kind of like a satanic twist on *Jeopardy!*

6. So complete is the subjugation of the liberal lemming's mind that they are literally incapable of noticing their own flagrantly religious and political expressions as anything but the completely benign norm for all of humanity. They literally do not realize that *their* opinion is *an* opinion. As William F. Buckley, Jr. put it, "Liberals claim to want to give a hearing to other views, but then are shocked and offended to discover that there are other views."

7. Expressing an anti-Christian opinion in the promotion of tolerance, acceptance, and unity is a natural and good thing, while expressing a Christian opinion on the same matter is almost always an open violation of goodness and decency at every level.

8. Perez and Paris Hilton are of roughly equal value to western civilization.

There are many more useful points that could be listed, to be sure, but the true nature of the new American thought police is revealed clearly enough by these eight examples. In a nutshell: Bible-believing Christians are, by definition, wrong and must be silenced. This is the guiding principle of the Secular Inquisition.

This movement has been underway in America for some time now. It continues to gather steam, having moved beyond its base of Statist media support and into the deeper fabric of the culture, primarily through the government education system. Its goal is, for now, the silence and suppression of Christian thought. As such, every Common Believer is a threat and legitimate target of the Secular Inquisition.

Any public expression of distinctly Christian thought must be met. It must be countered. It must be crushed. And soon, it must be *banned*.

There are those who would say that the last contention paints an overdramatic picture, that the author here is presenting a skewed take on reality for the sake of promoting alarm and implying the existence of an evil conspiracy against liberty, when in reality there is no such thing to be found. To these critics, we need only reply with a simple point north…to Canada.

The Crime of Christian

"In Canada, we respect freedom of speech, but we don't worship it."

CANADIAN BROADCAST STANDARDS COUNCIL

On April 29, 2004, Canada's governor general signed into law a measure that criminalized public expression in opposition to homosexual behavior, officially categorizing some orthodox Christian beliefs, when verbalized publically, as "hate speech." Welcome to the world of tolerance and inclusiveness, Perez Hilton style.

Dr. Albert Mohler Jr. addressed this seismic legal and cultural shift in an opinion piece featured at Crosswalk.com titled *The End of Religious Liberty in Canada*[6]:

> It's all over but the funeral. Free speech and religious liberty are now effectively dead in Canada, and recent developments across our northern border should awaken Americans to the peril of political correctness and its restrictions on freedom.
>
> On April 28, the Canadian Senate passed bill C-250 by a vote of 59 to 11. In passing this legislation, the Canadian Parliament added "sexual orientation" to the nation's laws criminalizing "hate speech." The end result is that the Bible may now be considered a form of criminalized hate literature and Christians who teach that homosexuality is sinful may face criminal charges.

This reality is worthy of our pause and careful consideration. The categorization of Bible content as hate speech deserving of punishment, constitutes state-sponsored persecution of Christians. This is what Canada has become.

Dr. Mohler concluded his warning to Christendom with the following:

> The pattern of criminalizing speech about homosexuals is spreading across liberal societies. In Sweden, pastors are explicitly warned that any sermons critical of homosexuality can lead to criminal charges. The same logic is spreading through the courts and legislatures of many European countries—and now has jumped the Atlantic to Canada.
>
> The truly threatening character of the Canadian legislation is further demonstrated in the fact that police do not have to charge persons with breaking a law. Any Canadian citizen can file a complaint against any other citizen, resulting in charges. At that point, the defendant is simply left to the dangerous whims of the liberal judiciary and governmental human rights commissions. The potential legal costs would alone intimidate some persons from talking about homosexuality.
>
> The most important part of the newly-revised criminal code reads: 'Everyone who, by communicating statements, other than in private conversation, willfully promotes hatred against any identifiable group is guilty of...an indictable offense and is liable to imprisonment for a term not exceeding two years.'
>
> During a recent debate, the Canadian attorney general refused to comment on whether or not the Bible is, in itself, hate speech. That matter, we are now warned, will be left for the courts to determined.
>
> We are fooling ourselves if we believe this threat to religious liberty will stay on the Canadian side of the border. This same logic is already accepted by many law professors

and judges in the United States. The passage of C-250 is a warning to us all. When free speech is denied and the preachers are told what they can and cannot say, religious liberty is effectively dead.[7]

Man has spoken. The spirit of antichrist and rebellion has spoken. The Canadian thought police have spoken: God's perfect Word on homosexuality is evil and its public proclamation can result in punishment by law.

Liberal fascism is on the march on both sides of the US/Canadian border. The Secular Inquisition is hardly confined by national boundaries. It is a global ideology simultaneously consumed and fueled by its overt hatred of truth and its author. The thought police are on a mission. As they march forward, they aim for nothing less than the total subjugation of our nation to their politically correct code...one individual at a time.

In subsequent chapters, we will further explore many of the numerous individual examples of this stormtrooper-style trampling of liberty. But before we go on to examine the stories of others, I would like to pull our focus back from the far flung fields of the cultural battlefield and into our own communities, homes, and individual lives.

We make this exploration for a purpose: It is vital that we realize our *personal* status as targets of the Secular Inquisition. You and I are anything but immune to this persecution. We are solidly locked into the enemy's crosshairs, each and every one of us, and for this, we must be *thankful*.

Yes, you read correctly. The Common Believer is to be thankful for biblically prescribed persecution.

As our Lord has called us to serve Him completely, He has called us to struggle. This is a price of our obedience to Christ in a God-hating world. This is a burden that our Lord has lovingly empowered us to bear. This is a quality that the Secular Inquisition simply cannot grasp or overcome.

The Price of Christianity

Indeed, all who desire to live a godly life in Christ Jesus will be persecuted, while evil people and impostors will go on from bad to worse, deceiving and being deceived.

2 TIMOTHY 3:12-13

If I had not done among them the works that no one else did, they would not be guilty of sin, but now they have seen and hated both me and my Father.

JESUS IN JOHN 15:24

Contrary to popular opinion, the call to Christianity is not an easy or simple thing to take up. The life of a Common Believer is difficult. *Impossibly* difficult. One of the first realities of Christian life that we are called to embrace is that, as a natural consequence of our living for Christ, we *will* be hated by this world.

This hatred is not optional. It is not avoidable. It's not a mere possibility, likelihood or probability. It is an absolute certainty and as such, it is something to which we should give some thought.

This reality required no explanation or revelation when Christ's church first formed after His earthly ministry. Hatred was the world's reaction to the first Christians. Persecution was as much a part of life for them as was eating or sleeping.

This persecution was not only endured by the first Christians, it was *celebrated*. Those who first promoted the Christian church viewed persecution as an essential beauty and privilege for the believer.

It is in this light that even the Secular Inquisition reveals itself to be an unwitting tool of the God it so despises. By persecuting the Common
Believer, as it is fervently committed to do, this movement offers each of us a precious and unique opportunity to glorify our Lord. What a wonderful confirmation this is of Paul's words in the book of Romans:

And we know that for those who love God all things work together for good, for those who are called according to his purpose. (Romans 8:28)

This price of true Christianity also gives us something of a barometer or measuring stick with which we can gauge our spiritual walk. We can know, for example, that if this world simply adores us in all that we say and do, then we are most assuredly *not* living for Christ. This world is in open rebellion against Him, and the more we reflect His will, the more we will be hated for it. This is as simple and clear a truth as any presented in Scripture.

Our reason for celebrating this truth rather than recoiling from it is that persecution from the world always offers the Common Believer a precious opportunity to glorify God that couldn't have come any other way.

These opportunities to glorify God through adversity come not only in direct response to the most flagrant displays of anti-Christian bias and persecution that a Common Believer may experience. They also come as we care for a hurting brother or sister, or as we comfort a non-believing friend in distress. They come as we patiently explain truth to children who struggle to grasp the nature of this world and the world to come. They come as we simply walk and talk with a concerned neighbor. The opportunities to glorify God through this time of cultural upheaval are as numerous as heaven's stars. This should be on our minds always as we endure, persevere, and bring light into a dark and dying world through the blessing of persecution.

The Common Believer's Daily Opportunity

Do your best to present yourself to God as one approved, a worker who has no need to be ashamed, rightly handling the word of truth.

2 TIMOTHY 2:15

Every issue of consequence should inspire in the mind of the Common Believer one simple question: What has God said about this? As we tackle the myriad concepts and ideas associated with the ongoing culture war in America, we must maintain a conscious devotion and fidelity to the Bible. It is our only reliable lifeline. Emotion, tradition, and personal preference cannot be allowed to guide us in any way contrary to Scripture, and resisting such inclinations is no easy thing.

What *is* easy for us to do is miss or mishandle opportunities to glorify God through our persecution by forgetting the principles at the core of biblical Christianity.

When we encounter the comically incoherent and hypocritical rants of a Perez Hilton or the hateful pronouncements of a Margaret Cho, we have to resist the emotional urge to respond in any number of wrong ways. While we can and must defend truth and, at times, do so in a fiery, passionate manner, we must never forget that these people are only acting according to their nature— *a nature that we shared completely before Christ imposed spiritual life upon us.* So when we face the slings and arrows inherent in culture warfare, we must never presume to operate from a position of moral superiority based upon anything of *our* doing. Our life, strength, purpose, and power have been given to us by Christ, and we must resist every inclination to separate ourselves from this truth in any attempt to stand "on our own two feet." Only through complete reliance upon and submission to our Lord in all things can we avoid the distractions and pitfalls that seek to trip up and trap every Common Believer.

When we observe events like the political frenzy surrounding Sarah Palin or the strange phenomenon that was the Miss California saga, it can be easy to lose sight of the core issues at the heart of all of the drama. It's easy to get lost in the fog of snippets, half-truths, and half-thoughts advertised as useful information in this era of the sound-bite and 24/7 "news" cycle.

We will more quickly find peace and success on the cultural battlefield when we focus on Christ. Common Believers can rest assured in the knowledge that God has provided answers to *every* essential question that we might face. With this knowledge comes responsibility. We cannot experience the true peace or joy He has made available unless we seek His will and *apply* it in our daily lives.

The acquisition of knowledge without the application of that knowledge is of no use at all. Only through submission to His revealed truth can we find true hope, peace, power, and purpose.

As we engage the culture and confront the Secular Inquisition, we are well served to hold close and contemplate the following biblical truths:

1. We are to *expect persecution.*
2. We are to *be thankful for persecution.*
3. We are to *pray for our enemies.*
4. We are to *defend truth.*

Each of these suspiciously simple-sounding points are of great weight and consequence. Each is worthy of lengthy contemplation and requires a life-long commitment to prayerful implementation. But don't let that frighten you off! As expressed earlier, the same Lord who has called us to accomplish these otherwise impossible tasks has also equipped us to do so. In recognition of this most critical and comforting of truths, we will add a fifth point to our list:

5. We *will be sustained and enabled through Christ to accomplish all of these things.*

It is this fifth point that makes the first four possible.

Always remember that the Secular Inquisition sweeping through contemporary American culture is no surprise to God. It was ordained by Him from the very dawn of creation. It is His tool. He *will* use it to His glory and our ultimate benefit.

Anticipating and Celebrating Persecution

Blessed are those who are persecuted for righteousness sake, for theirs is the kingdom of heaven. Blessed are you when others revile you and persecute you and utter all kinds of evil against you falsely on my account. Rejoice and be glad, for your reward is great in heaven, for so they persecuted the prophets who were before you.

JESUS IN MATTHEW 5:10–11

By lovingly warning us of the certain hatred we will inspire in this fallen world, our Lord has graced us with the opportunity to prepare.

As an essential early step in this preparation, we must come to embrace, however contrary to our nature the concept may seem, the biblical notion that the persecution we are assured to face is ultimately *for our benefit*. When this truth, as expressed by Jesus in Matthew 5:10–11, is fully grasped, the Common Believer's vision is sure to clear and their fear will give way to hope and anticipation. When we take an eternal perspective on persecution and actually come to agree that it is *always* to the glory of God, and therefore to our personal benefit as His people, we are then enabled to pray for our enemies and defend truth much more effectively.

And effective prayer is our greatest weapon in this culture war. As Hank Hanegraaff rightly described it, "Prayer is firing the winning shot."

Achieving Empathy and Sympathy through Prayer

You have heard that it was said, 'You shall love your neighbor and hate your enemy.' But I say to you, Love your enemies and pray for those who persecute you, so that you may be sons of your Father who is in heaven. For he makes his sun rise on the evil and on the good, and sends rain on the just and on the unjust.

JESUS IN MATTHEW 5:43–45

When we acknowledge that every rebellious, sinful man and woman engaged in the culture war on behalf of the enemies of Christ is only acting according to their nature and that we were once just as they are now, both sympathy and empathy become much easier to sincerely grasp as we heed our Lord's command to pray for those who persecute us.

As each of us reflects upon the state we were in before Christ claimed us as His own, every delusion of self-significance or independent personal capacity for good should evaporate. Hand in glove with this growth in knowledge will also come a heart for the lost so that they might too be found by Him.

This contrite, humble, God-fearing, and Gospel-fueled prayer will shake the world, one life at a time. It will break us of our arrogant notions of self-significance and allow for our transformation into the most effective culture warrior imaginable. The Spirit-filled, prayer-fueled Common Believer is the enemy most feared by the Secular Inquisition, and for the best of reasons. The fallen world's fear of the Fire Breathing Christian is a most reasonable thing.

Swim Deep, Make Waves!

For though by this time you ought to be teachers, you need someone to teach you again the basic principles of the oracles of God. You need milk, not solid food, for everyone who lives on milk is unskilled in the word of righteousness, since he is a child. But solid food is for the mature, for those who have their powers of discernment trained by constant practice to distinguish good from evil.

HEBREWS 5:12–14

For though we walk in the flesh, we are not waging war according to the flesh. For the weapons of our warfare are not of the flesh but have divine power to destroy strongholds. We destroy arguments and every lofty opinion raised against the knowledge of God, and take every thought captive to obey Christ.

2 CORINTHIANS 10:3–5

With the opportunity of persecution upon us, and proper prayer as our fuel, we have been placed by God and prepared by His Word and Spirit for battle. This is where things can get tricky. The challenge for the Common Believer here is great, particularly in a setting such as that presented in the contemporary United States of America. The problem in question is: This will be hard. Very hard. And hard is not popular these days in America or in American Christendom.

Yet hard is our path and there's absolutely no way around it. There's no shortcut, cheat, secret code, or letter from our parents that can excuse us from the studies we must pursue. There is no gimmick that can free us from this path. There is simply no escape: We *must* study our Bibles.

The purpose of this book is not to offer you a three-step plan to biblical literacy. You will find no magical acronym or memorization techniques promoted here, though I certainly do encourage memorization. The one thing that I would like to focus on and advocate in this book is as simple as it is difficult: individual effort.

There is nothing remotely similar in its ability to positively impact the life of a Common Believer. Sheer time and effort spent in and on the Word of God cannot be compensated for by any other activity. Only the dedicated pursuit of biblical knowledge will bring us the depth of understanding we require for personal growth so that we might engage the culture and claim victory for the Kingdom of Christ.

There is no workaround for this. It must be done "the hard way." That's the bad news.

The good news is that when you personally cross the threshold from *having* to study to *wanting* to study—and that day will come—you'll look back on even this bit of "bad news" as having been one of the most wonderful things to have ever come your way. As we mature and begin to actually grasp the individual sense of peace, joy and purpose already mentioned time and time again, we will come to celebrate that "bad news." As our hopes for what a Christian life *should* be become realized through the daily study and application of His Word, we will better understand and cherish the sentiments of Paul as he wrote to the church at Ephesus:

*"And he gave the apostles, the prophets, the evangelists, the shepherds and teachers, **to equip the saints for the work of ministry,** for building up the body of Christ, until we all attain to the unity of the faith and of the knowledge of the*

Son of God, to mature manhood, to the measure of the stature of the fullness of Christ, **so that we may no longer be children, tossed to and fro by the waves and carried about by every wind of doctrine, by human cunning, by craftiness in deceitful schemes.** *"*

EPHESIANS 4:11–14 (emphasis added)

When the Common Believer is equipped in this manner, an unstoppable soldier has just taken to the field of battle. With our eyes on Christ and our minds on His Word, we can accomplish anything...and we will.

When we face the raging storm of this culture war with our eyes firmly fixed on Jesus, we have nothing to fear. When we have nothing to fear, *we* can dictate the terms of engagement. When we dictate the terms of engagement, we proclaim and live truth rather than merely reacting to evil. All of this is made possible for each and every Common Believer and these are the things that make the culture war not only something that we can endure, but something that we can be thankful for as we engage, overcome, and bring Glory to God throughout the process.

As for the Secular Inquisition? Bring 'em on! They'll never know what hit 'em.

2

Change Has Come for America

A Culture at War with Christianity

You shall have no other gods before me.

EXODUS 20:3

"We are no longer a Christian nation—at least, not just."

BARACK HUSSEIN OBAMA

"Whatever we once were, we are no longer a Christian nation—at least, not just. We are also a Jewish nation, a Muslim nation, a Buddhist nation, and a Hindu nation, and a nation of nonbelievers." So proclaimed Barack Hussein Obama, first term Democrat Senator from Illinois, in the summer of 2006. Just over two years later, the nation he described would elect him as its leader.

In the same speech, delivered on June 28 before the Call to Renewal organization, Obama went on to say[8]:

And even if we did have only Christians in our midst, if we expelled every non-Christian from the United States of America, whose Christianity would we teach in the schools? Would it be James Dobson's or Al Sharpton's? Which passages of Scripture should guide our public policy? Should we go with Leviticus, which, uh, suggests slavery is okay and that eating shellfish is an abomination? Or we could go with, uh, Deuteronomy, which suggests stoning your child if he strays from the faith? Or should we just stick to the Sermon on the Mount, a passage that is so radical that it's doubtful that our own defense department would survive its application?

When we consider the profound deviation of the above sentiment from the expressed views of our first president, George Washington, and the vast majority of our nation's Founding Fathers, an understandable combination of confusion and anxiety can quickly wash over us. Release from this encroaching discomfort is most commonly and conveniently obtained through one simple, soothing mechanism: time.

In the 220 years that have transpired between George Washington's first inauguration and the election of Barack Hussein Obama, we find a tempting bit of cover. As we weigh America's fundamental shift from Christianity over a period of time well over two centuries in length, we have little trouble imagining that, over such a span, the whole thing was *inevitable*.

Change is natural, after all, and, with that concept embraced, it becomes quite reasonable to expect that we would move away from whatever it is that we once were, Christian nation or otherwise. In a culture programmed to exalt undefined change and chase after any new thing by the sheer virtue of its newness, we find a well-cultivated eagerness to jettison any old, steady, proven thing, no matter how good or even essential to goodness it may be. Thus, biblical Christianity was bound to go.

So it is that we are not only unsurprised by the dramatic and sweeping cultural change we see painted over the portrait of our nation's recent history, we are also unconcerned by it. By combining the perceived inevitability of this sort of change over time with our recent infatuation with newness, freshness, and contemporary relevance, we've crafted the perfect rationalizing mechanism by which we can allow for the dismissal of our personal role and responsibility in bringing about the very change in question.

Who can stand against such forces as the inexorable march of *change*? Just ask Hillary Clinton, John McCain, network "news" shows, and Joan Rivers.

We comfort ourselves by imagining that over these centuries there has been a slow, steady, and perhaps even unstoppable march of change at work in American culture. And said change, having been conveniently labeled inevitable, is then obviously something for which we *cannot* be held responsible. With this comforting bit of historical revision embraced, we are officially off the hook.

This liberating, if delusional, approach does much to obscure the nature and rapidly escalating rate of decline that has come to our nation in its very recent history. One way of illustrating this is to dismiss 200 of the 220 years between Washington and Obama, and focus for a moment on the year 1990, carefully considering the changes that have come in its wake.

In a mere twenty years' time—far less than spans even a single generation—our nation has experienced staggering levels of deterioration and decline. What's worse is that we have *pursued* the cultural carnage we now witness, often with great eagerness, volume and pride.

As we have abandoned the God of Scripture, we have openly courted personal, cultural, and national disaster. And lest we point our fingers at "them," whomever *they* may be—politicians, preachers, teachers, or businessmen—we do well to note and address the contribution that each of us have personally made to this rapidly disintegrating situation.

That's the process that we'll begin in this chapter: Identifying the worldview-shifting philosophical changes that have come to American culture as well as our role in their creation, both corporately and as individuals.

As touched on earlier, one thing that the self-help cults tend to get right is that the first step to solving a serious problem is admitting that it exists. Seems kind of obvious, I know, but these days we're constantly discouraged from acknowledging even the most frustratingly obvious of things when they don't conform to the progressive party line and presentation. Questioning anything *outside* of liberal orthodoxy is not only peachy, but very much encouraged, while questioning the foundations and assumptions of liberalism, well...that sort of critical thought and contemplation is anything *but* peachy. Heck, it's barely legal in many places.

As such pursuits are still tentatively allowed in America, we must take full advantage and have a careful, critical look at the change that has been brought to our culture by the progressive elites and their politically correct, properly programmed supporters.

Our tour will begin with a look into the short span of time between the fall of Soviet communism and the rise of an American variant as currently expressed by the Obama administration. By focusing on this most recent twenty-year sliver of our nation's history, we will gain clarity regarding the magnitude, intensity, and speed of the change that has been deliberately inflicted upon the United States. We will see what the religion of liberalism has wrought, not accidentally or as a result of blind, unpredictable, random change, but as a direct consequence of our acceptance and nurturing of a carefully crafted and decidedly counter-Christian worldview.

As we take a closer look at the change that has swept across our culture's landscape in these recent years, we will see that it isn't the shiny, new thing it's made out to be. This progressive path is as old as a once well-known conversation between Eve and the serpent in the Garden of Eden. This path is wide, many seek it, and it is as ancient as time itself. Its emergence as the preferred pathway for our culture has been long charted by the enemies of the church, and nearly every Christian in America has played some role in its establishment. So let's have a look at where two decades of war on God has brought us.

Twenty Years of War on Truth

"Because I have called and you refused to listen, have stretched out my hand and no one has heeded, because you have ignored all my counsel and would have none of my reproof, I also will laugh at your calamity; I will mock when terror strikes you, when terror strikes you like a storm and your calamity comes like a whirlwind, when distress and anguish come upon you. Then they will call upon me, but I will not answer; they will seek me diligently but will not find me. Because they hated knowledge and did not choose the fear of the LORD."

PROVERBS 1:24–29

"No people ever rise higher than their idea of God. Conversely, the loss of the sense of God's high and awesome character always leads to the loss of a people's highest ideals, moral values, and even what we commonly call humanity..."

JAMES MONTGOMERY BOICE

Twenty years ago I was a teenaged crewmember of the *Pacific Orion*, fishing commercially in the Bering Sea out of Dutch Harbor, Alaska. I had left my home in rural Arkansas to seek adventure and fortune in the high seas between the northern frontiers of the United States and the Soviet Union. Ronald Reagan's vice-president, George H.W. Bush, was in the first half of his term as president, Operation Desert Shield was underway in the Persian Gulf, and the Buffalo Bills were about to begin their historic four-year run of Super Bowl futility. The year was 1990.

The Reagan Revolution had come and gone, changing the nation and then the world. The American economy had rebounded from the smoldering wreckage of Jimmy Carter's "malaise days" and blossomed into the greatest engine for growth and opportunity that humanity had ever known. The Berlin Wall, constructed by progressive Marxists in Europe, was ordered down by Ronald Reagan, and it obeyed his command. The Soviet Union crumbled and tumbled into the ash heap of history. The Cold war was won.

The eagle was soaring, and just a few years after he appeared to be down for the count. America even seemed to once again embrace its identity as that biblically inspired shining city on a hill.

But despite its apparently miraculous recovery, America was far from healthy. Sure, she was healthier than the zombified state realized under Jimmy Carter and the progressive movement he led, but most living in the shining city on a hill, as Ronald Reagan had so beautifully described her, were much more interested in material success than fidelity to the one true God of Scripture.

This was no small thing. It was, as it always has been and ever shall be, *everything*.

Material success in a nation untethered to the Word of God predictably produced an explosion of narcissistic indulgence. God was spoken of more frequently, to be sure, but almost always in the vague sort of manner befitting your average ecumenical mystic or community organizer. God was everywhere, it seemed. But the specific Jesus of biblical Christianity and His essential gospel message to a dying world on the verge of a holy God's righteous judgment?

Not so much.

The Cancer of Statism

"Freedom is never more than one generation away from extinction. We didn't pass it to our children in the bloodstream. It must be fought for, protected, and handed on for them to do the same, or one day we will spend our sunset years telling our children and our children's children what it was once like in the United States where men were free."

RONALD REAGAN

"I once said, 'We will bury you,' and I got into trouble with it. Of course we will not bury you with a shovel. Your own working class will bury you."

NIKITA KHRUSHCHEV

In the '80s and early '90s, material success and spiritual ambivalence combined with restored national pride and the relentless advocacy of self-esteem to form an environment favorably inclined towards two culture-corroding cancers.

First, government grew, as cancers tend to do, at a frighteningly rapid clip. Fed by the increased revenues generated by massive tax-rate cuts and subsequent economic growth, the beast that is the U.S. federal system exploded in size. Even under the executive supervision of the most reviled "ultra-conservative" in memory, Ronald Reagan, the United States government grew faster than Michael Moore on buffet night. It was anything but pretty. As its scope and power expanded, the freedom and liberty of the American citizen axiomatically shrank.

The second malignancy to find fertile cultural ground for accelerated growth throughout the '80s and '90s was the new code of thought and conduct known as political correctness. With liberal orthodoxy left largely unchallenged beneath the surface of American thought, the massive machines of state-controlled education and media marched on in their establishment of various neo-Orwellian ideals and policies. Even as the Soviet Union was brought to its knees by the singularly insightful policies of the Reagan administration, former Soviet Premier Nikita Khrushchev's prediction of the "working class" scoring an ultimate victory for socialism in America crept steadily towards realization.

As American culture tried to dance with the God of Scripture somewhat anonymously and from a "safe" distance, the overt anti-Christianity of socialism couldn't help but capitalize on the opportunity presented by a nation disinterested in biblical submission.

At the end of the day, with neither the American nor Soviet worldviews in practice and explicitly exalting Christ or biblical Christianity, both became equally valid competitors for the secular spirit's attention. Both led to very bad places, albeit via different routes and at varying rates of speed.

While the Republican Party in general and Ronald Reagan in particular did much good for our nation at a most critical point in its history, and we should be thankful to God for all that was accomplished in that time, neither Republicanism nor Reaganism saved or can save this nation. Neither prevented the wild growth of a government racing towards hyper-socialism or the aggressive expansion of political correctness in the past, and neither will be able to effectively do so in the future, whatever the campaign ads and spin doctors might say. Those pinning their hopes for American renewal exclusively to a G.O.P. sweep in the 2010 and 2012 elections or a return to the policies and approaches of Ronald Reagan are merely charting an alternate course to oblivion. Theirs would be a path with far more material success, individual liberty, and earthly happiness, to be sure, but it would be a path to ultimate disaster nonetheless.

The good things realized by a return to conservative governing principles are only of lasting, genuine benefit insofar as they are shaped by and linked to our understanding of Christ and His perfect Word.

Is this a call for the top-down imposition of a theocratic caricature in America? Nope. Not at all.

It *is* a call for those who are submissive subjects of the King of kings to simply act accordingly in *all* things, including the realms of law and government. We of all people should know that true and lasting success cannot be realized any other way.

As Christ and the Gospel have been marginalized in our society, liberalism has metastasized, as it must and will always do in such a setting. Only when Christ and the Word of God are exalted in all areas of life (and yes folks, that includes the political) by those who claim Him as Lord can there be any real hope of reversing the cultural plunge that has come to America.

Only then will Ronald Reagan's shining city on a hill finally experience the kind of change that she so desperately needs. In order to properly prepare for the pursuit of God-centered change, we must be willing to take a careful, critical look at the alternative type of change currently gripping the nation.

The Inexorable Trajectory of Christ-less Hope and Change

"It will never be known what acts of cowardice have been motivated by the fear of not looking sufficiently progressive."

CHARLES PEGUY

When we ponder the quantity and quality of change that has come to every sphere of American culture over the roughly twenty years since Reagan as opposed as to the 220 since Washington, an entirely different picture comes into focus. With the comfort of "hundreds of years" removed from the equation, our imagined cover is removed and we are rightly inclined to become more than a bit concerned; maybe even panicky.

This is a good thing.

The lack of concern so naturally produced by our casual approach to Christianity, and therefore life in general, is something that we have to ditch, and ditch immediately. This is serious stuff and it's high time we started acting like it. We as Common Believers have been positioned and prepared for such a time as this, and unless we honor our obligation to Christ right here and right now, there is no reason whatsoever to believe that American culture as we have known it will endure for much longer.

America can end.

She can die.

Moreover, should America choose or be led to persist in her repudiation of God, she *should* die.

Unless the next twenty years produce a pronounced rebound from the trajectory charted over the last twenty, she must and surely will simply cease to be. With that reality in mind, let us pray that the fog of lethargy associated with the "America is forever" myth to which so many seem unconsciously subscribed will finally be forever banished. Shaking free of the "eternal America" delusion is essential to any serious pursuit of America's survival.

An early lesson to be learned as we begin this examination is that anything explicitly separated from Christ becomes, as an inevitable consequence of this segregation, incapable of any true and lasting good or positive result. This is the central theme that will be borne out as we examine the various changes that have come to American family, church, and culture ever since the progressive revolution began in earnest in the '60s.

Consider the progress made in redefining the following simple, yet profoundly impactful and culture-defining, words:

- **Love**—Separated from its biblical foundation, love has taken on a form best exemplified by the behavior of bad parents towards their child. It is accepting of everything and devoid of discipline. Modern appeals to this vague, watery "love" are commonly used to dismiss any clear biblical requirement for specific action by a believer whenever said action is challenging to another and may actually make them uncomfortable or unpopular. This is the primary mechanism by which we dismiss things like church discipline and holding teachers accountable for their doctrine. The pathetic irony of this situation is that we act in this biblically unloving manner in the name of "love."

- **Tolerance**—Hand-in-glove with the redefinition of love has come the perversion of tolerance. A word that, by definition, means a patient or permissive attitude towards things with which one does *not* agree or endorse, has been co-opted to better represent the politically correct charge to accept and embrace *everything* as equally viable and good. So it is that tolerance now means something akin to happy acceptance and universal qualitative equality in the minds of many.
- **Truth**—Where the Bible proclaims clear, essential truth to live by, ours is an age embracing but one truth: There is no truth. Well, okay, one truth and one contingency; the contingency being: If there *is* truth, it *cannot* be clearly defined and known.
- **God**—Scripture records God's issuing of Ten Commandments, the first four of which proclaim the exclusivity and necessity of the one and only true God, and require that we honor no other gods. At all. In any way. Ever.

We in America, however, are "progressively" encouraged to tolerate (now meaning accept and embrace) the equal goodness and viability of all gods (defined as anyone or anything that any person may or may not wish to worship) in a spirit of love (meaning loud, demonstrative acclaim without restriction or concern for discipline, growth, depth or truth).

Where once American culture largely embraced an explicitly biblical foundation for each of these terms, it now does not. Postmodernism has come, and in its wake every well-defined cornerstone concept and term has been turned into an amorphous, gelatinous bit of nothingness, ready to be sculpted and molded into anything by anyone at any time for any reason or no reason at all.

Stripped of their objective meanings as rooted in God's revealed truth, they have become weapons used in the destruction of the very virtues they once proclaimed.

The concepts of love, hope, truth, and even *change* are all rendered terminal malignancies once they are deliberately disconnected from the source and goal of all good things, the Sovereign Lord Jesus Christ. Any good thing, once critically compromised via the removal of Christ from its center, instantly becomes suitable for the promotion of all manner of evil.

No concept more profoundly exemplifies this truth in modern American society than that embodied by the word *progress*.

Progressive thought is all the rage. It advocates the legality of intentionally targeting innocent children for murder. It proudly aims to destroy and then remake the God-ordained institutions of marriage and family. It defiantly seeks the suppression of biblical truth at every turn and actively seeks to paint the Common Believer as an enemy of the new American way.

As we are learning time and again and across the spectrum of societal concern, progress without the glorification of Christ as its goal is *always* progress towards darkness and death.

We are living in the aftermath of sweeping successes realized by the enemies of Christ on three major fronts in the ongoing culture war. The collapse of one front has led to the compromise of another, and as the dominoes continue to teeter and fall, we find ourselves facing an increasingly desperate situation.

The enemy has experienced across-the-board breakthroughs and is at this very moment busily pillaging conquered cultural territory in three vital areas, one having led to the next:

1. **Progressive Christianity**: The Christ-centered, sheep-feeding, gospel-driven church in America has been largely replaced by a Christ-less, goat-defined, secular

business/purpose-model-driven approach to man-centered religion.

2. **Progressive morality**: With the church compromised, materialistic post-modernism and narcissism have become the primary ingredients of a new moral system in America.

3. **Progressive politics**: As biblical Christianity has been almost completely marginalized and the moral compass of our culture has been subsequently reset, the people of America have chosen to express their disdain for biblical truth in a most clear, powerful, and proud manner. The nation has freely chosen to embrace a brand of politics openly at war with the God of Scripture.

A compromised church has promoted the rapid and widespread corruption of morality throughout the land. This new church and morality have been employed by the enemy to form the staging ground from which the most clearly expressed systematic repudiation of biblical truth ever witnessed in our nation's history has been launched upon its own culture. There is no escaping the fact that the simple majority of America's voting populace has freely chosen to wage war on the God of Scripture through their vote. This spirit of "progress" has infected professing Christendom, redefined morality and given great strength to the new progressive political religion that even now sweeps from victory to victory in every sphere of American life.

These are the realities that the Common Believer must face as they take to the field of battle in the raging culture war. Progressive Christianity, progressive morality and progressive politics are enemies with which we must contend.

In the next section we will take a hard, honest look at these three areas of our compromise and the resultant secular "progress."

The Axis of "Progress"

3

The Goat-Driven Church

The Emergence of Progressive Christianity

"Behold, the days are coming," declares the Lord GOD, *"when I will send a famine on the land—not a famine of bread, nor a thirst for water, but **of hearing the words of the LORD.**"*

AMOS 8:11 (bold emphasis added)

"The Gospel is ours to proclaim, not to edit."

DR. JAMES WHITE

From the age of nine on through my high-school years, I grew up in the smaller-than-small town of Henderson, Arkansas. We had two gas stations and two restaurants; though one of each seemed to constantly alternate into and out of business. We'd have qualified as the classic "one stop-light town" if only we'd had a stop-light.

I went to school across Lake Norfork in Mountain Home, a town of about 7,000 at the time. I call it a town, though, from the prospective of a Hendersoner, it was a metropolis. They had fast food franchises and cable television there. For the folks in Henderson, Mountain Home was a big deal, though you'd never get most to admit it. (We are a proud people, you should know.)

Up until I was fifteen or so, the bus that picked my brother and me up for school had to make use of a ferry to cross the lake. For a kid that had spent his first eight years almost exclusively in the Chicago area, things like daily ferry rides from a town of 100 or so to get to a town of 7,000 or so inspired a tad bit of what one might rightly refer to as culture shock.

But this was a good kind of culture shock, if there can be such a thing. Henderson and Mountain Home came my way just in the nick of time. To this day, I adore and thank God for those places.

That said, one of the less-than-cool tradeoffs between Chicago and Mountain Home life was the disturbing plunge in theater quality. I had been a confirmed movie geek since I toddled my way into *Star Wars* and, to put it mildly, the theatres in Mountain Home weren't quite operating at or anywhere near the level I'd known as a kid. All things considered, this was a small thing. Very small. But I'll never forget the two tiny theater buildings operating on opposite sides of town, with their marquees loaded, lit, and aimed to entice all who passed along the town's main drag.

Each of the two theaters had two screens and an appropriate amount of marquee space for the four total flicks showing on 'em. That is, until sometime around 1990, when the Twin Lakes Twin Cinema, Mountain Home's cinematic stronghold on the eastern front, decided to up the ante and go to three screens. This was an event.

But before you get too wound up and cheering for little old Mountain Home and the inspiring expansion of theatrical options within her borders, it's important to note that, when the Twin Lakes Twin became the Twin Lakes Tri Cinema, it didn't add any square footage. The path to three screens was a humble one, consisting of building a wall right down the middle of auditorium number two, thus transforming it from one small screen into two tiny ones.

As a result, the marquee normally assigned the task of advertising for auditorium two suddenly found itself pulling double duty, squeezing two titles into the place where one had once sometimes barely fit. As you might imagine, this was an advertising approach fraught with danger.

All of the fears associated with the "new normal" in Mountain Home movie promotion were realized one day in early 1992, when the following appeared in bright lights, confounding many a highway 62 passer-by: "STOP OR MY FRIED GREEN MOM WILL SHOOT TOMATOES."

The listing for *Stop or My Mom will Shoot* was crammed onto the two-row display's left side. *Fried Green Tomatoes* was jammed into the right. And the requisite scrunching made for something of a beautiful thing—arguably a far more stirring artistic contribution to Mountain Home life than was made by either of the involved Hollywood productions.

The spacing of the two titles was seamless. They became one. It was brilliant.

Once again, the Mountain Home artistic community had outdone itself. It had provided a valuable teaching moment. In a most indelible manner, a vital truth had been boldly proclaimed that winter in black plastic letters: Context…is…*everything!*

Woe to the poor soul led to belief in such a thing as a fried green tomato-shooting mom. Woe indeed. Without the knowledge and appreciation of context, we are left wide-open to even the dumbest of possibilities. (If you think tomato-shooting-momism is wacky, check out Scientology.)

This was the lesson that the Mountain Home movie marquee taught me, and I share it with you now so that we both might remember the truth behind the tale. Context really *is* everything, and only when we know the true context of a word, snippet, verse, or concept can we have solid hope of avoiding even the most flagrant and idiotic of heretical perversions of the Christian faith.

If we don't seek and value *contextual* knowledge, we will fall prey to every lame show to come down the line.

Gimme That Show Time Religion!

"Much Christian pursuit of timeliness has become trivial. Following trends passionately but promiscuously, many Christian leaders have become trendy. Obsessed with the new, they have produced only novelty....Evangelicals were once known as 'the serious people.' It is sad to note that today many evangelicals are the most superficial of religious believers—lightweight in thinking, gossamer-thin in theology, and avid proponents of spirituality-lite in terms of preaching and responses to life."

OS GUINNESS

So, because you are lukewarm, and neither hot nor cold, I will spit you out of my mouth.

REVELATION 3:16

This chapter could, for the most part, be accurately summarized through the use of two words: "Joel" and "Osteen." Or, you could also go with "purpose" and "driven." Either pair works.

Long gone are the days when biblical Christians could expect the average church congregation in America to be built around the explicit, God-given charge to worship Christ and feed His sheep. The gospel message of a humanity deserving and precariously positioned on the verge of a holy God's wrath has proven far too uncomfortable for, well, practically *everyone*, so, quite obviously, it had to be shelved until it could be properly...um...*modified*.

You see, an unvarnished, undiluted biblical message epitomizes, as nothing else quite can, the modern unpardonable sin of being "not very marketable."

Nope, that whole "complete depravity of fallen man" and "all are deserving of Hell and in need of *the* Savior" routine doesn't play very well to those who are...you guessed it...depraved, deserving of hell, and in need of the Savior. In Bible terms (when we bother with such things), these folks are known as "goats." These goats are, according to Scripture, at war with God and in active rebellion against Him.

They are also now officially the tip-top target audience of most of the professing church in America. Yessiree, church in most places across the country these days is *all about the goats.*

This is *not* your grandfather's Christianity.

Or Martin Luther's or Charles Spurgeon's or John Calvin's or Jonathan Edwards' or The Apostle Paul's or, ultimately, Jesus Christ's. But then again, what did any of those guys know about goat-tending, anyway?

You see, what *we* in the modern American church want to do is get those poor, confused little goats into the building *any* way we can so that we can weave our magic, Madison Avenue-inspired, happy spell of market-researched psychological manipulation so that we can turn 'em *into* sheep.

How cool is that?

It's absolutely *brilliant*, no?

No.

And what about that whole "feeding of Christ's *actual* sheep" thing?

Fuhgeddaboutit.

If it makes the goats uncomfortable—and sheep food (aka: the depths of Scripture) *always* will—then it simply has to go. Remember: we're goat-focused here, and until those goats sprout wool and start to baa convincingly, all of our attention will, out of necessity, be aimed squarely and completely their way.

So the feeding of Christ's sheep has been, at best, back-burnered, and along with it any semblance of biblical fidelity to the charge of church leadership to make the feeding of Christ's flock a priority second only to His worship. The end result is a professing church whose direction and approach to everything is defined by the goats with whom she is completely obsessed.

A terrible thing happened shortly after we embraced this full-blown, across-the-board pursuit of the precious goat population.

We caught 'em.

Or, in actuality, *they* caught *us*.

Let me explain: As goats by their very unregenerate, unrepentant nature stand in stark opposition to true biblical Christianity, they tend, on a good day, not to value the Word of God much if any more than any other "good book" (whatever "good" means). With goat acquisition and accommodation displacing deep, undiluted Christ worship and the feeding of His sheep as the two primary motivations of the professing church, we have predictably witnessed a cliff-like drop-off in biblical literacy and fidelity within professing Christendom in America.

A Pathetic Christianity

"Everywhere there is apathy. Nobody cares whether that which is preached is true or false. A sermon is a sermon whatever the subject; only, the shorter it is the better."

CHARLES HADDON SPURGEON

This apathy-fueled biblical illiteracy was the first fatal blow struck to the professing church as a result of its idiotic goat fetish. But not only did this radical shift from Scripture- to goat-obsession seem to bother us little when it occurred, most of us still seem to not even realize that it's happened at all. That's just how goat-focused and defined the contemporary American church has become.

Rather than building corporate church worship around the *deep* worship and study of the Lord we claim to serve and adore, we instead construct Sunday events to appeal first and foremost to those who do not know Him and have no appetite—or stomach— for His truth. Rather than building a church around *feeding* the body of Christ so that non-Christians out in the world might be witnessed to by well-equipped, Spirit-filled, and spiritually mature Christians, we have chosen a much more secularly pragmatic route.

In these matters, we subject ourselves far more to the will of goats than the will of God, it would seem. The goat has become, in practice, our primary object of affection, all in the name of serving the God whom we have chosen to ignore.

But remember: We're all about the numbers, and 100 goats sure beats 20 sheep. Seven days a week and twice on Sunday!

So it is that those outside the body of Christ are now tenaciously pursued with countless secularly prescribed marketing and contact plans, with millions upon millions of dollars and millions upon millions of man hours, all spent in what has become the favored sport of American evangelicalism: The Chasing of the Goats.

Remember: *Goat means non-Christian.* As there is no middle ground, biblically speaking. Where Christ is concerned, *non-*Christian is another way of saying *anti-*Christian. They're synonyms. So it is perfectly accurate to say that, through the goat-driven policies of much of the professing church, we've witnessed the creation of a very large and booming "Christian" church in America that has become a church of, by, and for the *anti-Christian.*

Neat, huh?

One great irony here is that effectual, biblical evangelism is one of the first casualties of our infidelity to God's Word. In buying into the goat-driven secular approach to evangelism, we've not only compromised the deepening of our growth and worship of God, we have also promoted the decimation of the very systems by which *biblically prescribed evangelism* is most effectively accomplished. From the enemy's perspective, this is like a happy Satanic two-for-one deal.

By dismissing God's specifically prescribed design for church worship, growth, and evangelism, we have done more than any force on earth to assure that these goats *remain* goats, whether they do so from the comfort of their couches or a church pew on any given Sunday.

Think about it:

1. Church activities, strategies, worship services, and pretty much everything else are almost exclusively centered on a *perverted notion of evangelism* that places the attraction and accommodation of the goat as its guiding principle. We will

do *anything* to just get 'em in the building and keep 'em there.

2. With this principle in place, things like deep worship and growth in Christ simply cannot be vigorously pursued. *So they aren't.*

3. Christ's sheep are then left to starve or wander off in search of depth-cultivating food, as they are not being fed at church gatherings. Those who do remain in the congregation must either find spiritual food of substance on their own, outside the formal corporate church body, or remain in a perpetual state of spiritual infancy due to lack of nourishment.

Most choose the latter, though any combination of the two approaches always leaves a church body composed almost exclusively of spiritual infants.

One of several tragic results of this approach is that actual, biblically-prescribed evangelism, that being the natural outreach of well-fed, spiritually mature Christians as they interact with the world *outside the church* in their everyday lives, is left virtually impossible, a task abandoned through the church's own policy of feeding goats while starving sheep.

So in the name of evangelizing the Madison Avenue, purpose-driven way, we've managed to almost completely devastate our capacity to evangelize the biblical, Gospel-driven way. Neato!

We have a program for this, a program for that, and a program to meet the "felt needs" of any goat group that we encounter or imagine. We build weight rooms, workout centers, cafes, and basketball courts. We arrange for seminars on this, that, and any other thing that might have even the slightest little bit of secular appeal.

All of this is done while providing little to nothing in the way of support for the *explicitly biblically mandated* roles of fatherhood/manhood, motherhood/womanhood, and family as the gospel-driven, gospel-centered, and gospel-fueled centerpiece of true biblical Christian civilization. Where the Christ-centered education of children in *all* things is about as explicit a biblical mandate as you can find in Scripture, our churches are more than content to allow, support, and even encourage extra-biblical socialization programs for our children, rather than bump a serious, well-equipped home-schooling or Christian-schooling program or support system ahead of any of the numerous sports-related whatevers that always seem to find their way onto growth and building agendas.

Believe it or not, it wasn't always this way in the American church. But it is now. Appealing to a secular culture that is, by biblical definition, openly at war with Christ, has become the overall "growth strategy" for the church claiming Him as Lord. And there can be no doubt that this goat-centered growth strategy has yielded amazing results. Amazing, unprecedented, pathetic, and cataclysmic results.

While there are scores of terrible and completely predictable consequences that could be catalogued and elaborated upon where the goat-driven church philosophy is concerned, none has been more detrimental than the aforementioned acceptance and accommodation of biblical illiteracy. With the light and depth of Scripture radically marginalized and, in many cases, discarded entirely, the sheep have been left to starve, the goats have grown in comfort and control, and entire waves of wolves have found the warmest and most welcoming of arms waiting to escort them into church leadership positions.

Emergent Heresies

"As God can send a people or a nation no greater blessing than to give them faithful, upright and sincere ministers, so the greatest curse that God can possibly send upon the people of this world is to give them over to blind, unregenerate, carnal, lukewarm and unskilled guides."

GEORGE WHITFIELD

"I remember the first time I had feelings for Jesus. It wasn't very long ago. I had gone to a conference on the coast with some Reed students, and a man spoke who was a professor at a local Bible college. He spoke mostly about the Bible, about how we should read the Bible. He was convincing. He seemed to have an emotional relationship with the Book, **the way I think about** *Catcher in the Rye*."

DONALD MILLER, *BLUE LIKE JAZZ*, WHICH CAN BE HAD AT MOST "CHRISTIAN BOOKSTORES" (bold emphasis mine)

Two of the largest wolf packs to hit the American Christian scene have been the "word faith" and "emergent church" movements (though the emergents tend to blow through names for their movement faster than Al Gore blows through natural resources). So impactful and intriguing are these two groups that chapters seven and eight will be dedicated to their exploration. In the meantime, there are a few basic facts that must be acknowledged here so that the large-scale cultural transformation of American Christian political thought and theory over recent decades might be better understood. The first of these has to do with the conscious conversion of Christianity from a distinctive, well-defined and, above all else, Bible-based religion, into a more malleable, watery, warm, and welcoming form of spirituality or religiosity.

Turn on Christian television or walk into a Christian bookstore and you will, in most instances, be treated to a colorful display of goat-driven, seeker-sensitive, man-made religion with a Christian stamp of approval slapped on it somewhere. The point of the stamp—and it takes on various forms—is to assure the modern professing Christian that what he is looking at is, in fact, Christian.

With biblical illiteracy now an accepted and largely ignored epidemic, often times all that the garden variety congregant has to guide him in the selection of theologically sound material is this stamp, be it imagined, real or anything in-between. If an item is proclaimed to be Christian by Thomas Nelson, the Trinity Broadcast Network, or LifeWay Christian Bookstores, then that's that. It must be so.

It had better be, anyway, since John and Jane Q. Believer have been left utterly unequipped to test anything, including these "stamps," in light of deep Scriptural truth.

With the Bible essentially ignored in the average Christian's evaluation process, publishers, producers, and purveyors of product have been left with the responsibility to vet these items for their theological integrity.

You can imagine how well that's gone. Not that you have to.

As biblical literacy and fidelity have been abandoned, what was once the distinct and exclusive Christian worldview has been replaced by a wide range of much more seeker-sensitive, world-friendly, and imminently more marketable systems of spirituality. Christian bookstores are, most often, now much better described as *religious* or *spiritual* bookstores.

Just the way The Oprah likes 'em.

Goats *love* religion. Spirituality, too.

So do wolves.

Thus, the market for religious and spiritual stuff is enormous. This is precisely the market that has been tapped and dominated by both the emergent church and word faith movements' leaders as they have made their best—and, to date, wildly successful—attempt to reshape biblical Christianity into a much more politically correct form of mere spirituality and religion.

Where one group has built its membership around an appeal to good old-fashioned greed and covetousness (howdy to you, Misters Hinn and Osteen), the other has chosen to build upon a foundation of postmodern pseudo-intellectualism desperate to be perceived by others as spiritually deep, socially relevant, and excruciatingly cool. (Hey there, Brian McLaren and Donald Miller!)

All told, neither movement is based on anything new at all, however much they may attempt to market themselves as such. The lie at the heart of both movements is as old as lying itself: That man has an inherent power within to do or become something truly *good*—even great and god-like—through the exercise of his will.

In this we can say one thing for Satan: He *knows* his marketing. That original lie sure does have some legs! The Devil has his target audience down pat, to be sure.

The essential point here is that both the emergent church and word faith movements have actively undermined Scripture and paved the way for a man-centered counterfeit religion to emerge as the dominant system of belief within the professing Christian church in America. This is known, in devil-speak, as "spiritual progress." It's not too awfully hard to see why a devil might think of it that way, now is it?

A church compromised by its disinterest in biblical truth and its obsession with goat-friendliness is a church left in poor position to effectively oppose the implosion of morality in the greater culture at large. Thus, the enemy has actively, and so far successfully, acted to separate first the Bible from the professing Christian individual and then, by extension, biblical truth from the corporate church body. Through the continuation of this process, what was once biblical Christianity has been melted down and remolded into the shiny new religion and spirituality of the anti-Christian progressive movement.

This new "progressive Christianity," most vocally advocated by the emergent church movement, has, in a church climate steeped in biblical illiteracy and the subsequently unavoidable biblical infidelity, been stunningly successful in preparing the professing church in America for not only the tolerance of, but the *celebration* of, virtually every one of the flagrantly anti-Christian concepts that define the contemporary progressive *political* movement. In this, we see the lock-step unity of politics and religion from the progressive perspective.

From proclaiming the virtues of Marxism/socialism and the glories of non-Christian (meaning, of course, *anti*-Christian) religions, to exalting the will of man to stratospheric heights, the biblical foundation given the bride of Christ has been paved over and refinished throughout much of professing Christendom. By calling the sufficiency, credibility, and therefore the necessity of Scripture into question, the goat-driven church has been formally freed to endorse and support the most flagrantly anti-Christian of secular leaders and causes.

Welcome to progressive Christianity, the gatekeeper of progressive morality.

4

Dress Day and the Surrender of Moral Truth

The Emergence of Progressive Morality

"I did not have sexual relations with that woman, Miss Lewinsky."

BILL CLINTON

"This is—the great story here for anybody willing to find it and write about it and explain it is this vast right-wing conspiracy that has been conspiring against my husband since the day he announced for president."

HILLARY RODHAM...CLINTON

Few have personally embodied the progressive warping of the Christian political will in America as did professing Southern Baptist, William Jefferson Clinton.

With progressive Christianity embraced, progressive morality found a warm home and safe breeding ground within the walls of the professing church. The fatal fruit of the ensuing incubation process made itself known in a loud, pronounced manner during the fabled Monica Lewinsky scandal of the Clinton Administration in the late '90s.

Rather than re-hash the well-worn and quintessentially Clintonian tale here, I'd like to focus with some precision on one particular day during this crisis. We will call it: Dress Day.

We both know where this is going and I apologize in advance of getting there, but this is a place that we must visit if we are to understand a significant shift in our recent history, so...hold your nose, take a deep breath, and...*off to Bubba Land we go!*

Back to Dress Day...

This term is not necessarily intended as a reference to an objective, set date in history. Rather, Dress Day is the day on which any particular professing Christian voter came to the realization that there was, in fact, clear-cut, indisputable, genetic evidence of a sexual relationship between sitting President Bill Clinton and his young intern, known by him at the time primarily as "kiddo," and known to the entire world now as Monica Lewinsky. Different people heard this news at different times and while most Americans within *Drudge Report* range were all at once and on the same day in the loop where the dress revelation was concerned, there were some who straggled into the dramatic, disgusting details days and even weeks later.

The date on which one may have heard the news is not the point. Their reaction is. With this in mind, let's take a quick tour of the typical professing Christian Clinton supporter's thought process and stated positions during the Soiled Kiddo Crisis.

At the outset, Clinton supporters loudly denied even the fact of the relationship. After all, Bill said it was all a lie and Hillary was right there with him, standing by her "man" (though apparently refusing to bake him cookies). The whole thing was clearly a ploy of a "vast right wing conspiracy" that was gathering to ruin noble and virtuous Bubba by any means necessary.

That was the progressive party line, and virtually every professing Christian Friend of Bill toed it dutifully. They deplored the vast right wing deal and mocked those who would dare stoop to such depths as accusing Bill of doing *that* with or to Monica. Honestly, how could *anyone* responsible for the presentation of such a horror as the fabricated tale of ongoing adultery between their beloved Bubba and a young woman intern be anything but just the sort of evil creature that Hillary was shouting about from the White House rooftop?

Then a funny thing happened. And by funny, I mean terribly pathetic and tragic. The thing in question was the revelation of The Dress.

The Dress was real. Therefore, the Bubba/Kiddo over-a-year-long sex adventure was real. Apparently, Clinton critics were right: Bubba wasn't content to *figuratively* soil the Oval Office. He was just the intern-using, woman-hating, power-abusing cretin many had proclaimed him to be. Clinton had proven it all to be true in about as crude and pathetic a fashion as one could imagine.

And guess what? All of a sudden, the "horrible," "vulgar," and "disgusting" sexual affair once dismissed as fiction and now revealed to be totally and completely true, simply ceased to matter. It was nothing.

So what?

He did it.

Big deal.

It's *just* sex.

That's his *personal* life. It's none of our business. He's still a good President. What does morality have to do with good presidential leadership anyway?

And just like that, with a roll of the eyes and a shrug of the shoulders, what was once terrible, vile, and ugly was no big deal at all. The veil of faux-Christianity covering the face of many a progressive was left in tatters. But, true to form, they simply did...not...care.

In that moment, on Dress Day, as it dawned over the progressive-minded, professing Christian masses from coast to coast and sea to shining sea, the foundation of majority American thought was formally and fundamentally changed. We officially became a nation populated by a majority who simply dismissed the biblical moral component from serious consideration in their selection of leaders in particular and their political views in general, just as the progressive Christian movement had already encouraged them to do with their religion and spirituality.

The path paved through the professing American Christian church wound through the Lewinsky scandal and right on into a position of open contempt for biblical morality. There it camped. The route to this destination was anything but accidental. It was methodically charted and diligently followed. Through the imposition of and adherence to this carefully crafted course, the forces of change have achieved a long string of impressive victories for the progressive cause.

A "Progressive Morality" Breakthrough Event: The Dress Day Massacre

The ear that listens to life-giving reproof will dwell among the wise. Whoever ignores instruction despises himself, but he who listens to reproof gains intelligence.

PROVERBS 15:31–32

As the church has ceded its territory to secular seekers at an increasingly rapid clip in recent years, it has played no small role in laying the groundwork for previously unthinkable "progressive moral breakthroughs" throughout American culture. These moments of pronounced collapse act to punctuate the steady, gradual decline secured by the Gospel-fleeing trajectory advanced by the leaders we've chosen as our own.

Every now and again, amidst the standard and long-accepted rate of moral decline afflicting the culture, along comes one of these instances of compressed degradation. So intense is its expression that even those most acclimated and desensitized to the "normal" rate of moral disintegration tend to have their ears perk up. It's as though after a long, steady-rolling procession of tremors constantly rumbling about and shaking the moral landscape beneath their feet over days and weeks and months and years, lulling them ever-deeper into a state of apathy-fueled depravity, along comes an actual moral *earthquake*, and they manage to wake up for a moment.

Tremors do tend to forecast to earthquakes. We all know this. Yet, more often than not, we are surprised when the actual quake arrives and jars our world so profoundly.

Like on Dress Day.

It is likely that most professing Christian Clinton supporters were, on the day *before* Dress Day, quite confident in their moral position and strength. They knew that adultery was wrong. Moreover, they knew that it mattered where presidential leadership is concerned. They knew that a long-term sexual relationship between a President and a White House intern was a disgusting thing to even contemplate. They knew that such a relationship conducted *in the Oval Office of the White House* would be a most vulgar and flagrant insult to the office of the presidency, the people of America, and the dignity of the nation as a whole in the eyes of the entire world.

Most professing Christian Clinton supporters knew and agreed with these sentiments on the day before Dress Day. The fact of this moral knowledge and agreement is precisely the reason that they were so incensed with the "vast right wing conspiracy" for making the charges up in the first place. They were angry because they knew that the accusations made against Clinton accused him of the wanton violation of the most basic moral sensibilities known in the land, that those sensibilities mattered, and that they must be defended.

Then came D-Day.

And when this "progressive moral breakthrough" came in the form of the Dress Day earthquake, which was changed—the *moral* position of professing Christian Clinton supporters or the *political* position of professing Christian Clinton supporters?

One *was* changed.

Clearly and completely. And forever so, for most of those in this particular group.

In the face of this most glaring display of indecency and wanton demonstration of vacuous moral character, politics trumped morality. It wasn't even close.

Predictably, the leaders of progressive Christianity rallied to Bubba's side. This groundswell of support from the left's spiritual and religious icons was highlighted by the Reverend Jesse Jackson's spirited defense (*not* to be confused with a Holy Spirited defense). In his attempt to protect the Sacred Bubba, Jackson built upon the oh-so-biblically sound notion that since David was a man after God's own heart and David committed adultery with Bathsheba, the whole Bubba/Soiled Kiddo deal was not only no biggie in the negative sense, it may actually be a plus. In case that bit of fine biblical exegesis was somehow unconvincing (and how could *that* possibly be?), the Reverend Jackson also reminded us that in committing adultery, Clinton had only violated *one* of the Ten Commandments. That gave Bill a stunningly impressive .900 batting average for at least as long as we are unaware of what the other nine commandments say, so it's all good. (Yet if we *do* become aware of those other nine pesky pronouncements from on high, the whole Sacred Bubba Show quickly deteriorates into a "one down, nine to go" joke, which, when you think about it, is a perfect summary description of progressive theology in practice.)

Where once there was even a basic standard of decency in our leaders—a bottom-line expectation of moral standing—now there is not. At least not by biblical standards.

But by *progressive* standards? Oh yes, we wholeheartedly embrace and adore those! How else could we claim, out loud, that the party of the Kennedys and Clintons is *pro*-woman? C'mon, now.

The same path that wound through territories once separating us from the open embrace of publicly flaunted immorality through our chosen leadership led us right up to and on through the Dress Day moral massacre. We've come a long way, baby!

Yet, there is still far to travel for the sake of the progressive cause. Fortunately, or, if you're a biblically submissive Christian, tragically, we are now culturally equipped with the shiny new compass by which all are called to navigate to that mystical, Godless land once imagined by John Lennon. Emboldened by the breakthrough moment realized on Dress Day, we are well on our way to that place.

Abandon fidelity to biblical moral requirements in our leaders? *YES! WE! CAN!*

With our hearts increasingly hardened, our eyes see differently, our ears hear differently, and our minds think differently...a little more so with each passing day. Our perspective drifts ever-so-slightly on a moment-by-moment and thought-by-thought basis into an increasingly dark place.

We all know of the proposition that beauty is in the eye of the beholder. Now that the typical American beholder—even of the professing Christian variety—has embraced the progressive worldview and formally abandoned even the pretense of seeking to subject his thoughts, deeds, and actions, political or otherwise, to revealed biblical truth, they are left unrestrained. They are both able and willing to freely chase after the values defining the glorious new progressive age in which we live. And they tend to vote accordingly.

Welcome to progressive morality, the central plank of the progressive political platform.

5

Openly Mock the God of Christianity? *Yes! We! Can!*

The Emergence of Progressive Politics

"I think this is the kind of speech I think first graders should see, people in the last year of college should see before they go out in the world. This should be, to me, an American tract. Something that you just check in with, now and then, like reading *Great Gatsby* and *Huckleberry Finn*. Read this speech, once in a while, ladies and gentlemen."

CHRIS MATTHEWS, PRAISING A SPEECH MADE IN 2008 BY BARACK HUSSEIN OBAMA

"At the end, he drifted into wonderful, truly incredible pathos, concluding his oration with the word, 'Amen!' It seemed so natural that everyone was captivated and deeply moved. It was filled with such power and faith, was so novel and courageous, and had such power and stature, that nothing from the past bares comparison with it."

JOSEF GOEBBELS, PRAISING A SPEECH MADE IN 1933 BY ADOLF HITLER

During the national ascendancy of The One (also known as Barack Hussein Obama), there was no more devoted and awe-struck a worshipper than one Chris Matthews.

Not-so-stunningly, Mr. Matthews is employed as a high-profile journalist by the Statist media. Over the months leading up and into Obama's presidential run, Matthews once (that we know of) wept over an Obama speech and compared him to Jesus (who, on MSNBC, is now referred to as "the *other* One").

During MSNBC's February coverage of the primary campaign for the Democrat Party nomination for the presidency of the United States, the network's dozens of viewers were treated to the following Matthews masterpiece: "I have to tell you, you know, it's part of reporting this case, this election, the feeling most people get when they hear Barack Obama's speech. My, I felt this thrill going up my leg."

Who needs a Clintonian intern when you have the words of Barry O. to satisfy your every progressive dream? And who says that journalism is dead in the Statist media?

The fact that Matthews could blather on about his girlish crush over the air and still have a gig at the end of the day should have told us all we needed to know about the nature of progressive media in America. His leg-tingling thrill epitomized the media-based escort and coronation service arranged for The One as he went about his happy, teleprompted way to the White House.

All of this has been made possible by promoting a widespread aversion to depth and adoration of shallowness throughout contemporary American culture.

We chase after beauty without depth.

We chase after charisma without substance.

We chase after passion without just purpose.

We chase after journeys without destinations.

We chase after intellect without knowledge.

We do all of these things without regard for any biblical definition of the terms and, consequently, any ability to properly identify or avoid their perversion. Once the light of Scripture is hidden away and removed from the scene, all those left in the resulting darkness become slaves to their emotions, traditions, pet philosophies, and personal preferences. This is how you get from Reagan's Morning in America to Obama's Mourning of America in a mere two decades.

Any halfway marketable anti-Christian worldview has always been able to produce such things as passion, beauty, charisma, and intellect, albeit in perverted form, in great quantity while encouraging their pursuit in every manner distinct from biblical direction. This is nothing new. The progressive leadership of the day oozes with the counterfeit attributes that we've come to adore. With our Bibles long closed and discarded, we are dazzled by the lies.

When we do catch up to the progressive leaders that we've chased after for so long and we wish to embrace them completely, having determined them to be good by every fraudulent standard or measurement, we stand ready to give them the official professing Christian stamp of approval. We're cocked, loaded, and ready to validate. Call it a holdover from our *actual* Christian history or a tip of the hat to the reasonable guilt inspired in those still left with a functioning conscience. Whatever the case, we in America still tentatively prefer to at least call and consider our leaders to be Christian in some watery, vague sense of the term.

In this culture at its present stage of transformation, progressive leaders are more than happy to accept that unmerited Christian tag. So, for now anyway, they grab the easily claimed title and run.

Put another way, "name it and claim it" isn't just for charismatic, prosperity preaching heretics anymore. Claiming Christianity is a *very* politically hip thing to do, so shrewd politicians latch onto that tag as their default setting all the time. Most of their supporters do the same, all with full knowledge in most participants' minds that the tag in question is roughly equal in legitimacy to the tags of implied Christianity attached to those books at LifeWay and programs on TBN.

With biblical illiteracy entrenched in the professing Christian church and the subsequent drift of American culture to a place far away from a Bible-based worldview, *everyone* is left empowered to claim Christ and Christianity. *Anyone* can claim Jesus…and they do.

Christianity, Christ, Jesus, God, truth, justice, and love have all been deconstructed so that they might then be properly rearranged and conformed to the orthodoxy of a new religion awaiting its formal inauguration just over the horizon's edge.

Progressive Christianity has, through its abandonment of biblical fidelity, empowered progressive morality, giving it a sway over American culture that it could never have otherwise achieved. The progressive church and its progressive morality represent twin pillars of a movement that has, through carefully coordinated exploitation, positioned itself for something of a slingshot move into absolute cultural dominance.

Abandon the Word of God as our guiding light? *YES! WE! CAN!*

Mock His truth and proclaim its repudiation at every turn? *YES! WE! CAN!*

Defend the legality of murdering innocent children by the millions? *YES! WE! CAN!*

Destroy and remake the God-ordained institutions of marriage and family? *YES! WE! CAN!*

Is *this* the sort of change that a professing Christian can believe in? Apparently so.

Welcome to the wonderful world of progressive politics.

The God Jesus and His Perfect Word

I am the way, and the truth, and the life. No one comes to the Father except through me.

JESUS IN JOHN 14:6

"The difficult thing about any religion, including Christianity, is that at some level there is a call to evangelize and proselytize. There's the belief, certainly in some quarters, that if people haven't embraced Jesus Christ as their personal savior, they're going to hell."

BARACK HUSSEIN OBAMA

While many may and often do lay claim to the name, words, and work of Jesus in pursuit of decidedly counter-Christian agendas and goals, their success is almost entirely dependent upon a high level of biblical illiteracy in the target audience. As we've covered, this is a problem with deep inroads into professing Christendom in America. I repeat and emphasize the fact of this profound issue only because it is far and away the single greatest scourge of our age.

Fortunately, the solution is as simple as…*reading the Bible.*

Well, maybe it's not quite that simple. Reading is one thing. Absorbing is another. And none of this counts for much without application, also known as that most politically incorrect of concepts: *submission.* Without submission to revealed truth, said truth will *not* set one free.

Knowledge or intellectual assent is never enough. The Devil himself knows exactly who Jesus is, and it sure isn't helping him much. So it is that every Common Believer is charged with the responsibility to read, learn, and come to know Scripture so that they might "hold fast to that which is true" and "test all things" in its light. And there is no more important a thing to know than the true identity and nature of the Jesus of biblical Christianity. His sheep know Him. They hear and obey His Word. Goats and wolves do not.

For the Christian, Christ is God, Savior, and Lord. Jesus is the *exclusive* path to eternal life. For the wolves and the goats leading, defining, and supporting the progressive cause, Jesus is...*any* alternative to these things.

All Scripture is breathed out by God and profitable for teaching, for reproof, for correction, and for training in righteousness, that the man of God may be competent, equipped for every good work.

2 TIMOTHY 3:16–17

"Which passages of scripture should guide our public policy? Should we go with, uh, Leviticus, which suggests slavery's okay? ...Or we could go, uh, with, uh, Deuteronomy, which suggests stoning your child. ...Or should we just stick to the Sermon on the Mount, a passage that is so radical, that it's doubtful that our own defense department would survive its application? Folks haven't been reading the Bible."

BARACK HUSSEIN OBAMA

For the Christian, the Holy Bible is the perfect Word of the all-powerful and Sovereign Creator of the universe. It is divine rather than human in origin and our submission to its clearly reveled truth is essential to any successful pursuit of peace, prosperity, happiness, fulfillment, and joy. Apart from this submission, there is no true Christianity. Apart from this submission, there is no true life.

For the wolves and the goats leading, defining, and supporting the progressive cause, the Bible is confused, confusing, cloudy, self-contradicting, and simply cannot serve as an absolute guide to anything of significance—certainly not as an authoritative standard by which we must define our political thoughts and actions.

> *Therefore God gave them up in the lusts of their hearts to impurity, to the dishonoring of their bodies among themselves, because they exchanged the truth about God for a lie and worshiped and served the creature rather than the Creator, who is blessed forever! Amen.*
>
> *For this reason God gave them up to dishonorable passions. For their women exchanged natural relations for those that are contrary to nature; and the men likewise gave up natural relations with women and were consumed with passion for one another, men committing shameless acts with men and receiving in themselves the due penalty for their error.*
>
> Romans 1:24–27

> *I am not willing to have the state deny American citizens a civil union that confers equivalent rights on such basic matters as hospital visitation or health insurance coverage simply because the people they love are of the same sex—nor am I willing to accept a reading of the Bible that considers an obscure line in Romans to be more defining of Christianity than the Sermon on the Mount.*
>
> Barack Hussein Obama

Now please ask yourself: Is it or is it not a difficult thing to categorize Barack Hussein Obama as, based on his own thought out and freely offered words, *distinctly* non-Christian in his worldview?

What has Barack Hussein Obama *told us* about his view of the Bible? What has Barack Hussein Obama *made clear* as to his desire or willingness to *submit* to the Bible as his guide in all—or *any*—things? What has Barack Hussein Obama conveyed to you and to me regarding his current relationship with the author of true justice, peace, righteousness, and joy?

In Mr. Obama, we see the fruition of the entire progressive movement in America. He is the very embodiment of progressive Christianity, progressive morality, and progressive political thought as they merge to compose the epicenter of cultural change. He is the realization of their collective vision in many profound and disturbing ways.

He claims Christianity while sarcastically repudiating every clear teaching of Scripture that does not conform to his will. His open mockery of God's perfect Word is usually delivered with a smirk and a chuckle. And now, in no small part due to the active support of millions of professing Christians in America, this man has been propelled to the pinnacle of power in a nation that was founded upon the very principles that he aims to mock, ridicule, rebuke, and repeal.

He has been proudly and enthusiastically elevated to the position of national leader in the United States of America.

By professing Christians.

Winning the Change War

Finally, be strong in the Lord and in the strength of his might. Put on the whole armor of God, that you may be able to stand against the schemes of the devil. For we do not wrestle against flesh and blood, but against the rulers, against the authorities, against the cosmic powers over this present darkness, against the spiritual forces of evil in the heavenly places. Therefore take up the whole armor of God, that you may be able to withstand in the evil day, and having done all, to stand firm. Stand therefore, having fastened on the belt of truth, and having put on the breastplate of righteousness, and, as shoes for your feet, having put on the readiness given by the gospel of peace. In all circumstances take up the shield of faith, with which you can extinguish all the flaming darts of the evil one; and take the helmet of salvation, and the sword of the Spirit, which is the word of God.

EPHESIANS 6:10–17

This is where progressive Christianity, progressive morality, and progressive politics converge. This is the course that was charted back in the '60s and successfully re-emphasized just twenty years ago.

The American family, church, culture, and leadership has been infiltrated and overrun by the enemy, and that enemy has had virtually unfettered reign for decades. In the wake of this "progress," we see devastation and decline for as far as we dare look. This is the smoldering, enemy-overrun cultural landscape in which biblical Christians are now called not only to live, but do battle.

How much of an apocalyptic bummer is *that*? I mean, this scenario is daunting, to say the very least. It's a scary place to be.

And had we been left to our own devices, this spot in which we find ourselves should and would certainly be impossibly daunting and scary. We'd be, without a doubt, totally and completely doomed.

Yet, by the grace of the one true God we worship and serve, we are given in this dark and dying world something beautiful beyond comprehension and specifically tuned for maximum impact in the life of each and every individual Common Believer. With this gift held firmly in hand, we cannot only survive, but thrive. We have been called and equipped *perfectly* for every battle to come. In what many may see as an impossibly intimidating and frightening culture war, ours is the ultimate weapon: The perfect Word of God.

Remember, as recorded in the book of Matthew (16:18): The gates of Hell *will not prevail* against Christ's church. This is *not* a statement of Christians making a successful defense of *anything*. It is a clear declaration of aggressive, and unstoppable, *offensive* power.

We are to be on the march.

We are to be active agents of and for God-centered change.

When a Christian is armed with and submits to undiluted biblical truth, he is invincible. He will recognize every lie and treat it accordingly. He will know when a "change" being advocated is a change that will lead towards God or away from Him. He will recognize every wolf and treat them accordingly. He will know when a "leader" is seeking to lead towards God or away from Him. He will know and wield the sword of the Spirit, which is the Word of God (Eph. 6:17).

He will seek out and destroy every stronghold of the enemy. He will know that there *is* an enemy, that this enemy *has* strongholds, and that God has commanded that those strongholds be annihilated. The gates of Hell itself *cannot* stand against him. He will fight the good fight, wage the perfect war, and glorify Christ with every breath and step taken along the path to victory.

Now you know why *real* Christians scare progressives. Not only do they scare 'em, but they *should* scare them.

You and I, as biblical Christians, will absolutely mortify the leadership of the progressive movement for as long as we draw breath, and doubly so when we speak while exhaling. You can take that to the government-owned bank. This spirit of progressive fright won't be inspired by some wacky call to drama or a paranoia-fueled demonstration of rage or anger. Nope, nothing of the sort. It'll be automatic. Our unique ability to strike fear in the heart of the progressive is an autonomic attribute. We don't have to do anything but be who we are in order to frighten them this way. By simply *being*, we scare 'em to death. It's that fundamental.

So it is that every single solitary Common Believer will frighten the enemies so clearly described by God the Holy Spirit in His Word. Quite naturally then, we would expect the progressive movement to do anything within its power to thin our ranks.

The biblically submissive and empowered Christian soldier is an opponent—the *only* opponent—against whom the progressive movement sweeping through our culture simply cannot stand…which is precisely why at every turn, in every realm, and at every opportunity, the progressive movement aims to separate man from God's perfect Word.

Love Your God and Know His Enemies

Let love be genuine. Abhor what is evil; hold fast to what is good.

ROMANS 12:9

O you who love the LORD, hate evil! He preserves the lives of his saints; he delivers them from the hand of the wicked.

PSALM 97:10

God has enemies. He hates them and their works.

If we are to wage war effectively against these enemies, we must not flinch from the first essential task of *identifying* them. Some of that work has hopefully already been accomplished here, and there's more to come in subsequent chapters. The processes of target acquisition and opposition research are vital aspects of any war effort, after all.

To that end, Scripture provides us with many clear guidelines. As we learn His Word and grow in our knowledge of and relationship with Him, we will naturally find ourselves more and better equipped to properly identify every phony god, counterfeit Christ, and man-made religion that comes down the progressive pathway. In time, detecting deceit and deceivers will become another autonomic ability. Like breathing and offending progressives. It'll be effortless. And with it in place, we'll see and smell the opposition coming a mile away.

As most of us are far from that place and level of maturity as believers, the next chapter will be dedicated to applying several biblical principles of discernment to various progressive and counter-Christian leaders and movements currently seeking to undermine and corrupt the church of Christ. We will see, in their own words, crystal clear expressions of opposition to the perfect Word of Christianity's God.

Facing an enemy—just taking a straight, unwavering *look* at him—can itself be an incredible challenge. Most of us retain something of that "kid afraid to look under the bed" element throughout our lives. This is quite normal and natural. Yet, if victory over that enemy is to be achieved, these fears and apprehensions must be overcome. The enemy must be faced. So take a deep breath, pray—*always* pray—and come along as we now take that straight, unwavering look together.

But before we dive too deeply into the sea of false prophets and leaders, there is one particular enemy behind the enemies that we must now face. He must be known so that his offspring might be better understood and engaged.

But be ye warned: This is an adversary so unthinkably deceptive, sinister, and vile as to represent a singular evil, the likes of which has not been (and cannot be) even so much as imagined or seriously contemplated in the minds of most men. The ability to even see him accurately requires nothing short of the miraculous act of spiritual regeneration that God grants His people. The unregenerate mind cannot so much as glimpse this enemy in his true form.

He is an absolute master of darkness. We're talkin' darker than Damien, more horrible than Hitler, and more frightfully disturbing than Hannibal Lechter or Barney Frank.

His is an evil so potent, a darkness so complete, that, were in not for the Spirit of God Himself dwelling within us, we would surely fall before him. We would be nothing more than a powerless plaything in his hands; a tool to be deployed at his slightest whim. And we would *love* him for it, so corrupting are his charms.

For decades now he has been chosen by many among us as the chief guide to progress and change for our families, our churches and our nation. Given these roles, he has orchestrated the implosion of a once God-honoring and vibrant culture. He is a truly great and terrible opponent.

He is, of course, Mr. Potato Jesus.

The Rise of
Mr. Potato Jesus

6

Imagine there's No Clarity…
It's Easy if You Try

The Progressive Assault on Revealed Truth

*See to it that no one takes you captive by philosophy and
empty deceit, according to human tradition, according to the
elemental spirits of the world, and not according to Christ.*

COLOSSIANS 2:8

In 1971, John Lennon released the hit single, *Imagine*. The song
went on to become an anthem for the progressive movement and is
widely regarded as one of the most influential songs of all time.
Lennon commented that *Imagine* was an "anti-religious, anti-
nationalistic, anti-conventional, anti-capitalistic song, but because
it's sugar-coated, it's accepted." Lennon's wife, Yoko Ono, later
added, "It's not like he thought, 'Oh, this can be an anthem.'" It
was "just what John believed—that we are all one country, one
world, one people. He wanted to get that idea out."

And get it out he did. In the nearly four decades since *Imagine* became a reality, its proclamations of peace, prosperity, and progress distinctly *apart* from the God of Scripture evolved into something of a hymn for the progressive spiritualist. It's as pervasive as elevator music and perceived to be just as benign. Practically every American under the age of sixty knows the tune and most of the lyrics by heart.

Over time, the anthem's clear message has become equally familiar. In the years since *Imagine*'s emergence, its vision of a Christ-less paradise has metastasized from a fringe notion mostly confined to a counterculture rebelling against...well...*anything*, on to a more broadly accepted concept and finally, at this present time, an assumption. American culture has, for the most part, happily conformed to the God-less dream postulated in *Imagine*.

Tearing down established notions of God, His Heaven, His Hell, and every truth associated with any of these concepts has become the epitome of cool in a culture more openly at war with Him by the minute.

Shelving God is cool. Essential to the cause, too.

Feigned depth is cool.

The denial of truth is cool (and, it should be noted, has also become the preferred method of feigning depth).

Avoiding theology, doctrine, and dogma is *very* cool.

Jesus is love!...and that's all you need to know.

How you define "Jesus" is up to *you*.

How you define "love" is up to *you*.

How you define "is" is, well, *tricky* according to some.

The only truth to be known is that truth cannot be known. You can bet everything on that one.

With these hip, new standards of postmodern coolness established, any significant obstacles to subsequent waves of cultural change were removed, and this cool new thing was enabled to roll right on through the breach.

Other gods?

Cool!

Other religions?

Oh yeah! Cool, too.

Christ-less "education"?

Cool.

Darwinian evolution?

Cool.

Coveting the property of another?

Cool.

Che Guevara, the Dalai Lama, Ted Kennedy, and Bill Clinton?

Yep, all cool.

Socialism is cool.

The "right" to murder a baby for any reason or no reason at all is cool.

Homosexuality is cool.

"Gay marriage" is…you guessed it: *Cool!*

The drug-drenched, "free-loving," Christianity-abhorring, counterculture of John Lennon's dream is now the very essence of cool, and not just amongst garden variety pagans roaming the American countryside. Nope, not at all. In sad reality, what we have here is the new cool as embraced by the professing church of Christ in America.

Lovers of *Imagine*'s progressive themes have in recent years accumulated scores of cultural victories to celebrate, including many within professing Christendom.

Lovers of the Christ of Scripture…not so much.

Cult Week at Henderson First Baptist

Train up a child in the way he should go; even when he is old he will not depart from it.

PROVERBS 22:6

When I was twelve, I was regenerated by God. I have no idea why. I'm just glad to be here.

As a result of His unmerited favor, I repented and became a member of His church. I couldn't possibly grasp what had happened at the time, but one thing that I did recognize was a deep desire to know more about it. A *lot* more. I wanted to know *everything*.

All twelve-year-olds want to know everything and by sixteen they usually do, so I realized it was high time for me to kick things into gear and start gathering intelligence, particularly where this amazing, new, life-changing experience was concerned. I was a kid on a mission.

My grandmother, Ruth (known alternatively as Gram, The Gram, Yes Ma'am, or Keyser Söze), was thrilled with recent events at Henderson First Baptist, as you might imagine. She was the one taking my brother and me to church every Sunday and most Wednesdays, so when we became members of the church, she was one giddy Gram.

Shortly after I was baptized, there came an intriguing Sunday announcement from the pulpit: The church would be hosting a series of studies over the coming week nights, each featuring an examination of prominent cults in America. Nights one and two were to be dedicated to the Mormons and Jehovah's Witnesses, respectively.

This sounded very cool to me, in an oddly curious monster/sci-fi flick kind of way, so I begged Gram to take me to the grand event.

"Can we go to Cult Week? Please! Please! *Pretty* please? C'mon, Gram…what could be more fun than *Cult Week?* Cult Week! Cult Week! Cult Week!"

I was like a little Cult Week cultist right there. In hindsight, it's kinda creepy, but Gram was happy to oblige, so away we went.

I don't remember what the order was, but Monday and Tuesday nights were indeed dedicated to the Mormons and Watchtower Society, exactly as advertised, and after the end of night two, I was very suspicious. Not of the cultists, but of the Baptists.

The absolute lunacy of what I had just heard over the course of two evenings in that little white building tucked into the woods just off Highway 62 left me more than a tad skeptical. There was just *no way* that people actually *believed* those things. It was impossible. Surely I had been given an inaccurate description of Mormon or Witness theology.

This stuff wasn't just dumb; it was *Godzilla* dumb.

I smelled Baptist propaganda.

I mean, who believes that, if they're a good enough guy down here, one day they will be rewarded by becoming the god of their own little planet, over which they will have eternal celestial sex with their numerous spirit wives, and that the spiritual offspring generated by said celestial sex will then become the souls that go on to populate the bodies of the people on the planet that they're a god over? And who believes that the God of Scripture was once a man just like any of us guys down here and that, once upon a time, He went through the same process in order to get to where He is now? How do you get more polytheistic than *that*?

I liked a loopy sci-fi plot as much as the next kid, don't get me wrong, but this stuff was flat out *nuts*. We're all potential gods in waiting? The God of Christianity was once just a man, and a boy, like me? Jesus and Lucifer were *brothers*?

Well, okay, it's fair to say that I occasionally saw flashes of Satan in my little brother at the time, but beyond that one point, the so-called theology I'd just heard about was just too goofy to take seriously. It was weird and wacky to such an extreme that it couldn't be real. Who would possibly buy into it as serious?

Well, Mormons would, apparently.

This I discovered in subsequent weeks as I got my hands on some reading material and did my best to learn all about Mormonism and Watchtower theology from the perspective of Mormons and Jehovah's Witnesses. It was an amazing experience. I read their own words in their own publications and then took to Dr. Walter Martin's *The Kingdom of the Cults*, which became, for me, something of a "moment" in book form. Reading Martin's work fed my fire and gave me a first solid glimpse into the world of anti-Christian beliefs in which we live.

Apparently, the Jesus preached at Henderson First Baptist stood in complete contrast and opposition to every man-made religion in the world. It all makes perfect sense when you think about it, of course, but I hadn't.

Until Cult Week.

We're not in Arkansas Anymore

"Believing in God is important, but what about God believing in us?…maybe if we had more insight into the culture that Jesus grew up in and some of the radical things he did, we'd understand the faith that God has in all of us."

PROMO MATERIAL FOR ROB BELL'S *DUST* VIDEO

"Although fallen persons are capable of externally good acts (acts that are good for society), they cannot do anything really good, i.e., pleasing to God (Rom. 8:8). God, however, looks on the heart. And from his ultimate standpoint, fallen man has no goodness, in thought, word, or deed."

JOHN FRAME

A few years back and about two decades removed from Cult Week, I'd relocated to southwestern Missouri after long stints in the Seattle and Little Rock areas. I had just begun the process of finding my new church home, and in the course of my comprehensive sweep of all things Baptist in the area, I visited Second Baptist Church in Springfield, Missouri.

It was one of the larger churches I'd ever attended; thousands came every week and the building was ginormous. It had meeting areas and study rooms everywhere. There was a café, a beautiful retail bookstore, and even a full blown, stage- and juice/food bar-equipped club right there inside those walls. It was one bowling alley and indoor roller-coaster away from material perfection.

I even remember getting lost one evening while seeking out the "Summit Room," which turned out not to be on the third and top floor, where I was looking, but rather was located in the basement. Go figure. Navigating that monstrosity for the first time was like trying to find your way around the starship *Enterprise* without the benefit of having ever seen *Star Trek*.

As a Baptist boy who was first brought to faith and growth in a church congregation of about 60 regulars in size, finding my way around the gargantuan construct that was the Second Baptist building was awkward, but fun. The people were open and kind. They asked questions and seemed genuinely interested in every answer. By the time they had grasped the basics of my bio, they were able to suggest over half a dozen different groups and ministries that I might want to give a whirl.

It was a very warm welcome. There was no way for me to even scratch the surface of what might be happening at Second Baptist in one visit, so I decided to make an effort to find out more and see what God might have for me to do there.

Heck, how could any self-respecting geek pass up a chance to explore and maybe find a home on board the *Enterprise*?

Red Alert

"When people say that all we need is the Bible, it is simply not true."

ROB BELL, *VELVET ELVIS: REPAINTING THE CHRISTIAN FAITH*, WHICH CAN BE HAD AT MOST AMERICAN "CHRISTIAN BOOKSTORES."

All Scripture is breathed out by God and profitable for teaching, for reproof, for correction, and for training in righteousness, that the man of God may be competent, equipped for every good work.

2 TIMOTHY 3:16–17

On my second or third evening visit to Second Baptist, following a contemporary worship session featuring an acoustic guitar and some uplifting, happy songs, the informal assembly of a couple hundred or so was treated to a video presentation. The video featured a speaker by the name of Rob Bell. He was a silky smooth thirty-something and was there to tell the good Baptists gathered 'round the screen something new about Jesus.

As we all know—or should know—anytime anyone claims to have something "new" for you where Jesus is concerned, they're probably not about to reveal a new truth about the biblical Jesus of Christianity. What they're about to do is introduce you to a newly reconstructed version *of* Jesus—one that suits them far better than the Christ of Scripture. There's a big difference between the two, obviously, and we'll get into that more later, but for now, back to Rob.

His presentation was compelling, so long as you hadn't actually read a Bible. He was articulate and passionate. He even wore the magical "I'm cool and hip and can relate to young people" square-framed glasses. The crowd, consisting mostly of younger people, ate it up.

Rob shared with the assembled Baptists his vision of Jesus, humanity, and what the former thought of the latter[9]:

Rabbis were the most honored, respected, revered people anywhere. I mean, the best of the best of the best were the only ones who got to be Rabbis, and this Rabbi comes down the beach and says to you, "Come follow me!" Well, what's he really saying?

"What's Jesus *really* saying?" I remember thinking, and probably mumbling, as I shifted in my seat. "What's Rob *really* smoking?" seemed the better question. That or maybe, "What's Rob really *selling?*"

These frustrating thoughts were amplified by the fact that absolutely *nothing* that had so far emerged from Bell's mouth was *distinctly* Christian in the biblical sense. Oh, he used the name of Jesus and painted pictures with vaguely Christian-ish colors, but none of the focus was ever on core biblical truths from an actual orthodox Christian perspective. Worse still, whenever Bell was anything close to clear, it was in the presentation of expressly unbiblical and anti-Christian sentiments.

As harmless curiosity shifted to alert suspicion, I began to simultaneously wonder who was, right then and there at Second Baptist, thanking God for providing Rob Bell so that they might finally know what Jesus had *really* said.

Right on cue, Rob the revelator continued: "What he's really saying is, 'I think you could do what I do.' All of this, to me, has huge implications for how we understand Jesus. I mean, faith in Jesus is important, but what about Jesus' faith in us?"

And with that, all I could see behind the polished presentation and super-hip metro-sexual guide to postmodern anti-Christianity was a sea of waving red flags (and *red* flags were appropriate in ways that we will also get into more later).

I couldn't believe I was sitting in a Southern Baptist church in the Ozarks listening to *this*. My inner Walter Martin was about to have an aneurism.

Hell's Bells

Now the serpent was more crafty than any other beast of the field that the LORD God had made. He said to the woman, "Did God actually say, 'You shall not eat of any tree in the garden'?" And the woman said to the serpent, "We may eat of the fruit of the trees in the garden, but God said, 'You shall not eat of the fruit of the tree that is in the midst of the garden, neither shall you touch it, lest you die.'" But the serpent said to the woman, "You will not surely die. For God knows that when you eat of it your eyes will be opened, and you will be like God, knowing good and evil."

GENESIS 3:1–5

We're all greatness in waiting. Jesus came to convince us of that. We have the power within ourselves to create paradise on earth. We can do what He does and *He* has faith in *us*.

For those of you still reading who are not named Benny Hinn, Joel Osteen, or [insert major TBN contributor here], there's an excellent chance that you too have detected the peculiar odor of a very particular and ancient lie rotting at the core of Rob Bell's shiny new video production.

We're all great, we can do anything, Jesus is our nonjudgmental pal...yada, yada, yada.

For the gazillionth time, yet another rehashed version of the same ol' lame fave of Satan was brought to the masses.

This time, the masses were (physically, if not mentally or spiritually) attentive Baptists. This time, the sin-friendly theological rehash came courtesy of one Rob Bell.

We might as well have just been subjected to a theological pitch by Rob Zombie, yet the assembled evangelicals soaked it up and many seemed to think it was just about the coolest thing ever. Ears were tickled, egos were stroked, the Gospel was trampled, and the crowd was huge.

I felt really, *really* weird.

In a way, it was like Cult Week all over again. Only this time, the overtly anti-Christian, unbiblical perspective in question wasn't being presented for the purpose of preparing the bride of Christ for battle against it.

Nope, this time, the counter-Christian perspective in question was actively *promoted* by the professing church of Christ. It was all a part of the show.

You know, from a secular perspective, maybe that place didn't need a bowling alley or indoor roller-coaster to achieve worldly perfection after all. It had the philosophy of Rob Bell, and that was surely more than enough to compensate.

The Cool New Christ-less Christianity

Who does Peter lose faith in? Not Jesus; he is doing fine.
Peter loses faith in himself... I've been told I need to believe
in Jesus. Which is a good thing. But what I'm learning is that
Jesus believes in me....God has faith in me."

ROB BELL, *VELVET ELVIS: REPAINTING*
THE CHRISTIAN FAITH

But false prophets also arose among the people, just as there
will be false teachers among you, who will secretly bring in
destructive heresies, even denying the Master who bought
them, bringing upon themselves swift destruction.

2 PETER 2:1

There's little argument left to be made that virtually every counter-Christian perspective on every aspect and area of life has been packaged, repackaged, re-repackaged, and relentlessly marketed with great success to the culture in which we live. This sort of evangelical secularism has come to dominate virtually every segment of society, including the professing Christian church.

The penetration of unbiblical thought has been so pervasive and deep that much of what falls under the umbrella of contemporary American Christianity has, for the most part, become just another tool of the enemy.

I think that, for me, the reality and gravity of the situation didn't really hit home until I sat through and subsequently contemplated the whole "Rob Bell experience" at Second Baptist. I'd lived in

Seattle for years and would have had little trouble understanding how something that nutty might become popular up there. But here? In southern Missouri? The Ozarks? The Heartland of America?

Yes, apparently in the Heartland of America...and at a Baptist church, to boot.

There's no denying it: Christ-less Christianity is on its way to becoming just as cool in America's heartland as Christ-less *anything* has already become in the Pacific Northwest.

The wolves we were warned of have been welcomed with open arms to help tend the sheep. And heck, if they can boost our attendance and make us a few bucks in the process, it's all the better. We're all about the numbers, and this cool new brand of religion definitely delivers those. So, with pews filled and building funds financed, off to the postmodern, post-Christian races we go.

One of the things that I find both annoying and ironic about the whole deal is the *sameness* of it all; its uniformity, conformity and predictability. It's so very tired, lame, stale, and old in every basic and bad sense. Yet it's being sold—and successfully so—as something bright, shiny, and new. The same old, ever-marketable, and appealing ingredients from time immemorial have been once again remixed to crank out yet another "interpretation" of what is, in essence, basically just the same old thing. Kind of like a "new" item on a Taco Bell menu.

While pretending to hawk some brainy new insight or twist on reality that will supposedly open up a mystical and heretofore unknown doorway to unlimited human potential, all that the Rob Bells of the world are actually pitching is garden variety postmodern political liberalism and socialism dipped in a vat of steaming eastern mysticism.

That's it.

Really.

It's *that* tired, old and lame.

And man, is it selling. And by selling, I mean literally, as in, "like hotcakes."

This hotcake-like sales phenomenon has very much extended into the professing church in America, particularly among its younger members. The twenty- and thirty-something Christian sets are sucking this swill down as fast as NOOMA can crank out Bell product and Zondervan can craft materially profitable alternatives to God-honoring literature.

Counter-Christianity (which is another way of saying *anti*-Christianity, as there is no middle or neutral ground to be had where the biblical Christ is concerned) has absolutely, positively become *very* cool in America.

Cool like soul patches and squared glasses. Cool like free love, drunkenness, and giggle-as-you-go blasphemy. Cool like jazz.

7

? > ! (or: soul patches gone wild)

The Wannabe Artists Formerly Known as the Emergent Church

"I confess I enjoyed being different. I got more attention by being the hippie guy than I had when I was normal. I felt better in a lot of ways, more superior, because I was no longer sheltered. I had been in the world, and **the world had approved of me.**

They were cute, these little Christian people. I liked them. They reminded me of my roots, where I had come from all those days ago, before my month in the woods with the pot smokers and the hippies and the free love for everybody."

DONALD MILLER, *BLUE LIKE JAZZ*
(bold emphasis mine)

Do not love the world or the things in the world. If anyone loves the world, the love of the Father is not in him.

1 JOHN 2:15

Meet Donald.

Donald wasn't popular for most of his life. As a result, popularity became something of an idol to him. (And, let's face it, most of us are right there with him.)

Donald became a liberal and is now very proud of his liberalism. Excruciatingly proud.

Donald can't stand conservatives, mainly because they are so darned judgmental. He is more than happy to judge them for this again and again and again.

Donald can't stand biblical Christians for the same reason, only more intensely so than garden variety conservatives, and is even happier to rail against them loudly, proudly, and redundantly.

Donald enjoys pouting far too much to allow even the most rank of hypocrisy to get in the way.

Donald likes "hippie culture." A lot.

He has "never experienced a group of people who loved each other more" than a gaggle of pot-smoking, promiscuous hippies that he once hung out with for a month in the woods.

Donald needs to get out more.

Donald has little trouble with the notion of others practicing homosexuality. Actually, he thinks they're quite cool.

Donald has little trouble with communism. He has communist pals and thinks they're cool too.

Donald is a socialist…at the very least. Socialism, at the very least, is cool to Donald.

Donald can't stand Republicans. He'll tell you all about how not-cool Republicans are if you'll just give him the chance, and probably even if you don't.

What about Christian ethics, rules, and principles, you ask?

Donald *hates* 'em. He sees them as, at best, problems to be solved; obstacles to be overcome.

So, in order to help overcome the obstacle of biblical Christianity, Donald wrote a book. It's called *Blue Like Jazz*, and it's sold well over a million copies in just a few years' time.

Neat, huh? But wait, *there's more!*

You can almost certainly pick up a copy of Donald's masterpiece at your local Christian bookstore. Thousands upon thousands of professing Christians have done just that. Because, you know, anything *advertised* as Christian must actually *be* Christian, right? And anything that sells hundreds of thousands of copies to professing Christians must be good. Right?

…and this is Your Christianity on Drugs!

"I began to understand that my pastors and leaders were wrong, that the liberals were not evil, they were liberal for the same reason Christians were Christians, because they believed their philosophies were right, good, and beneficial for the world. I had been raised to believe there were monsters under the bed, but I had peeked, in a moment of bravery, and found a wonderful world, a good world, better, in fact, than the one I had known.

The problem with Christian community was that we had ethics, we had rules and laws and principles to judge each other against…**Christianity was always right**…And **I hated this. I hated it with a passion.** Everything in my soul told me it was wrong."

DONALD MILLER, *BLUE LIKE JAZZ*
(bold emphasis mine)

Or do you not know that the unrighteous will not inherit the kingdom of God? Do not be deceived: neither the sexually immoral, nor idolaters, nor adulterers, nor men who practice homosexuality, nor thieves, nor the greedy, nor drunkards, nor revilers, nor swindlers will inherit the kingdom of God.

1 CORINTHIANS 6:9-10

So we've established that when he's not frolicking in the forest with Mary Jane and Che Guevara, Donald Miller writes flamboyantly anti-Christian books that professing Christians across America then proceed to gobble up and digest by the hundreds of thousands. And this goes on while his good buddy Rob Baal (thank you, *Wretched TV*) produces the most wondrously trendy and polished of heretical videos to have ever been eagerly welcomed by and played in evangelical churches across the fruited plain.

Add to these two seeker-sensitive juggernauts such spiritual gurus as author/"musician" Brian McLaren, who has expressed the belief that Christians should hold a five-year moratorium on even taking a position on homosexuality, and teacher Phyllis Tickle, who views this wonderful Miller/Baal/McLaren-led movement as nothing short of a God-ordained "new reformation" of Christianity, and you end up with what's been commonly known as "the emergent church movement," "the emerging church," "the emerging conversation," or any other number of boringly similar and constantly emerging monikers.

At any rate, in a tip of the hat to the musician-wannabe theme pervading everything from Jazzy, Elvisy book titles, to Brian McLaren's ear-punishingly progressive *Songs for a Revolution of Hope: Everything Must Change* album, from here on out this crew will be known as The Artists Formerly Known as The Emergent Church. Having secured a name for the name-eschewing movement, it's time to have a good, long gander at what Phyllis Tickle calls the "new reformation."

Every 500 years or so, Tickle asserts, God *really* shakes things up and changes what we call "Christianity." Big things happen. Paradigms are shifted. Doctrines are challenged. The parameters of precious relevance are reset.

This process tends to bother the unenlightened and under-anointed amongst us, of course, but that's just the way these reformation deals go, so don't sweat it. It's all a part of this 500-year-ish cycle that God is so into.

And whaddaya know, right on cue, roughly 500 years after Martin Luther and John Calvin came along to reform the church by bringing her *back* to the perfect Word of God as her infallible and completely *sufficient* guide in all things, here come the Millers, McLarens, Baals, and Tickles to help us down the good and godly path to the *next* stage of Christian "reformation."

So, when you really think about it, Miller, Baal, Tickle & Co. are simply carrying on in the most excellent tradition of...Luther and Calvin. Oh yeah, that's the ticket. It all makes perfect sense.

I did mention that these "new reformers" tend to be cool with the whole pot-smoking hippie culture thing, right?

The Tickle Me Baal Reformation

"I had never felt so alive as I did in the company of my liberal friends. It isn't that the Christians I had been with had bad community; they didn't, I just liked the community of hippies because it was more forgiving, more, I don't know, healthy."

DONALD MILLER, *BLUE LIKE JAZZ*

There are some things in them that are hard to understand, which the ignorant and unstable twist to their own destruction, as they do the other Scriptures. You therefore, beloved, knowing this beforehand, take care that you are not carried away with the error of lawless people and lose your own stability.

2 PETER 3:16–17

Apparently, gateway drug theory finds much in the way of validation here, as it's hard to imagine mere pot-smoking providing the necessary cerebral obliteration required to compose, much less promote, this idea of a Tickle Me Baal Reformation. (It goes a long way towards explaining *Songs for a Revolution of Hope: Everything Must Change* as well.) Something heavier than pot—*much* heavier—simply must have been involved.

At any rate, what we've been left with in the wake of this movement's stunning success is a cracked foundation in the professing church and a wide swath of corruption cut primarily through the twenty- and thirty-something segments of professing Christendom in America.

Tens of thousands of Christians, many of whom are attending the most purportedly orthodox of protestant denominational churches in the most conservative regions of the nation are being spoon-fed a steady diet of McLaren-esque philosophy and Rob Baal videos.

And who is doing the feeding? Why, church leadership, of course.

In another of a long line of pathetic and desperate attempts to "connect" with those who reject the Gospel for which the martyrs gave (and give) their lives and find relevance to a culture at war with Christ, much of contemporary American church leadership has latched onto the emergent church movement and its comically/tragically unbiblical worldview as a vehicle by which they can ride to relevance and what Phyllis Tickle would call reformation.

And what is the Tickle Me Baal Reformation aiming to reform, exactly? Well, as Phyllis has alluded to and we have already seen, pretty much *everything*.

The fundamentals are being shaken up; the basics are being realigned. The very foundation of Christian thought is being revamped from corner to corner. Christianity is being deconstructed so that it might be reconstructed in a manner that conforms to the ideals of The Artists Formerly Known as the Emergent Church.

The Christian worldview is being comprehensively redefined through this process. And to shed a little light on the pervasiveness and depth of penetration that this "new reformation" has achieved in professing American Christendom, I'd like to share an experience I recently had right here near my home in the southwestern Missouri Ozarks.

Comrade Oxymoron and the Deconstruction of Christianity

Beware of false prophets, who come to you in sheep's clothing but inwardly are ravenous wolves.

MATTHEW 7:15

"If you don't know the difference between fleece and fur, then you're going to lose your spiritual arm right up to your elbow."

DR. WALTER MARTIN

Did you know that "Christian worldview" is an oxymoron? Me neither. (And don't worry; it isn't.)

Yet just last December I spoke with a professing Christian who actually believed that the very notion of a "Christian worldview" was indeed oxymoronic (Worldview being defined here as: "The overall perspective from which one sees and interprets the world." I hope that such a definition isn't too jarring or confusing.). He said this to me. Out loud.

He explained to me that "worldview" meant "a view from a worldly perspective," and that, as such, a Christian shouldn't have a worldview. I laughed. He didn't.

I explained what the word "worldview" actually meant. Then crickets chirped for a moment before he moved along with his presentation.

Worldview meant whatever he wanted it to mean. Hadn't I gotten the memo? Or the Brian McLaren book? Or the Rob Bell video? Or the...you get the emerging picture...

He was in full-blown progressive deconstruction mode, and man, it was *bizarre*.

At any rate, he was quite detailed in his pitch to dismiss the credibility of the Christian worldview concept. This was no off-the-cuff, heat-of-the- moment, bit of conversational fumbling, mind you. Nosirree, it was a carefully constructed response to the clear and present threat that this man perceived in the mere acknowledgment of a Christian worldview (that is, if such a thing were to actually exist, anyway).

It's probably a good idea to pause here and make note of one vital truth that is made plain any time someone claims that a particular thing does not exist. *Anyone* dismissing the notion of a clear, coherent, biblical Christian worldview is admitting, if nothing else, that they do not hold to a Christian worldview. This is a biggie.

While such an admission is useful to acknowledge, those who would make that sort of self-incriminating assertion are going about the process of defining and defending their counter-Christian position in a particularly cowardly and deceptive manner. Rather than own up to the fact that, yes, there *is* a clearly defined biblical Christian worldview to which they simply *will not* individually conform, they seek instead to escape personal responsibility by dismissing the concept as a standard by which *anyone* can be expected to live. In strict theological terms, this is known as "lame."

It's not enough for them to personally deny or refuse submission to the Christian worldview. They want to take it away as an option for you, too. Or anyone, for that matter. And if this ridiculous contention is allowed to stand, its proponent will claim and build upon a victory founded on two delusional principles:

1. With "Christian worldview" dismissed as a concept, they cannot possibly have any personal obligation to honor it.

2. With the Christian worldview removed from legitimate consideration, any individual even claiming to make an argument from said perspective can be just as easily dismissed.

Once the notion of "Christian worldview" has been deconstructed in such a manner, the Christian walk is left completely open to interpretation, or, more accurately, perpetual, never-ending *re*-interpretation. This is an intentional vacuum crafted for intentional use in the intentional redefinition of Christian life.

What's left at the end of such an exercise?

Well, pretty much anything you want, theologically speaking.

And that's precisely the point.

This is just the kind of counterfeit religion that fallen mankind and the brave new "reformers" love. It's Mr. Potato Jesus brand spirituality.

You can claim all of the nice, warm, fluffy, non-threatening and harmless bits about Jesus and Christianity and anything else that you like while at the same time retaining the full freedom to dismiss the pieces that don't conform to the will and comfort-level of the little god you've crafted in your mind. Back in the day, this was known as "idolatry."

God hates idolatry. (And yes, that's "hates" in the present tense.)

Since there's really nothing new in any of this, you might be wondering why I'm making such a big deal about the fact that I managed to bump into a person in America who openly embraces a fundamentally anti-biblical worldview. This hardly seems newsworthy. We are living in post-Christian America, after all.

But here's the rub: This guy *preaches*. He's a deacon...at a Baptist church...in the Bible Belt Buckle. So it is that this man *must* be held accountable, and *to a much higher standard* than the garden-variety professing Christian roaming the countryside.

I didn't make that rule. God did.

As Mr. Oxymoron and I continued our conversation, I poked and prodded around his worldview. We talked about books and politics, mainly. Throughout the discussion, he offered nothing in the way of orthodox Christian positioning or defense on a single, solitary major issue of the day, and I tried to wiggle a bunch of 'em into our little chat. Most disturbing in all of this was that he seemed not to be bothered in the slightest by any of the issues he routinely took passes on. He was unmoved by nearly every one of 'em. In his mostly evasive, dispassionate responses, it seemed clear that he felt little if any compulsion to bring his views in line with orthodox, biblical Christianity.

Every subject I touched on, from homosexuality to infanticide, and the requirement of biblical Christians to oppose both, was met with indifference. He had no interest in even addressing those things.

However, he did manage along the way to get in some kind, complimentary words for The Artists Formerly Known as The Emergent Church. He was particularly keen on *Blue Like Jazz*. Go figure.

Yep, Miller's *Jazz* was a surefire hit where Mr. Oxymoron was concerned, and it seemed to matter much more to him than any of the major cultural issues of the day that we'd touched upon, at least at that point in the conversation.

Yet, a little later in our chat, there was one issue that finally got his pulse going. There was a single defense that he leapt to make. There was one issue that brought an otherwise sedate Mr. Oxymoron roaring to life.

And what was it, you ask? Making the intentional murder of innocent children illegal? Nah, as I mentioned, Mr. O. saw no reason to take a firm (or even squishy) stand there.

Combating the legitimization of homosexuality in accordance with God's clearly stated disdain for the "lifestyle"? Nuh-uh...no big deal, that.

Nope, the sacred cow that required Oxymoronic defense was neither of those things. Children can be legally murdered at a clip that'd make Nazi Germany blush and homosexuality can be legitimized at every cultural turn, regardless of any crystal clear thing that God may have had to say on either matter, but there was one thing—one glorious and beautiful concept—that simply *had* to be defended when attacked: *Socialism.*

Yes, *socialism* was the one and only thing we touched upon that Mr. Oxymoron felt compelled to defend. At that moment, I could feel Donald Miller smiling. He must've been *so* proud.

Comrade O. had found something worth fighting for. Just when I was beginning to wonder if all the Bible, baby-murder, and homosexuality talk had actually put him into a boredom-induced coma, he rebounded thoroughly.

There was finally an issue that inspired some passion in the man. Socialism was clearly a favored concept...much more real and defensible to him than that ridiculous "Christian worldview" thing. This was where Comrade Oxymoron had to make a stand.

And lest any of this be taken as some sort of unintended, anomalous response to the emergent message, let's take a closer look at more of Southern Baptist Comrade Oxymoron's preferred worldview source material.

Painting Over Christianity

"Life in the church had become so small," Kristen says. "It had worked for me for a long time. Then it stopped working." **The Bells started questioning their assumptions about the Bible itself—"discovering the Bible as a human product," as Rob puts it, rather than the product of divine fiat.** "The Bible is still in the center for us," Rob says, "but it's a different kind of center. We want to embrace mystery, rather than conquer it." "I grew up thinking that we've figured out the Bible," Kristen says, "that we knew what it means. **Now I have no idea what most of it means.** And yet I feel like life is big again—like life used to be black and white, and now it's in color."

"THE EMERGENT MYSTIQUE," CHRISTIANITY TODAY, NOVEMBER 2004 (bold emphasis mine)

"The notion of evil itself does not fit in the postmodern scheme of things. If we can't know anything for certain, how can we judge anything evil? Therefore postmodernism's one goal and singular activity is the systematic deconstruction of every other truth claim."

JOHN MACARTHUR, *THE TRUTH WAR*

Meet Rob.

Rob likes to deconstruct and reinvent Christianity.

Rob thinks that's cool.

You may remember him from such hits as *Velvet Elvis: Repainting the Christian Faith* (book), *Jesus Wants to save Christians: A Manifesto for the Church in Exile* (book), *The Gods Aren't Angry* (tour/DVD), *Sex God* (book) and, as witnessed and transcribed by yours truly, *Cult Week Flashback Night at Springfield Second Baptist*. When he's not cranking out the printed or digitally produced heresies, he takes 'em straight to the itchy-eared masses as the founding pastor of Mars Hill Bible Church in Grandville, Michigan.

Rob thinks that Phyllis Tickle is dead-on with the whole "new reformation" thing. Yet Rob also openly rejects the central truths of the *actual* Reformation. Weird, huh?

Well no, not really, once we accept the difficult but obvious fact that little Rob Baal likes the idea of a "new reformation" precisely because he cannot abide by the core tenants of the *actual* Reformation and he wants to do something about it.

So a-"reforming" he goes. And along the happy trail to anti-Reformation reformation, Baal rolls out some silly little tricks. By that, I mean goofy gimmicks like: "God never changes, nor do the central truths of Christianity. But our understanding of those truths is in constant flux."

This cute little Baal-ism is taken from the synopsis of his book, *Velvet Elvis: Repainting the Christian Faith*, as posted at the Zondervan website. The gimmick on display here is how Rob is able to pay lip-service to the unchanging central truths of God and Christianity in the first half of a sentence while snatching its practical reality away in the second. If "our understanding" of truth is in constant flux, then, practically speaking, the "truth" in question is just as much in flux. Objective, universal truths of Scripture are massacred by such an approach…and deliberately so.

Rob also likes to hypothetically dismiss essentials of the Christian faith and then pretend that the Christian faith could remain viable without 'em, thereby transforming the specific essential article under consideration into an optional nonessential.

He happily plays with the essential truth of the virgin birth of Jesus this way in the pages of *Velvet Elvis: Repainting the Christian faith*:

What if tomorrow someone digs up **definitive proof** that Jesus had a real, earthly, biological father named Larry, and archeologists find Larry's tomb and do DNA samples and **prove beyond a shadow of a doubt that the virgin birth was really just a bit of mythologizing the Gospel writers threw in to appeal to the followers of the Mithra and Dionysian religious cults that were hugely popular at the time of Jesus**, whose gods had virgin births? But what if as you study the origin of the word *virgin*, you discover that the word *virgin* in the gospel of Matthew actually comes from the book of Isaiah, and then you find out that in the Hebrew language at that time, the word virgin could mean several things. And what if you discover that in the first century being "born of a virgin" also referred to a child whose mother became pregnant the first time she had intercourse?

Could a person keep jumping? Could a person still love God? Could you still be a Christian?

Is the way of Jesus still the best possible way to live?

Or does the whole thing fall apart?

I affirm the historic Christian faith, which includes the virgin birth and the Trinity and the inspiration of the Bible and much more. I'm a part of it, and I want to pass it on to the next generation. I believe that God created everything and that Jesus is Lord and that God has plans to restore everything.

But **if the whole faith falls apart when we reexamine and rethink one spring, then it wasn't that strong in the first place**, was it?"[10] (Bold emphasis mine.)

Isn't it funny how, all of a sudden, Rob has some "definitive proof" and can actually present some things as "proven beyond a shadow of a doubt," all for the purpose of crafting another limp hypothetical aimed to inspire nothing but doubt and the tolerance of doubt regarding the necessity of one essential (and, by extension, many essentials) of biblical Christian faith?

And howsabout Rob's nonchalant assumption that the gospel writers would *ever* submit to the acquisition of popularity over the truth of the Spirit-delivered Gospel as they recorded the words given them from above?

Can't you just *smell* the Baal in that?

Can you hear an echo? I can. It carries that original lie reverberating once again. These days it seems to get louder almost every time Rob exhales.

"Did God *actually* say?"

Everything must be questioned. Nothing can be answered in any concrete sense. The only thing you can be certain of is that there is no certainty, and this liberating bit of info should make you happy. Like Rob.

It really is quite amazing the way that these smiling, giggly, soft-spoken teachers go about utterly dismantling the core of Christianity, isn't it? Yet this sort of stuff rolls right out of emergent mouths all of the time.

Normally the expression of these Baal-isms would be more of an adventure in funny-but-sad humor, but with so many left uneducated and vulnerable to this entry-level, sleight-of-mind fluff, we are seeing these sorts of ideas actually gaining currency at an alarming pace within the professing church. What would once have been instantly dismissed by any intelligent, informed and attentive hearer as acutely idiotic doubletalk is now perceived by many as the expression of some sort of deep spiritual insight.

Think of it this way: Remember those "new" Taco Bell menu items we touched on earlier? Imagine them being pitched as something transcendently and revolutionarily significant; an amazing evolutionary advance in the human culinary experience. Now imagine that pitch *working*. That's where we are with this, folks.

What's most disturbing isn't the flagrant denial of core Scriptural truth, it's that these "new reformers" are able to blaze this Bible-repudiating trail so effectively from *within* the church. As The Artists Formerly Known as The Emerging Church roll along, they torch their way through truth the way Sherman blew through Georgia. All while the gatekeepers and shepherds invite them right on in to do it. Like on Flashback Night at Springfield Second Baptist.

Relevance is a pricey thing these days. And, apparently, we are more than willing to pay.

The Universal Lameness of McLarenism

"Although I don't hope all Buddhists will become (cultural) Christians, I do hope all who feel so called will become Buddhist followers of Jesus; I believe they should be given that opportunity and invitation. I don't hope all Jews or Hindus will become members of the Christian religion. But I do hope all who feel so-called will become Jewish or Hindu followers of Jesus.

Ultimately, I hope that Jesus will save Buddhism, Islam and every other religion, including the Christian religion, which often seems to need saving about as much as any other religion does. In this context, I do wish all Christians would become followers of Jesus, but perhaps this is too much to ask. After all, I'm not doing such a hot job of it myself."

BRIAN MCLAREN, *A GENEROUS ORTHODOXY*[1]

For certain people have crept in unnoticed who long ago were designated for this condemnation, ungodly people, who pervert the grace of our God into sensuality and deny our only Master and Lord, Jesus Christ.

JUDE 1:4

Meet Brian.

Brian is what qualifies as "a leader" amongst The Artists Formerly Known as The Emergent Church.

Brian just *loves* to mock biblical Christians and orthodox Christianity.

Brian thinks clarity is overrated, which explains why he thinks biblical Christians and orthodox Christianity are overrated.

In *A Generous Orthodoxy*, Brian elaborates on this cornerstone principle of McLarenism: "I have gone out of my way to be provocative, mischievous, and unclear, reflecting my belief that clarity is sometimes overrated, and that shock, obscurity, playfulness, and intrigue (carefully articulated) often stimulate more thought than clarity."

More thought? Hmmm. ...Is *more* always better?

Where does *quality* come in?

Ah, but before we even allow ourselves to go too far down that track, we must remember: qualitative statements are hard to nail down when your one and only truth is that there is no knowable truth. What works for you might not work for me, don't ya know, so let's just ditch this notion of objective, universal standards of better and worse; right and wrong; and good and evil, shall we?

This is how we overcome the problem of quantity vs. quality.

With quality dispatched, we are left with quantity as the winner by default.

So we then seek *more* conversation...

More dialogue...

More stories...

More paths...

More religions...

More gods.

All are welcome. Everything ultimately fits right in. It has to. Everything can—and must—be accommodated. Once the filter of objective quality as expressed through the perfect, sufficient Word of God is dismissed, we are left to drown in a sea of relativism hand-in-hand with every other adherent to the subsequently inescapable faith of Universalism. Neat, huh?

Ultimately, at the end of the day, Universalism is the name of this game. Everything's okay. Well, everything but the exclusive claims of biblical Christianity.

And you thought Brian didn't have a point.

A Non Kind of Christian and His Propaganda War

"What makes postmodern ministry so easy to embrace is that it doesn't demonize youth culture—Marilyn Manson, *South Park*, or gangsta rap, for example—like traditional fundamentalists. Postmodern congregants aren't challenged to reject the outside world."

"GENERATION: A LOOK INSIDE FUNDAMENTALISM'S ANSWER TO MTV: THE POSTMODERN CHURCH," *MOTHER JONES* (JULY–AUGUST 1998)

"I drive my car and listen to the Christian radio station, something my wife always tells me I should stop doing ("because it only gets you upset"). There I hear preacher after preacher be so absolutely sure of his bulletproof answers and his foolproof biblical interpretations. . . . And the more sure he seems, the less I find myself wanting to be a Christian, because on this side of the microphone, antennas, and speaker, life isn't that simple, answers aren't that clear, and nothing is that sure."

BRIAN MCLAREN, *A NEW KIND OF CHRISTIAN*

Brian's "new kind" of Christian is, as we are seeing with increased clarity every time we consider his own words, actually a "non kind" of Christian. Or, simply and accurately summarized, a *non*- and therefore *anti*-Christian.

Certainty cannot be had, much less proclaimed or preached. Of this, you can be certain. (You paying attention, Comrade Oxymoron?) The more certainty is conveyed by a biblical Christian, the less the likes of Brian want to be one.

Even the expression of strictly defined terms of significance can send the Tickle Me Baal Reformers off the rails, particularly those dealing with less-than-warm-and-fuzzy theological concepts like a holy God who views all of those who are unregenerate as "children of the devil" and utterly deserving of his wrath, which will ultimately be poured out upon them.

These are but a few of the many biblical certainties that cause Brian to pout, whine, moan, and record terrifying—both musically and theologically—CDs. Exposure to the certainties of biblical Christianity seem to make McLaren nuttier by the day.

Many clear teachings of Scripture simply must be jettisoned if this "new reformation" is to ultimately succeed.

Sin. Hell. Wrath. These are no-nos. You just don't go there if you wanna fully emerge into relevance. There's nothing quite like preaching the *whole* Gospel to send a wannabe emergent into an apoplectic fit. What's a "New Kind of Christian" supposed to do with the whole "depravity of man" and "coming judgment of a holy God" routine, anyway? Talk about a buzzkill.

At the very least, those bummed out by the crystal clear truths of Scripture can take some comfort in the fact that they are not alone. If history has taught us anything, it's that heresy loves company.

The situation presented by The Artists Formerly Known as The Emergent Church is certainly no exception. The Tickle Me Baal Reformation has a large, powerful and perhaps even unlikely ally in their war on biblical truth.

Donald, Phyllis, Rob and Brian…meet Joel, Benny, and the gang

8

Naming and Claiming our Christian Candyland

With Evangelicalism Like this, Who Needs a Whore of Babylon?

"When you were born again the Word was made flesh in you....Don't tell me you have Jesus. You are everything He was and everything He is and ever He shall be....Don't say, 'I have.' Say, 'I am, I am, I am, I am, I am.' That's why you never ever, ever, ever ought to say, 'I'm sick.' How can you be sick if you're the new creation? Say, 'I'm healed!' Don't say, 'I'm a sinner.' The new creature is no sinner. I'm the righteousness of God in Christ."

BENNY HINN

Though he slay me, yet will I trust in him

JOB 13:15

One summer day in 2005, I realized a fear that I believe lurks in the minds of most men and women who've given mortality much thought. This moment came as I was standing in the Intensive Care Unit at St. Vincent's Hospital in Little Rock, Arkansas, watching, for the first time, a machine help my wife to breathe.

We'd been in the hospital for many days already. I.C.U. was not a new experience. But seeing her this way was something very different. It was hard.

She was awake and aware, but her eyelids were heavy. She was so very tired. But that didn't last.

It wasn't long after that day that Kristi decided she didn't need help to breathe anymore, so she pulled the respirator tube out. She'd had enough and was, at that point, a little more angry than scared, I think.

As you might imagine, the hospital staff expressed serious concern over the whole episode, but, in light of her display of determination, they were willing to give Kristi a little time without the respirator. If she remained stable, the machine would be kept at bay. If she was to falter, the respirator would, like it or not, be returned to her service.

Kristi embraced the challenge and proceeded to improve by the hour. In this, there was finally a moment of tangible triumph. Kristi had won a battle, but there would be many more to come, and the challenges heaped upon her would sometimes come from surprising places.

Several on the paternal side of Kristi's family had become, at some level, captivated by Word Faith Mythology. For those who are not well versed in the expressed worldviews of Word Faith luminaries such as Joel Osteen, Benny Hinn, and Joyce Meyer, one core tenant of this system of belief is that Christians need never be physically ill. Sickness is not something that a Christian must endure. In the minds of Joel, Benny, Joyce & Co., all genuine Christians have complete power over illness and, as a result of this power—a power expressed through the spoken, omnipotent "word of faith"—they are able to deny sickness any footing in their lives.

Christians can simply speak whatever they want, health-wise, into or out of their lives.

Ironically, *biblical* Christians are *always* sickened by the expression of such views, but I'm getting ahead of myself…

As if metastasized breast cancer, chemotherapy, extended I.C.U. stays and battles with respirators weren't enough, Kristi had to also contend with Word Faith Mythology as heaped upon her by confused family members.

If only she had enough faith, she would be healed. Or maybe it was my faith holding up the guaranteed-healing program. One could never be certain. Apparently, the only thing we *could* know for sure was that if there was enough faith had and spoken on her behalf, Kristi would be just fine. That was a guarantee. So say the Word Faith Mythologists.

However well-intentioned a purveyor of such metaphysical tripe might be, it is an easy thing to see the pain inflicted on the already suffering through the imposition of such a heresy as this. It is difficult to imagine a more vulgar perversion of God's truth to be deliberately aimed from one professing believer to another in such a dark and challenging time.

But even in this, as the Sovereign of Scripture has made plain from the start, there was purpose. This was another challenge that God had equipped Kristi to conquer with grace. Just as she had inspired so many through her handling of everything from diagnosis and surgery to chemo and mechanical respiration, so, too, was she enabled to present a Christ-centered response to the man-centered mythos of the Word Faith movement.

When relatives would quote particular verses out of context and insist on their "new" meaning equaling a genuine, real-deal guarantee direct from God to Kristi for perfect physical health, she would patiently listen. When a Word Faith "Pastor" would roll into town and drop by to pray a certain kind of prayer over her—the kind that, when done just the right way and with just enough faith, would make Kristi physically well—we would let him do so…with the clear requirement that he "keep it orthodox Christian," as I explained it to him.

This was more than a hassle, of course, but it was a trauma that Kristi and I had to endure at this time because biblical Christianity has lost vast expanses of territory to heretical movements such as that found in Word Faith. The greater this mythology's influence grows, the more biblical Christians will suffer.

But at the end of the day, Kristi knew the score. She knew that God was God; His plan was purposeful and had been crafted by Him as such from before the dawn of time; and that sometimes that perfect plan of His called for our great suffering here and now. This gave her peace and strength when the Word Faith adherents in her family knew only panic and confusion. Her resting in the full revelation of God's perfect Word made it all—even the "prayers of guaranteed healing" aimed at telling God what to do—not only endurable, but glorifying to the God she so dutifully served.

One of my most treasured possessions is Kristi's Bible, which bears the marks of her diligent study over the last years of her life here. The notes, highlights, and underlines never cease to amaze when I revisit them. Her depth of understanding was a beautiful thing, even more so as it was born though the most challenging of trials.

She was far from perfect clarity on why these things had happened to her. But she had more than *enough* clarity as to the purpose of such suffering. It was this that gave her grace to deal kindly even with those who had brought this most vile of man-centered mythologies to her during a time of great trouble. She knew that they meant well and were terribly deceived. And she knew the truth. This was a magical formula.

Did we believe that God could miraculously heal? Absolutely! Kristi and I know and worship the God who literally spoke the cosmos into existence, has decreed every moment of His history, and will have no trouble whatsoever seeing to it that He will be completely glorified in every single solitary second of that vast span of time. He is in complete control of everything. He is sovereign. Put another way: He is *fully* God.

Even knowing this, we were shaky, frightened, and frustrated. This frustration was frequently aggravated, to say the least, by the barrage of "if only you'd have enough faith" moments that seemed to always be right around the corner, courtesy of some destructively delusional family members and friends.

Their confusion and co-option into the Word Faith Mythology movement is but one example of many thousands that are endured annually within American Christendom. As with most accessories available to Mr. Potato Jesus, the Word Faith mythos has great appeal. It offers us a whole lot of power, after all, and the benefits literally encompass everything for which a fallen mind could yearn. But make no mistake: This most alluring of options is dangerous to and through its rotten, Christ-deposing core.

When we play god, however we go about the process and whatever hopes, dreams, or ideals we claim as our inspiration for doing so, at the end of the day, we lose everything of value. And Mr. Potato Jesus keeps right on smiling.

As with The Artists Formerly Known as The Emergent Church, Word Faith Mythologists bring a particular skill set to Team Potato Jesus. In order to get a better feel for these particular adversaries, we'll now take a look at Word Faith Mythology as expressed by some of its best-known advocates. (You might wanna keep some Tums handy.)

The Word Faith Mythos

"It is vital for us to understand that it is illegal for Satan to put sickness on us, and there is no good reason to let him do it….It was illegal for Satan to kill Jesus, but he was able to do it because Jesus allowed him. Why? Because Jesus was going to use Satan's illegal action to bring salvation to the world! So it's illegal for Satan to bring sickness on us, and we must stand against it. The moment we begin to recognize the symptoms of sickness, we need to stand against them— we need to resist them in the same way we would resist the temptation to sin."

JOYCE MEYER

You know it was because of a bodily ailment that I preached the gospel to you at first, and though my condition was a trial to you, you did not scorn or despise me, but received me as an angel of God, as Christ Jesus.

GALATIANS 4:13–14

Meet Joel, Benny, Kenny, and Joyce. They have quite a thing going.

They are *very* powerful people. More like little gods, you might say. Or little versions of the big one. Or maybe not even that limited.

They have quite a message, too; that being that you, too, can attain this God-like power over life and creation. Health, wealth, comfort, and fame…you can have it all! And then some! But only if you have enough faith.

God awaits your spoken command, so that He might obey. Think: Genie in a bottle, only with no limits on the number of wishes. Pretty cool, huh? I knew you'd like that one...people always do. I know it certainly appeals to my ego and desires. As we covered earlier, Satan *knows* his market. We'll get more into that later, but, for now, let's dive back into the Word Faith Mythology press kit.

You see, God is bound by your faith. Faith is a force awaiting your manipulation. It is a most formidable force, and words are the containers of that force. Words dictate the direction that this force of faith takes. They completely determine the effects of this faith. Therefore, you literally have the power to speak good things into existence by simply realizing and acting upon this truth.

When you speak according to this truth, God will hear and obey, *as He must*. Always remember: You're the one in control here.

While methods of style and delivery may differ, this is the core of Word Faith Mythology. With the nature of this core revealed, there can be no doubt that Word Faith Mythology is an enemy stronghold. As such, it must be annihilated.

Poison with a Smile

"It's not enough to simply see it by faith or in your imagination. You have to begin speaking words of faith over your life. Your words have enormous creative power. The moment you speak something out, you give birth to it. This is a spiritual principle, and it works whether what you are saying is good or bad, positive or negative."

JOEL OSTEEN

"False teachers are God's judgment on people who don't want God, but in the name of religion plan on getting everything their carnal heart desires. That's why a Joel Osteen is raised up. Those people who sit under him are not victims of him; he is the judgment of God upon them."

PAUL WASHER

Mr. Potato Jesus loves you. All he wants is to be your pal. He's your buddy. Your amigo. He's your nonjudgmental confidant and ever-encouraging friend. He's always got a smile and never a word of condemnation. He's so absolutely, positively, universally wonderful that he knows nothing of sin and can't bear to think that anyone might actually deserve eternal punishment. He only ever has the nicest of things to say through his picture-perfect smile.

Did I say Mr. Potato Jesus? I meant Joel Osteen. Or maybe Stuart Smalley. But since Stuart's teeth aren't *that* good and he isn't a leader within the Word Faith Mythology movement (at least not yet), and Joel is, we are compelled to give Mr. Osteen the nod and have a gander at his views on Christ and Christianity.

While he uncritically embraces Word Faith Mythology whole (health; wealth; name it and claim it; blah, blah, blah…), he has crafted some memorable moments in the annals of heretic history through his, um, *interesting* descriptions of views widely held within the movement. One peach of an example came as the Guy Smiley of you-can-do-it evangelicalism delivered a most memorable Easter message. Join me now as we relive his description of a battle that he believes Jesus had with Satan in Hell following the crucifixion (and yes, he means this *literally*, folks):

For three days Jesus fought with the enemy. It was the battle of the ages, light versus darkness, good versus evil. But thank God Satan was no match for Jesus.

He grabbed Satan by the nap [sic] of his neck and He began to slowly drag him down the corridors of hell. All beat up and bruised because He wanted to make sure that every single demon saw very clearly that Jesus was indeed the undisputed Champion of all time![12]

And you thought *South Park* had bad theology.

Of course, wacky as all of this seems (or had better seem, anyway), it is par for the course where Word Faith Mythologists are concerned. Joyce Meyer has not only embraced the same particular brand of lunacy as expressed by Osteen, she takes the craziness a step further by making it an essential test for Christian orthodoxy. As Joyce put it: "There is no hope of anyone going to heaven unless they believe this truth I am presenting: You cannot go to heaven unless you believe with all your heart that Jesus took your place in Hell."[13]

Here we see the peculiar and even goofy brand of evil lurking behind that Guy Smiley façade. While there is something silly about the Osteens and Meyers of the world, there is nothing the least bit funny about their vivid denials of the sufficiency of Christ's death on the cross.

The Insufficiency of Christ's Crucifixion

When Jesus had received the sour wine, he said, "It is finished," and he bowed his head and gave up his spirit.

JOHN 19:30

"If Jesus had preached the same message that ministers preach today, He would never have been crucified."

LEONARD RAVENHILL

While Joyce and Joel may have visions of a *Celebrity Deathmatch* featuring their mythological Jesus and Satan in Hell, the Jesus of biblical Christianity is nowhere to be found in such pathetic flights of fantasy. The Christ of Christianity *completely* finished the work of atonement on the cross.

This is as foundational a matter as there can be to the biblical Christian worldview. It *should* be unthinkable that any professing pastor—much less one leading the largest mega-church in America—would find anything remotely resembling a warm response as he spouted such heretical views.

Yet there he stands...and smiles: The Great Joel Osteen. The most recognized evangelical in the land. Arguably the best known "Christian leader" in the nation. He stands and delivers flagrant repudiation of the atonement of Christ on the cross from his Houston pulpit and is rewarded with thunderous applause.

What might somebody like, I don't know, maybe the Apostle Paul, have to say about this? How might *he* react to Joel's "teaching"? I'm thinking we might see something close to Smiling Osteen's farcical *Deathmatch* depiction actualized were such a

144

meeting to take place between him and Paul. Now *there's* a pay-per-view event for the ages: **Paul vs. Joel**! (I think they could even use Joel's "light versus darkness" and "good versus evil" taglines in all of the required pre-event promos.)

While even this small sample of Osteen and Meyers should help to illuminate the roach-infested corridors of Word Faith Mythology, we really must trudge through a bit more before we can have a solid feel for the depth and breadth of heresy driving this pervasive cancer within the professing church. After all, Joyce and Joel are but two within a large pack of ravenous, if smiling, wolves.

The God Who Fails

"I was shocked when I found out who the biggest failure in the Bible actually is....The biggest one is God....I mean, He lost His top-ranking, most anointed angel; the first man He ever created; the first woman He ever created; the whole earth and all the fullness therein; a third of the angels, at least—that's a big loss, man....Now, the reason you don't think of God as a failure is He never said He's a failure. And you're not a failure 'til you say you're one."

KENNETH COPELAND

I saw the Lord sitting upon a throne, high and lifted up; and the train of his robe filled the temple. Above him stood the seraphim. Each had six wings: with two he covered his face, and with two he covered his feet, and with two he flew. And one called to another and said: "Holy, holy, holy is the LORD of hosts; the whole earth is full of his glory!" And the foundations of the thresholds shook at the voice of him who called, and the house was filled with smoke. And I said: "Woe is me! For I am lost; for I am a man of unclean lips, and I dwell in the midst of a people of unclean lips; for my eyes have seen the King, the LORD of hosts!"

ISAIAH 6:1–5

The god of Word Faith Mythology is a failure. He is a tool. But hey, at least he's *your* tool…that is, if you know and are willing to apply the simple rules that will make him dance.

The God of biblical Christianity is completely sovereign over *all* of His creation—every bit of it. Every financial crisis and cancerous cell in His creation is always a tool used purposefully by Him to bring about His glorification. He is omnipotent, omnipresent, and omniscient. He is self-sufficient and unchanging. He needs nothing from us and always acts according to His own will according to His pleasure for the purpose of bringing Himself glory. He is the source and goal of every good thing and is utterly unencumbered in any matter by the will of any angel, demon, or man.

In Word Faith Mythology we see yet another in a seemingly infinite sea of examples where the "problem" of a sovereign God is concerned. Virtually every wrong theological turn begins with a misunderstanding or perversion of the nature of God, and far and away the most problematic attribute of God, from fallen man's perspective, is His sovereignty.

His total Lordship over all that is—every thought, item, and action—simply cannot be allowed to stand. Therefore, it is universally opposed by every counter-Christian worldview and system of belief.

Put another way, total sovereignty is one option that you will *never* find in a Mr. Potato Jesus Playset. It scored the only absolute zero in the history of Team Potato Jesus test marketing.

While Kenneth Copeland's description of God as a failure will rightly sound an alarm in the mind of any informed biblical Christian, it shouldn't really come as much of a surprise. By this, I mean that such lowering of God from His perch of perfect sovereignty is the norm where all counter-Christian systems of belief are concerned. In the wake of this demotion, the notion of God as a failure of some sort permeates, of necessity, each and every counterfeit version of Christianity.

The Seesaw Principle

So that we might get a better feel for the pervasiveness of this God minimizing doctrine, I'd like to make use of "The Seesaw Principle" as described by Dr. Donald Grey Barnhouse:

We have long since adopted the old-fashioned method of the seesaw to test all doctrines. When children are riding two ends of a plank on a seesaw, we know that if one end is down the other is up, and if the first is up the second is down. So it is in the matter of all doctrines. There is an entire set of doctrinal interpretations, which exalts man and abases God, and there is another set that exalts God and abases man. We may be absolutely sure that the path of truth, **in every case**, exalts God. How far did man fall? Only part way, say some, so that he still has the power within his lovable self to lift himself back to God. Man is up in that interpretation, and God is down. But did man fall all the way, so that not one man could ever have been saved unless God had moved to do it all? That abases man to the place where God has said he is, but it exalts God, and that is the true interpretation of the Word of God. The same rule of interpretation may be applied to all the doctrines in theology.[14] (emphasis added.)

In light of Dr. Barnhouse's seesaw test, we can clearly see that Word Faith Mythologists have indeed radically exalted man through the axiomatic reduction of God's sovereignty. But it is worth noting that the vast majority of contemporary professing American Christians do the very same thing, only to a lesser extent.

Where Word Faith Mythologists or The Artists Formerly Known as The Emergent Church may seek to yank the God of Christianity far from His perch of 100% sovereignty, the typical, more conventional professing Christian in America also seeks to exalt his will over God in at least some—or at the very least, *one*— matter of significance. All who employ this approach, even to the slightest extent, find themselves in the same super-huge and ever-growing camp.

This is the ultimate Big Tent experience. All dwelling therein reject the absolute sovereignty of God. In doing so, they all qualify for a Team Potato Jesus t-shirt, too.

This is a dangerous place to be, of course, so the examination of Word Faith Mythology and emergent theology may serve us far more than originally expected. How many professing American Christians of any stripe actually believe that God is sovereign over *their* individual will in *all* matters and is *never* bound by it? Food for thought...

Now, back to this particular take on a controllable god: The idea of a god who is somehow subject to the will of man is an essential first step towards constructing an even *better* god who will more readily do our bidding, grant our wishes, and indulge our desires.

This god will give us health. He will give us wealth. At the end of the day, he will do any and every thing that we wish, when we wish, and in the manner we wish. Once we embrace the notion of our will having *any* binding power over God in *any* way at *any* time, this is the path that we are on.

The Artists Formerly Known as The Emergent Church and Word Faith Mythologists may be well on down the trail, comparatively speaking, but when we seek to move God down from His actual position of complete sovereignty, even an inch or in a single matter, we join them on the same road.

You can confirm this by simply reading any copy of the *Mr. Potato Jesus Owner's Handbook*. The step-by-step process of self-serving god assembly is all covered right there, not that we aren't able to figure it out intuitively. Such pursuits come quite naturally to fallen man, after all. Just ask Kenneth Copeland and Benny Hinn.

Health and Wealth by Your Command

"You have a covenant with Almighty God, and one of your covenant rights is to a healthy body."

KENNETH COPELAND

"I'm sick and tired of hearing about streets of gold. I don't need gold in heaven. I gotta have it now! I mean, when I get to glory, all my bills will be paid, brother. I won't have bills in glory! I won't need to worry about bills in glory! I gotta have it here!"

BENNY HINN

The pursuit of personal health and wealth right here and right now is anything but difficult to understand. Where The Artists Formerly Known as The Emergent Church are zoned in on appeasing their collective ego through the exaltation of a Marxism-driven, socially-focused counterfeit gospel, the Word Faith Mythologists opt instead for a more primal, basic appeal to naked greed and gluttony. In ways, these two groups could be said to be camping under opposite sides of the tent, but any way you slice 'em, these favored tools of Mr. Potato Jesus are built upon the same basic foundation: A rejection of the perfect God, Word, and Spirit of biblical Christianity in favor of a god, message, and movement of their own making.

It's important that we acknowledge just how thoroughly these groups have come to infiltrate and subsequently define contemporary American Christianity. In many cases, the names and faces discussed in the last three chapters of this book are the names and faces most closely associated with Christianity in America by most of the nation's population.

Rob Baal and Donald Miller are wildly popular in the professing church. Joel Osteen is even *bigger*. Joyce Meyer, Benny Hinn, and Kenneth Copeland each have very large and thriving "ministries."

Like it or not (and you shouldn't), these are the faces of Christianity in America. They've entertained us into oblivion by tickling our egos and scratching our itching ears through an endless parade of books, videos, tours, and presentations aimed at one thing: The exaltation of man through the debasing of God. It is difficult to imagine any force from outside the church successfully doing even a large portion of the damage that has been done by these movements from within.

With evangelicals like these, who needs a Whore of Babylon?

Entertainment...Potato Jesus Style

"I hope you have become nauseated with the tawdry entertainment that passes for the true worship of God in many of our churches and, like the saints of the past, are longing for more of the deep truths of the inerrant Word of God."

JAMES MONTGOMERY BOICE

"Entertainment is the devil's substitute for joy."

LEONARD RAVENHILL

A Missionary Alliance pastor named A.W. Tozer summarized the pathetic state of the church this way:

The church has surrendered her once lofty concept of God and has substituted for it one so low, so ignoble, as to be utterly unworthy of thinking, worshipping men. This she has done not deliberately, but little by little and without her knowledge; and her very unawareness only makes her situation all the more tragic. This low view of God entertained almost universally among Christians is the cause of a hundred lesser evils everywhere among us. A whole new philosophy of the Christian life has resulted from this one basic error in our religious thinking.

With our loss of the sense of majesty has come the further loss of religious awe and consciousness of the divine Presence. We have lost our spirit of worship and our ability to withdraw inwardly to meet God in adoring silence. Modern Christianity is simply not producing the kind of Christian who can appreciate or experience the life in the Spirit. The words, 'Be still, and know that I am God,' mean next to nothing to the self-confident, bustling worshipper in this middle period of the twentieth century.

This loss of the concept of majesty has come just when the forces of religion are making dramatic gains and they are more prosperous than at any time within the past several hundred years. But the alarming thing is that our gains are mostly external and our losses wholly internal; and since it is the **quality** of our religion that is affected by internal conditions, it may be that our supposed gains are but losses spread over a wider field.[16] (Bold emphasis added.)

Pastor Tozer recorded this observation in 1961. A generation later, in 2007, the trajectory identified in his words was confirmed in the writings of a leading pastor in the American church, John MacArthur, who observed:

I am convinced that the greatest danger facing Christians today has infiltrated the church already. Countless false teachers already have prominent platforms in the evangelical movement; evangelicals themselves are loathe to practice discernment or question or challenge anything taught within their movement; and many leading evangelicals have concluded no doctrine or point of theology is worth earnestly contending for. **The evangelicalism *movement* as we speak of it today is already doomed.** It stands roughly where the mainstream denominations were in the early part of the twentieth century when those denominations began formally excommunicating conservative voices of dissent from their midst – and sounder evangelicals began actively separating from those denominations en masse."[17] (Bold emphasis added.)

With every inch of biblical truth surrendered, we've continued our long descent into secular "progress," and we are now very near the end of this wide and welcoming path. Our destination is in sight. Our church buildings are huge and growing. Building fund plans are always cocked and loaded. Our books sell like hot-cakes. Rob Baal's efforts to convert Christians and Donald Miller's tales of forest frolicking with the Manson Family are all the rage. Our marketing campaigns are brilliant. We've made every conceivable appeal to God-hating minds, and this purpose-driven path has paid off handsomely, enticing millions upon millions of goats to fill our pews. Our smiles are broad, our message is catchy and our relevance is way, way up. After all, who could possibly refuse the invitation to live their best life now?

The world loves us. And we love us, too.

While many professing Christians are quite pleased with this progress, Mr. Potato Jesus is *ecstatic*. And when Mr. Potato Jesus is that happy, you know it can't be good. But victory has not been secured. The conquest is not complete. He knows this.

Even now, while seeming to be perched on the very precipice of ultimate victory, Mr. Potato Jesus is nervous. He's anxious. Don't let the extra-large, tacked on plastic smile fool you. (I mean Potato Jesus' ; not Joel Osteen's, though you shouldn't let his fool you either.)

For all of the truth-destroying progressive success realized by the likes of Rob Baal, Donald Miller, and Brian McLaren; for all of the rank appeals to greed and gluttony advanced by Smiling Joel, Benny Hinn, Joyce Meyer, and Kenneth Copeland, there still stands one opponent that, when deployed in the field of battle, will overturn every heretical vision of every counter-Christian preacher, teacher, follower, and foot soldier.

At this moment, there are very few of these open opponents to satanic "progress," but that will soon change. And the very thought of this terrifies Team Potato Jesus.

Every Christian's War

He must hold firm to the trustworthy word as taught, so that he may be able to give instruction in sound doctrine and also to rebuke those who contradict it.

TITUS 1:9

"We want again Luthers, Calvins, Bunyans, Whitefields, men fit to mark eras, whose names breathe terror in our [foes'] ears. We have dire need of such. Whence will they come to us? They are the gifts of Jesus Christ to the Church, and will come in due time."

CHARLES SPURGEON

It's an easy thing to imagine that the responsibility to overcome enemy strongholds and defend the hard truths of Scripture are duties reserved for preachers, teachers, and leaders within the church. This is a lie. And Team Potato Jesus would very much like for you to believe this lie.

So, do you?

Believe it, I mean.

I once did.

I once thought of all of those spiritual warfare and defense of Scripture obligations as, at most, a mere option for the "normal Christian." Moreover, I assumed that typical Christians would not pursue these things, since, in doing so, they would immediately be on a path out of the "normal Christian" category. And that path just didn't look comfortable, you know? It looked hard.

Whenever these things were spoken of from a pulpit, I automatically redirected the commands delivered into my mind's optional folder. You know, the folder right next to the trash bin.

Pastors and church leaders do indeed have unique responsibilities. They must be held to a higher standard. Yet, while this is true, *every* Christian man, woman, boy, and girl is to be held to a high standard as well. This is not optional. Never has been; never will be.

While it is not optional, it is beautiful in countless ways. Gospel-driven pastors, teachers and people—Common Believers, all—are each individually called to a hard and narrow path by their Lord. The cost of taking this path is great. It is measured in lost friendships, severed family relationships, decimated social positions, lost credibility with the world and, in many cases, the loss of physical life itself. This is the path of the Common Believer.

It is the *only* path of the Common Believer.

These sheep led by these shepherds are the forces—the *only* forces—that, as Spurgeon said, will "breathe terror into our foes' ears."

Why? Because their everything is and will always be centered on the bold, unapologetic proclamation of the undiluted Gospel of Jesus Christ. This is the one and only truth that makes people free. When this proclamation is made, God is honored and people are saved.

When this proclamation is tweaked, modified, compromised, and betrayed for the sake of comfort, marketability, and peace with a

God-hating world, we mock Christ and escort vast crowds of professing Christians to the very gates of Hell. We mock the martyrs and end up with the heart of The Reformation trampled to death by much beloved "new reformers" like Rob Baal and Phyllis Tickle. We complete the shift from Sola Scriptura, which is the classical Christian concept of complete reliance on the sufficiency of Scripture in *all* things, to Sola Cultura, which exalts the anti-Christian culture in which we live as the first and last authoritative filter of every thought, idea, and action that we might take. If this Scripture-based to culture-based transformation is complete, the ruler of this world will take complete ownership of the professing church.

With this death knocking at the door of contemporary Christendom in America, the next section will be spent examining several specific fronts in the culture-wide war against biblical Christianity.

As we consider all of the concepts to be covered in these coming chapters, we're well served to keep the wide chasm between the Christ of Word Faith Mythology and the Christ of biblical Christianity firmly in the forefront of our minds.

The Christ of Word Faith Mythology has so very much to offer his followers in this life—everything from cars, homes, rings, coats, and exotic travel to health, popularity, and comfort in every sphere of human existence.

The Christ of biblical Christianity offers only two things: A cross to die on. And eternal life with Him.

SECTION FOUR:

War

.

9

On Family Value

The Common Believer's Defense of the Home Front

Now concerning the matters about which you wrote: "It is good for a man not to have sexual relations with a woman." But because of the temptation to sexual immorality, each man should have his own wife and each woman her own husband.

1 CORINTHIANS 7:1–2

Let marriage be held in honor among all, and let the marriage bed be undefiled, for God will judge the sexually immoral and adulterous.

HEBREWS 13:4

When Dr. Laura Schlessinger described gay and lesbian parenting as "inferior" to heterosexual parenting in a newspaper column printed in May of 1997, the reaction of those kind, loving folks at Forces of Tolerance HQ was swift, brutal and merciless.

For daring to take a stand that would elevate the God-ordained family model even *slightly* above the homosexual alternative,

Schlessinger was savaged. She was branded a bigot, painted as a reactionary fanatic, described as a threat to the progress of civilization, and directly equated with Adolf Hitler. You know, the usual.

It really should come as no surprise that the cornerstone of human civilization—an institution ordained by God even before He commissioned the earthly church—would be squarely in the crosshairs of every foot soldier, lieutenant, and general engaged in waging the progressive war against biblical Christianity.

The impact of radical liberalization has been plain as day for as long as I've been alive. More often than not, this new spin on "progress" has come to define life itself—in every area and at every turn.

My parents were typical professing American Christians in the 1970s. They attended a Methodist church that was roughly as attached to biblical truth as Bill Clinton is to a wedding vow. They divorced when I was four and my brother was one, after my father ran off with another woman, who was pregnant with my soon-to-be-born half-brother.

Ah, good times. Can't you just *feel* the progress?

Anyway, my mother won custody of Dale and me, though she was ill-equipped to raise children after the breakup of the marriage. Consequently, he and I ran wild, pretty much doing whatever we wanted, whenever we wanted, however we wanted.

It was a few years into this toys-and-cookies-on-demand lifestyle that I remember sitting up one night—no doubt way too late—and rolling through the channels on our television. Without much of a father influence around, I had become a sci-fi and monster flick kind of geekchild, and happily so. I was surely churning through the TV programming in search of a Godzilla movie or Dracula flick. I just loved those things. And they went great with Cheetos. (But then again, what didn't?)

What I found was something much, much better. Something completely new. Something much more violent. Something much more...*manly*. In a split second, I went from bored and searching to utterly captivated.

I can only imagine what the look on my face must have been as I sat spellbound by the vicious collision I'd just witnessed between two armored warriors locked in pitched battle, the lightning quick blow from one sending the other helplessly somersaulting through the air. It was magnificent!

The pain inflicted on the vanquished combatant was clear from the expression of humility and defeat etched across his face. The victor stood proud, having won the day completely, claiming ownership of the field of battle at least for that moment through the brutal incapacitation of his beaten enemy. This was impressive stuff.

The conqueror strutted off the field triumphantly. The crowd cheered. And from that moment forward, I was a miraculously converted Oakland Raiders fan.

As wonderful and precious as this memory is to me, and as thoroughly as the silver and black still courses through my veins, this is *not* how boys should be introduced to *anything*.

How ridiculous is it that, even as I wrote this little snippet the first time, I didn't even notice the fact of television being allowed to introduce a child to something—anything—in an unsupervised setting. And this little diddy was set in the 19*70*s, folks. Just ponder for a moment what millions of unsupervised children in America are going to experience *tonight* by way of the ever-present, perpetually-active Idiot Box.

It's not just a babysitter anymore. It's more. Much, much more.

It's a teacher.

It's a tour guide.

It's a parent...sometimes both.

It's the greatest mass mega-marketer of virtually every vice known to man.

It's *that* bad.

For the most part, the center and heart of family has been broken. It's been abandoned and has long since died throughout the great majority of our disintegrating civilization. Where once a Bible served as the centerpiece of an American "living" room, now occupying that prime position is the audiovisual gateway to hell that is contemporary television. And it is doing all it can to kill us. Fortunately, ours is a God who is all about restoration, regeneration and *resurrection*.

Resurrection is just what the family concept needs in America, and that makes our God just perfect for this situation. Through Him, and *only* through Him, the otherwise impossible task of family renewal in America is well within reach.

These families—God-ordained and God-defined families—are essential, and we can have them again. But only if we submit to His instruction and take up His standard.

Let's take a moment to remember how impossibly beautiful family can actually be, so that we might carry with us at least one precious glimpse of the treasure awaiting us on the other side of the necessary struggle to come.

When Children Really Mattered

Grandchildren are the crown of the aged, and the glory of children is their fathers.

PROVERBS 17:6

Like arrows in the hand of a warrior are the children of one's youth.

PSALM 127:4

Once upon a time, men were men, women were women, and both seemed to not only be okay with this, but they liked it quite a lot. More than a lot. They *loved* it. And they loved each other. All in a manner approved by the Southern Baptist Convention, of course.

Consequently, they loved their life. All of it. Not all of the time, maybe, but close enough to seem crazy from a contemporary perspective.

These men and women would come together to build homes; not the brick or wood kind, but the people kind. They would then seek to have and raise children. Many children. As many as they could have…and then they'd want more.

They loved their homes.

They loved their children.

They loved their God, and it was their love of and devotion to this God that had made all the rest of it possible. Life was good.

Older family members were lovingly tended to and taken care of by the younger. Their wisdom was treasured. Little boys and little girls basked in the glow of their stories, experience, and hard-earned depth.

They all lived, loved and laughed together.

They even ate together.

Are you feeling sick yet?

Is this all just a little too *Little House on the Prairie* for you? Or maybe a lot?

Don't sweat it; that's a normal reaction to the sight of God's plan for families in action from a contemporary secular perspective. It happens   all the time. It's called "improper emotion sickness," and while Dramamine doesn't do much for this form of disorientation, there is a solution, so try to relax. We'll get to it shortly.

This is just a hyper-Rockwellian fantasy spin on history, you might be thinking. But you'd be wrong. And I think you know it already. I think that we all do. All Common Believers, anyway.

We all know that God gave us something of matchless beauty and power in His ordination of the family, and that we, as we tend to do with every good and precious thing entrusted to our care, have profoundly trashed it in every way imaginable (and then some). So we like to pretend that those vivid, detailed family pictures painted in His perfect Word are completely detached from reality; rendered impossible by the "more factual" representation dictated by the prevailing views of the time in which we now live. We'd never say it out loud—God's Word being "completely detached from reality"—but we definitely think it. And we act accordingly.

We divorce at rates in perfect harmony with the openly anti-Christian folk roaming the landscape. We pursue relationships and romance in the same distinctly unbiblical manners so highly esteemed and advocated by the culture. We know that homosexuality might *technically* be a problem, but we love *Will & Grace*. We value children like the culture, meaning: We murder and defend the right to murder innocent babies just as the world does.

When we do let them live, we abdicate our responsibility to raise and educate our children, instead shipping them off to government-controlled schools for Christ-less "education."

We define success just as the world does, exalting the pursuit of careers, education, titles, cars, and houses well above the pursuit of a large and growing Bible-centered and happy home.

In short, we *are* the world. There is no discernable, substantive difference. So what is the solution to all of these profound problems and "improper emotion sickness" too?

Is it a new ten- or twelve-step program?

Maybe a cool set of acronyms to help you memorize a new ten or twelve step program?

Could it be a cool new hip and relevant ministry aimed at helping you realize your best family now by repainting your Christian faith with a bluesy, jazzy new perspective?

Nope.

It's just the Bible.

Sorry folks; that's the only real thing I've got to offer here. (And no, I'm not really sorry at all…and you won't be either.)

Celebrating and Defending the God-Ordained Family

He answered, "Have you not read that he who created them from the beginning made them male and female, and said, 'Therefore a man shall leave his father and his mother and hold fast to his wife, and the two shall become one flesh'? So they are no longer two but one flesh. What therefore God has joined together, let not man separate."

MATTHEW 19:4–6

"There has only been one man in history who did not have a family. Interestingly, this man's 'aloneness' was the occasion upon which God first used the phrase, 'it is not good...' (Genesis 2:18) Moreover, God soon remedied Adam's aloneness by making 'a helper fit for him' (Genesis 2:18 ESV). Since then, we have all been born into families."

VODDIE BAUCHAM

Would you like for your great-grandsons and great-granddaughters to *never* be introduced to anything through unsupervised interaction with a television, the Internet, or whatever the next technological treat to come down the pike may be? Would you like for them to experience a happy, vibrant and stable home life? Would you like for them to know God fully and aim to honor Him in all things?

If so, then you and I can begin laying the groundwork for this fantasy scenario's realization by submitting to every pronouncement God makes through His perfect Word where the subject of family is concerned.

This will include horrifyingly politically incorrect things like...*gasp*...*defining gender roles* and then defending those definitions from the inevitable assault that they will inspire from The Forces of Tolerance and progress.

We'll have to actually say that those who disagree with God are...*wrong*.

This is where the breastplate piece of that "whole armor of God" set will come in real handy. Calling homosexuality wrong, for example, will always inspire the swiftest of responses, and it won't be pretty. Just ask Dr. Laura.

Advocates of homosexuality have a seething disdain for the God of Scripture and those who would dare give voice to His truth. So be prepped and primed for those reprisals; they *are* coming. Remember Perez Hilton? (S)He's, like, out to get you.

And that's scary in ways so creepy that I'm just gonna leave it there and move along...

We all know that there's a war going on, and we all ought to know that this war, at least from the enemy's perspective, extends right on into our front doors, through our living and dining rooms, and straight into our bedrooms.

The home front in this war is literally the home front. Our only defense on this front, as with every other, is contained in the perfect Word of God.

In the next chapter, we will take a look into the single sphere of humanity most often used as the gateway through which the whole is corrupted.

10

On Sexual Counterrevolution

The Common Believer's Defense of the Sacred

"You will see a time when we as a nation finally recognize relationships between two men or two women as just as real and admirable as relationships between a man and a woman."

BARACK HUSSEIN OBAMA, IN A 2009 ADDRESS
TO THE HUMAN RIGHTS CAMPAIGN

"Physicality and sensuality are not one and the same, and when they are made identical, the reduction is fatal to the senses. The only way to transcend the physical and the sensual while retaining their essential features is to bend them to the sacred."

RAVI ZACHARIAS

I knew that the end was near when, as I was perusing through a small bookstore in the lobby of Northpoint Church in Springfield,

Missouri, I came across a most remarkable "Scripture study aid": *Girls Gone Wild, Bible Style.*

It was a CD-Set.

For sale.

At an *evangelical* church.

In the Bible Belt Buckle of America.

I remember thinking clearly at that moment that the apocalypse was upon us.

It was in the following moment that I realized this should be anything but surprising.

After all, worldly "seekers" just don't seem to be all that sensitive, at least in a good way, to what Christ's church has traditionally offered since His ascension, so it's only natural that we've opted to revise and update our approach a little. You know, spice things up a bit.

Or maybe *a lot.*

With grade-A, nose-to-the-grindstone commitment and five-star, Guy Smiley enthusiasm, we've pragmatically swapped out truth in favor of something *much* more comfortable. Something warm, fuzzy, fluid and friendly. Something we can wrap our minds around and to which our targeted audience can relate. Something sensible to the rebellious mind. Something much more marketable and—dare I say it?—much more *sexy.*

For those of you Puritan-types out there, please do try to restrain yourselves and remember: Times have changed. People have changed. We need to adapt to the culture if we are to have any hope of making it our friend and playmate. So *everything* needs to be on the table. The ends justify the means.

If the culture has become sex-obsessed, then so be it. We can play that game, too. And we can play it *well.*

We can clone *any* secular approach, copy *any* man-made marketing move and mimic *any* worldly trend that might endear us to the culture with which we so desperately seek a connection.

We'll do *anything* to encourage and nurture a bond with the enemies of Christ…and we have.

The Marketing of Mr. Potato Jesus

"You adulterous people! Do you not know that friendship with the world is enmity with God? Therefore whoever wishes to be a friend of the world makes himself an enemy of God."

JAMES 4:4

Surveys and temperatures have been taken. Studies and focus groups have been done. Every secular marketing concept has been digested; every Hollywood approach absorbed. And at the end of the day, a grand new strategy has been hatched.

This is a plan built around a shiny new message and a non-judgmental, friendly new god. His name is not holy. We print it on t-shirts, bumper stickers and posters, shoe-horning it into every Madison Avenue-spun secular mold imaginable. He must be sold, after all, and what better way to accomplish this noble task than to cloak him in counterfeit Coca-Cola, Calvin Klein, and McDonald's logos?

If we could dip him in chocolate and put a bow on his head, we surely would. *Anything* to entice the poor, lost sinner—um, I mean "understandable mistake maker"—to choose wisely, of course.

All's fair in love, war, and evangelism.

There's no denying that sex sells, and we're all about the numbers. *Numbers, numbers, numbers!* Numbers are good.

Numbers are success. Numbers are the goal. Size matters most. More is always better, and ever-increasing quantity is the new gold standard for evangelistic success. Hitting those targets, filling those pews, selling those tickets, books, albums and god-wear have become favored ways of spreading the seeker sensitive message.

The warm, welcoming new god of happy accommodation has arrived: Welcome, once again, to the world of Mr. Potato Jesus. People just *love* the little guy!

And how could they not? After all, he's equipped with all of the accessories that you could possibly want, and you have the power to effortlessly discard those that you don't.

But wait! *There's more!*

He comes with one arm locked into a supportive thumbs-up pose and the other cocked and loaded, ready to back-pat on command. He's got a gleaming smile, optional sovereignty, and a selective judgment meter on his back so that you can choose the sins he "understandingly tolerates" as well as those he doesn't (and fear not, that last setting has and defaults to a zero option). And every Mr. Potato Jesus ships with its very own made-to-scale copy of *Girls Gone Wild, Bible Style.*

Can you see the brilliance here? Are you getting some clarity as to the genius of it all? Has the culture-winning potential of this carefully crafted new god become apparent?

He nails *every* marketing point, accommodates *every* felt need of his audience, and appeals to *every* demographic group in the known universe, including San Francisco and Amsterdam. No wonder he sells so well.

It's easy to see why this is the god chosen by much of contemporary American Christendom to reach the world. It's even easier to see why the dying world, when it is reached by *this* god, is not only unmoved to repentance, but actually emboldened to chase even harder after oblivion.

Selling the Sexual Revolution

"Any view of the human will that destroys the biblical view of human responsibility is seriously defective. Any view of the human will that destroys the biblical view of God's character is even worse."

R.C. Sproul

Mr. Potato Jesus rode to power on quite a wave. His ascension was made possible by a spirit of rebellion natural to man and increasingly prevalent in the American church. Harmless though he may seem, he is anything but. He's actually nothing short of a revolutionary—a rebel's rebel, you might say. His reign is dedicated to fanning the flame of this revolution and furthering its cause in every area of life.

Most brilliantly, he's taken his cue from us. His agenda is *our* agenda—at least insofar as our agenda falls in line with the natural desires of our rebellious heart. His every success has come by way of encouraging us to relax, enjoy, and leave the heavy lifting to him. No need for troublesome things like doctrine or dogma.

And, puh-leeze, *do* leave the theology to the theologians, m'kay?

Mr. Potato Jesus is on *our* side. He understands what makes *us* happy. With this spirit of shallow, fluffy pseudo-Christianity enabled and embraced, his revolution has flourished.

One of the greatest triumphs of this counter-Christian revolution has been the enemy's "opening of the Christian mind" in the area of human sexuality. Through the simplest of appeals to desire and narcissism, Mr. Potato Jesus & Pals have crafted a wide and enticing path to personal destruction and corporate corruption.

Thus, the church has been crippled and American culture at large plunged deep into darkness.

Sex in the City on the Hill

"The most dangerous thing you can do is to take any one impulse of your own nature and set it up as the thing you ought to follow at all costs. There is not one of them which will not make us into devils if we set it up as an absolute guide."

C.S. LEWIS

This is where much of the American church is at.

As with all issues under consideration, we must first look to ourselves so that we might recognize how profoundly we've failed to live up to the message we are charged to proclaim. On the subject of sexuality, we've clearly dropped the ball and in doing so, have greatly aided in orchestrating the current nightmare scenario confronting contemporary American culture.

Our contributions have been born of a basic infidelity to the clear teaching of Scripture combined with an arrogance that comes quite naturally.

An imagined sense of condescension inspiring superiority can easily creep into the spirits of biblically submissive believers. As we succumb to the notion that we have somehow remained above the fray by simply avoiding the physical indulgence of inappropriate sensual desires, we delude ourselves, destroy our witness, and do great damage to our personal relationship with the

God we claim to love. We are prone to forget that even a lustful *thought* is as an adulterous act and a sin against Him.

Our Savior has given clear warning in this regard:

> *"You have heard that it was said, 'You shall not commit adultery.' But I say to you that everyone who looks at a woman with lustful intent has already committed adultery with her in his heart."*

MATTHEW 5:27–28

So when we see a *Girls Gone Wild, Bible Style* CD set being actively promoted and sold by an evangelical church, we are presented with powerful evidence that the new Mr. Potato Jesus brand of religion embraced by much of evangelicalism has done far more to connect professing Christians with anti-Christian standards and attitudes than it has called fallen man to repentance and repudiation of sin.

The results of this approach to cultural engagement were as predictable as they are depressing. A cursory glance across the landscape of professing Christendom in America reveals stunning parity with the secular population of the nation where the most horrific consequences of corrupted sexuality are concerned, including:

- Adultery—The professing church is riddled from top to bottom with extra-marital affairs and counter-Christian sexual practices.
- Divorce—The professing church experiences divorce rates right in line with those of the secular population.
- Abortion—Hundreds of thousands of innocent children are intentionally targeted for murder by professing Christians in America each and every year.

The price paid by the church as well as the culture at large in the wake of the sexual revolution is impossible to overestimate. The necessity of a sexual counterrevolution is therefore also impossible to overstate.

In pursuit of this goal, it is important that we take a survey of the cultural battlefield—get the lay of the land, so to speak. While it is not the purpose of this chapter to delve deeply into the subject of human sexuality, it is important that we take note of the significant connection between the spirit motivating the compromised church and those who drive the counter-Christian culture at large.

With a secular path increasingly undertaken by much of the professing church, it's getting harder to differentiate between that which is of Christ in the culture from that which is overtly opposed to Him. In order to try and get a proper fix on the issues in play here and the trajectory that's been charted, we will consider two culture-shaping segments of the population:

1. Contemporary media leadership
2. Contemporary political leadership

In surveying both of these groups, we will compare their advocated views on sexuality with those of biblical Christianity. Then, we will return to Mr. Potato Jesus, *Girls Gone Wild, Bible Style*, and see how this mix has come together to impact the thoughts and actions of the professing church. Finally, we will prescribe a biblical solution for the mess in which we find ourselves.

The Morality of Media

"He who marries the spirit of the age soon becomes a widower."

DEAN INGE

Do not love the world or the things in the world. If anyone loves the world, the love of the Father is not in him. For all that is in the world—the desires of the flesh and the desires of the eyes and pride in possessions—is not from the Father but is from the world. And the world is passing away along with its desires, but whoever does the will of God abides forever.

1 JOHN 2:15–17

Contemporary American media has, in its presentation of anything from news and history programs to sporting events and sitcoms, come to epitomize the counter-Christian worldview. Whether spewing forth Statist propaganda via CNN and MSNBC or promoting the "progressive" party line through *Will & Grace* and *Family Guy*, the mainstream, pro-State media is as committed a counter-Christian force as the civilized world has ever seen.

As one would expect, the individuals responsible for the production of this never ending parade of Orwellian bilge tend to embody the very radical, leftist views so favorably represented on the programs in question.

In the fall of 2009, two well-known media figures were the focus of stories that provided much in the way of insight into both the elites empowered to steer American popular culture and those who compose said culture. The unexpected autumn dramas of David Letterman and Roman Polanski shed a great deal of light onto the prevailing media view and its impact on our civilization. The depth and breadth of the ugliness revealed in that light should give us pause.

On September 26, 2009, Roman Polanski was arrested by Swiss police on charges related to the 1977 rape of a 13-year-old girl. Polanski had pled guilty to the charges at that time but fled the United States after learning that, despite the plea, he would still be sentenced to significant time behind bars. This turn of events came as a bit of a surprise to the Hollywood set, as Polanski had been at large for over thirty years, producing film after film and even winning an Academy Award for *The Pianist* in 2003.

Polanski had admitted to drugging and raping a 13-year-old girl, yet upon hearing the news of his arrest, the outcry from Hollywood was loud in his defense.

"We stand by and await his release and his next masterwork," said Debra Winger. She added, "We hope today that this latest order will be dropped. It is based on a three decade old case that is all but dead, except for a minor technicality."

Harvey Weinstein added, "We are calling every filmmaker we can to help fix this terrible situation."

CNN provided the following reported on Hollywood's reaction to the arrest of a child rapist:

Polanski's friend, Swiss filmmaker Otto Weisser, was among the first to publicly run to his defense.

'This is for me a shock. I am ashamed to be Swiss, that the Swiss is doing such a thing to brilliant fantastic genius, that millions and millions of people love his work,' Weisser said upon learning the director had been detained by Swiss authorities. 'He's a brilliant guy, and he made a little mistake 32 years ago. What a shame for Switzerland.'

By Tuesday, more than 130 heavyweights in the movie industry had taken up Polanski's cause.

An online petition has been signed by directors such as Marin Scorsese, Woody Allen, and Pedro Almodovar, as well as actors.[19]

Hmmm... enlightened/progressive older guy... 13-year-old girl... drugs... forced sex... Things like ACORN become a more than a tad easier to understand when we get these little peeks into the liberal mindset, do they not?

The position of Hollywood was clear, if not unanimous: Roman Polanski, admitted child-rapist, should not have been arrested. He need not be formally punished for drugging and then having forced sex with a 13-year-old girl.

About a week after the Polanski arrest came news that David Letterman had engaged in numerous affairs with staffers from his show. This had all come to light as a result of a blackmail attempt that was being made against Dave in order to secure silence on the matter. Rather than pay the two-million dollar fee demanded, Letterman decided to admit to everything and let the chips fall where they may.

For those fortunate enough to be out of the loop where things like late-night American comedy are concerned, David Letterman is the host of a nightly show on CBS. He is a comedian who was, by most accounts, quite funny in the eighties and early nineties.

Whatever one may think of Letterman's comedy, morality, or basic common sense, it must be admitted that he does know his crowd. He decided to preempt any breaking news on the potentially destructive and embarrassing story by addressing the matter directly to his studio audience during the normal process of taping his show. While the affairs were certainly newsworthy in and of themselves, it was the audience's reaction to Letterman's live, on-stage admission that was revealing and more than a tad creepy.

When, in response to the blackmailer's charge that Letterman had had sex with women who work on the show, he reported to the audience that, "Yes, yes I have," the assembled *Late Show* audience responded with...*laughter*. Even Dave seemed somewhat taken aback by this disturbing twist.

One was left to wonder for a moment if Roman Polanski was directing.

What just a generation ago would have rendered a career impossibly damaged now inspired *laughter* from a crowd. This, taken in along with Hollywood's overwhelmingly supportive stance in favor of child-rapist Roman Polanski, gives us more than a glimpse into the minds, motives, and results of progressive liberalism as practiced by contemporary media elites.

And these elites, it should be noted, support a particular political party and adore a particular political messiah with a zeal not witnessed in this world since Bill Clinton discovered Craigslist.

For these fine folks, big government is beautiful, biblical Christianity is an obstacle, and Barack Hussein Obama is The One.

The Morality of the Ruling Political Class

On every side the wicked prowl, as vileness is exalted among the children of man.

PSALM 12:8

In October of 2009, during an address to the pro-homosexuality/bisexuality/any-kind-of-sexuality "Human Rights Campaign," President Barack Obama made the boldly anti-Christian pronouncement that, "You will see a time in which we as a nation finally recognize relationships between two men or two women as just as real and admirable as relationships between a man and a woman."

Those with ears to hear took notice. Among them was Dr. James White of Alpha and Omega Ministries, who observed,

"In this speech—I keep getting close to saying *sermon*—and I think there might be some ways in which that is an appropriate term to use, because clearly he is seeking to change worldviews. And he clearly believes that there is one worldview that is superior to another worldview. That worldview that he thinks is superior is an anti-Christian worldview.

It is not surprising to hear Barack Obama enunciating anti-Christian rhetoric, though he ends his speech, shockingly enough, in front of this particular group, by saying, 'Thank you for the work you're doing. God bless you and God bless America.' Evidently, what God is supposed to bless America with is this new understanding of morality and ethics."[20]

Southern Baptist leader Dr. Albert Mohler responded to the Obama address as follows:

"Those words represent a moral revolution that goes far beyond what any other President has ever promised or articulated. In the span of a single sentence, President Obama put his administration publicly on the line to press, not only for the repeal of the Defense of Marriage Act, but for the recognition that same-sex relationships are 'just as real and admirable as relationships between a man and a woman.'
It is virtually impossible to imagine a promise more breathtaking in its revolutionary character than this—to normalize same-sex relationships to the extent that they are recognized as being as admirable as heterosexual marriage."[21]

It really is difficult to imagine a more pronounced, frontal assault on Christianity than that which emerged from President Obama in this speech. His contempt for the teachings of Scripture could not be clearer. His commitment to open rebellion against God could not be bolder.

In the same Hollywood and media elites who provided the casts of the Polanski and Letterman sagas, Obama has powerful allies in his war on biblical truth.

The Corrosiveness of a Secular Embrace

For this is the will of God, your sanctification: that you abstain from sexual immorality; that each one of you know how to control his own body in holiness and honor, not in the passion of lust like the Gentiles who do not know God; that no one transgress and wrong his brother in this matter, because the Lord is an avenger in all these things, as we told you beforehand and solemnly warned you. For God has not called us for impurity, but in holiness. Therefore whoever disregards this, disregards not man but God, who gives his Holy Spirit to you.

1 THESSALONIANS 4:3–8

"It is difficult to resist the conclusion that twentieth century man has decided to abolish himself. Tired of the struggle to be himself, he has created boredom out of his own affluence, impotence out of his own erotomania, and vulnerability out of his own strength. He himself blows the trumpet that brings the walls of his own cities crashing down, until at last, having educated himself into imbecility, having drugged and polluted himself into stupefaction, he keels over, a weary, battered old brontosaurus, and becomes extinct."

MALCOLM MUGGERIDGE

With a culture driven by media and political elites committed to the overthrow of every God-given principle and truth, one would hope that the church of Christ would see the clearly defined battle lines, identify the threat posed by her enemies, and take to the field of battle with bold determination and commitment to the cause of Christ.

In doing so, one would be wrong.

Sadly, with the Mr. Potato Jesus brand of Christianity having achieved prominence, the church has been catastrophically compromised and rendered largely ineffective against the tide of evil washing over the land. Nowhere is this more evident than in the church's accommodation and even embrace of secular standards of sexuality.

So it is that we must begin a Christ-centered sexual counter-revolution from within the church so that we might have hope of one day bringing this life-saving perspective to the culture at large.

Certainly, this must seem an impossible task from our perspective as we survey the smoldering wreckage of the perpetual Red Light District that is contemporary American culture on the sexual front. And, in the strictest human sense, it *is* impossible. But as we've seen before and will see again, ours is a God who specializes in miracles such as this.

Through repentance and submission to Him, we can conquer even this most intimidating of cultural battlefields. And we must.

The Christian's Call to Sexual Counterrevolution

The impossibility of this cause's success if attempted under our own power is not something that can be overstated. Only through a return to the God of Scripture and a complete repudiation of the Mr. Potato Jesus brand of religion that has led us so far away from truth can we have any hope whatsoever of restoring our culture in this vital area.

In this pursuit, there are three things that we can do to greatly impact the culture war for Christ and His people:

1. **Revive a spirit of personal responsibility.** We must remember that each of us who have entertained even a lustful *thought* have sinned against God. We have no room to boast.
2. **Restore a spirit of vigilance.** Knowing that we are inclined toward sexual temptation by our fallen nature, we must remain guarded and protective of each and every one of our thoughts and actions.
3. **Reclaim and proclaim God's matchless gift of human sensuality.** We can no longer stand by as the enemy seeks to abduct and redefine every God-given gift in the realm of human sensuality and sexuality.

In our application of these simple yet profound principles, we can reclaim the beauty of our God-made sexuality, restore the culture in which we live, and bring glory to our sovereign Lord and savior.

Reviving Personal Responsibility

"You have heard that it was said, 'You shall not commit adultery.' But I say to you that everyone who looks at a woman with lustful intent has already committed adultery with her in his heart."

MATTHEW 5:27–28

The success of our sexual counterrevolution hinges upon our embrace of individual responsibility for both our future actions as well as our past sins.

We are all guilty at some level. As such, we have no room to boast of anything even remotely resembling true purity. Additionally, this reality should compel us to refrain from self-exaltation over those whom we diametrically oppose in the culture war on matters of sexuality.

However dark, vile and depraved they may appear to us, our hearts were no less black before Christ imposed life upon them. Remembering this will not only glorify God, but inspire us to more sincerely and successfully empathize with those we engage in this culture war.

Restoring a Spirit of Vigilance

So flee youthful passions and pursue righteousness, faith, love, and peace, along with those who call on the Lord from a pure heart.

2 TIMOTHY 2:22

Most of us, if we're honest, have vast knowledge of just how corrupt we are by nature. Even when we try—and try *hard*—we feel the pull towards evil on a moment-by-moment basis. Our relentless drive to sin really is quite amazing.

As Christians, however, we are equipped to resist these urges and inclinations. This is a great blessing that brings equally great responsibility.

The things to which we expose our eyes, ears, and minds have a profound impact on what we are, both intellectually and spiritually. Our spiritual and intellectual health is determined by what we feed our spirits and minds, just as what we eat has an unmatched influence on our physical health.

Vigilance is essential. Guarding what Hank Hanegraaff calls "the eye gate and the ear gate" is a must to any person seeking genuine personal improvement through obedience to God's perfect, loving standards. Keep a constantly running inventory of the things you are seeing, hearing, and even thinking. Be aware of the things to which you expose your mind.

Pay attention to:

- o   What you read.
- o   What you watch.
- o   What you seek in entertainment.
- o   What you desire.
- o   What you think.

Yes, even and perhaps *especially* what you think. We do have control over such things, contrary to popular and Mr. Potato Jesus's promoted opinion. Aside from the occasional spark that pops into our mind, we have complete control over our thoughts. The more we exercise this control the more we will even find those unhelpful, spontaneous sparks fading from the scene. Also, the more exclusively we feed our minds with healthy subject matter, the less those "random" negative sparks will emerge.

The practice of the one good thing will *definitely* lead to the establishment of the other. In time and with patient, dedicated practice, even our thoughts can be brought in line.

The challenge here is great, and at first it may seem to be yet another *Mission: Impossible* scenario. But just as our Lord has called us to these high standards, so too has He equipped us to attain them, and as we progress along this difficult path, we will find it easier and easier to continue in that progress. With practice and the formation of good habits, we will find the peace of mind and spirit that we once thought impossible.

In this, we will live life more fully, all to the glory of God.

Celebrating a Sexuality worth Fighting For

Let him kiss me with the kisses of his mouth! For your love is better than wine; your anointing oils are fragrant; your name is oil poured out; therefore virgins love you. Draw me after you; let us run. The king has brought me into his chambers.

SONG OF SOLOMON 1:2–4

The notion that counter-Christian culture is liberated, free, and unrestrained to pursue unfettered wonder, joy, and awe-inspiring experiences the likes of which those poor, restricted little simpleton Christians will never know is one of the most idiotic and pathetic lies ever dumped into an uncritical mind.

With shattered spirits, broken bodies, destroyed families held fast in one hand and countless diseases, phobias, and psychoses gripped in the other, it's hard to imagine anything resembling a coherent argument coming from those actively engaged in a counter-Christian pursuit of sexual or sensual expression. Their loud proclamations of liberating lifestyle choices and open-minded sexual practice cannot even begin to overcome the tragic and tangible evidence available for inspection to anyone capable of critical thought.

When it comes to physical intimacy, sensuality, and matchless heights of experience in every good sense, we as Common Believers have what the fallen world can only dream of.

Consider God's perfect Word in *The Song of Solomon*:

If you do not know, O most beautiful among women,
follow in the tracks of the flock,
and pasture your young goats
beside the shepherds' tents.

I compare you, my love,
to a mare among Pharaoh's chariots.
Your cheeks are lovely with ornaments,
your neck with strings of jewels.

> Others - *We will make for you ornaments of gold,*
> *studded with silver.*

She - *While the king was on his couch,*
my nard gave forth its fragrance.
My beloved is to me a sachet of myrrh
that lies between my breasts.
My beloved is to me a cluster of henna blossoms
in the vineyards of Engedi.

> He - *Behold, you are beautiful, my love;*
> *behold, you are beautiful;*
> *your eyes are doves.*

THE SONG OF SOLOMON 1:8–15

God made our bodies. God made our spirits. God crafted *The Song of Solomon*.

God-given desires, hopes, dreams and fantasies are made by Him, for us, and all to His glory. Only in our submission to His perfect will, we are fully empowered to experience peace, joy, and fulfillment.

What train-wreck of a warped Hollywood scenario can compete with *that*?

When we make a clear, forceful case for biblical sensuality, we cannot lose. It is mainly when we are intimidated into silence that the enemy makes his gains.

He confiscates beautiful terms, claims them as his own, perverts them completely, and then scatters the freshly corrupted concepts about the cultural landscape, proclaiming them to be the "real thing." We cannot allow this to stand.

When we exalt the *true* beauty of sex and sensuality as crafted by God for our benefit and enjoyment, we will inspire Christians as never before, bring change to the culture in which we live, and win battle after battle in the coming sexual counterrevolution.

Viva la Counterrevolution!

There are a few keys to success in the sexual counterrevolution so pivotal to our victory in the greater culture war. Our relevance to this culture will not come as a result of a willingness to accommodate or conform to its standards. Our relevance as Christians will come as the sheer force and intensity of our *opposition* to the standards of rebellion against God is made clear.

This clarity will come not through the volume of our protests or the frequency of our complaints. It will come as a result of our daily living out the sexually pure path that we have been called to walk by the one we claim as Lord.

We cannot proclaim a gospel that seeks to skip over shame and expect anything but disaster. We must profess a gospel that *indicts* man—a gospel that induces shame. Not for the sake of shame, but so that repentance might be earnestly inspired and salvation sought and appreciated, all by the sovereign grace of God.

This is the only path He has for those who are drawn to him. There is no easy way. There is no shortcut or cheat around the essential experience of shame. And shame is one accessory that is utterly foreign to the Mr. Potato Jesus Religion Playset that the compromised church so eagerly promotes.

We must cling to *Song of Solomon* and ditch *Girls Gone Wild, Bible Style*. This is the change that is required of us, and it cannot come soon enough.

God-hating, self-glorifying narcissism has come to define even much of Christian American culture and it is killing us. This narcissism has led us from God to self, from light to darkness and from true freedom into bondage. And now this narcissism has a body count.

11

On Murderous Narcissism

The Common Believer's Defense of the Innocent

If God is dead, somebody is going to have to take his place. It'll either be megalomania or erotomania; the drive for power or the drive for pleasure.

Malcolm Muggeridge

When I was a boy, I developed a keen interest in World War II history, particularly the European theater. The unparalleled scale and drama of that tumultuous time captivated me. I can remember as a fourth grader purposefully seeking out every book on the subject made available in the public and school libraries and absorbing them with an intensity that certainly would have served me well were I to have applied it to the areas of study that were actually assigned to me in those early days. This infatuation grew over time and blossomed into a deep, relentless sort of fascination that has held sway to this very day.

I often wondered what it must have been like to live in Germany in the 1930s during the ascent of the political savior Adolf Hitler. I pondered the dire economic situation, the crushed national pride, and the desperate longing for restoration to greatness that had permeated the nation's psyche and paved the way for its enthusiastic embrace of a messiah. How wonderful must it have been to see one's cherished homeland redeemed and restored to prominence all through the iron will and masterful execution of one "great man"!

I also found it intriguing to imagine what life might have been like on the allied side of the fence in late 1941 and early 1942 as the black forces of Nazi Germany and Imperial Japan were on the march with the wind at their backs. Nation after nation had fallen under the relentlessly advancing jackboot of fascism in Europe and it surely must have seemed then as though the ultimate victory of evil was something frighteningly close to inevitable. The world was coming to an end.

What must it have been like to awake from this horror having achieved what once seemed to be an impossible triumph over evil only to find the ensuing rapture and thrill of victory so profoundly tainted by the unfathomable revelations that were to follow? Those first post-war glimpses into the minds and souls of our brothers and sisters in the Third Reich must surely have inspired a dread on par with and quite possibly worse than the nightmarish prospect that had loomed over the collective consciousness of the allied powers during the darkest nights of 1941.

In reading of and grappling with these heavy things, several questions emerged and perplexed me to a point so far beyond frustration that I resigned myself at an early age to the notion that these answers were simply not to be known. They were not to be had. These were sure to be eternal mysteries for any rational mind, since to believe otherwise would be to acknowledge a logic or sensibility of some sort that would or could somehow make sense of it all and therefore bring to the table a form of justifying rationale.

Yet this resignation could not silence the questions. How? Why?

How could such a thing as Hitler's Nazism rise to dominance in a once Christian nation on the very cutting edge of civilization?

Why would an imminently rational, scientifically inclined people come to embrace a worldview so overtly evil and utterly devoid of positive philosophical substance?

How could a people so renowned for their intellect and work ethic find themselves so completely enslaved to group-think and plunged into oblivion?

Why did the purpose of life come to require the pursuit of death?

These are questions that I contemplated over and again in endless forms for many years. These are questions that I no longer ask. As a man now in my thirties, I have no need for them. At long last, I have found the answers.

The people of Martin Luther's Reformation became the nation of Adolf Hitler's Third Reich in much the same way that the people of the American Revolution have become the nation of Barack Obama's "Yes We Can (insert whatever you like here)!"

Today's United States of America holds all of the answers to what I once considered the dark mystery of history that was Nazi Germany.

I now know how it is that a nation flush with pride over its technological advancement and material accomplishment can enthusiastically surrender its humanity for the sake of bettering mankind. I now know that it is a relatively simple and easy thing to define the inconvenient or unattractive life out of existence figuratively and rhetorically so that it might one day be done away with literally. I now know that a nation that is Christian in name only is no farther from hellish barbarism than that which openly professes allegiance to a pagan god or no god at all.

The reason for this once illusory key to understanding coming into focus so that it might be grasped is perhaps the most terrifying part of it all, in that the reason is *reasonable*. It is logical. It makes sense. Perfect sense.

However impossible this may have seemed in my youth, I now know that the paths of historic Germany and contemporary America are founded on a solid, clear and powerful line of logic. It all begins with one simple, all-encompassing and worldview defining principle: There is no God.

Killing God: Our Essential First Murder

The fool says in his heart, "There is no God." They are corrupt, doing abominable iniquity; there is none who does good.

PSALM 53:1

"I believe that humanism is the second oldest religion in the world—man endeavoring to live in Eden without the boundaries set by God."

RAVI ZACHARIAS

Even the casual survey of a cultural landscape shaped by the likes of Britney Spears, Kanye West, and Madonna quickly reveals the defining characteristic of our age: A burning desire to live in a world without rules. A life free of externally imposed standards is the dream that finds unfettered expression across the cultural landscape, from Perez Hilton's anti-Christian rants and Marilyn

Manson's Bible-shredding (literally) tirades to Lady GaGa's "wardrobe" and MoveOn.org's incessant push to, well, *move on* past absolutely *anything* even the least little bit challenging to the "progressive" cause without pronouncing judgment of any sort (judgments against Christianity exempted, of course).

This situation brings to mind an image of Lieutenant Frank Drebin from the *Police Squad* television series and *Naked Gun* films. In one scene from the first movie, a fleeing bad guy literally finds himself straddling a rolling missile as it careens directly into a fireworks warehouse, causing just the kind of ridiculously dramatic, loud. and sparkly explosion one might imagine. This all occurs in broad daylight. As the burning warehouse showers the sky with every conceivable form of Fourth of July goodness and the area rumbles with the thunderous fury of a million loosed M-80s and thousands of firecracker bricks, there stands lieutenant Frank Drebin, addressing the quickly massing crowd of stunned, curious onlookers with a wonderfully deadpan, "Alright, move on. Nothing to see here. Please disperse. Nothing to see here...."

This is where we are.

We see the sky exploding. We feel the earth shaking. We stand in awe at what we witness unfolding before our eyes. Yet as the world burns around us, the Statist media and cultural elites tell us that, at the end of the day, it's really not such a big deal.

Nope, not at all. There's nothing to see here.

Our pursuit of unobstructed self-gratification has come to dictate nearly every facet of our lives, including our vision. As such, we've become more than willing to play along with those who would wave us past the smoldering carnage that is our cultural landscape, and on to the next shopping season, pennant race, or blockbuster flick.

All of a sudden, Lieutenant Drebin doesn't look so silly anymore. Not by a long shot. He seems quite inspired, actually. He's on to something with this whole "move on" thing. Just ask

Bill Clinton, James Carville, Al Gore, Hillary Clinton, or any other sexual-predator/sexual-predator-enabler prowling the political scene.

What the powerful have, everyman tends to want. The ability to pursue sexual pleasure without restriction or consequence is certainly no exception. If this pursuit requires the banishment of God and His laws from our minds, then so be it.

With Him out of the picture, everything becomes possible. Every fantasy, hope, and dream, no matter how bleak or bankrupt it may appear to some, becomes not only possible but worthy of pursuit to many. All of this occurs in an environment where there are no absolutes and there is no objective truth. Anything goes.

In strict sociological terms, this is known as "a problem." It's bad. *Really* bad.

Every impulse is indulged, every perversion is justified, and every inclination is validated at the altar of self-actualization. Anything that might impede or impair our ability to pursue any self-centered desire must be done away with immediately, if not sooner.

The first step that was required in the pursuit of this fantasy of a world without rules was the elimination of the real world's rule-maker.

To that end, we have killed God, or at least put Him as far out of our mind, both collectively and individually, as we can manage. What German philosopher Friedrich Nietzsche called our killing of God has served as an essential opening act—the prerequisite murder for an infinite onslaught to follow. In his *Parable of the Madman*, Nietzsche painted a picture of post-Christian culture's rise in the West:

> "Have you not heard of that madman who lit a lantern in the bright morning hours, ran to the market place, and cried incessantly: 'I seek God! I seek God!'—As many of those

who did not believe in God were standing around just then, he provoked much laughter. Has he got lost? asked one. Did he lose his way like a child? asked another. Or is he hiding? Is he afraid of us? Has he gone on a voyage? emigrated?— Thus they yelled and laughed.

The madman jumped into their midst and pierced them with his eyes. 'Whither is God?' he cried; 'I will tell you. *We have killed him*—you and I. All of us are his murderers.'"[22]

With the creator of life and purpose abandoned, humanity's value has been catastrophically compromised. All things have become possible.

At first this may seem to be great news: "All things have become possible." To the secular and depraved mind, it is wonderful news indeed.

In *The Voyage of the Dawn Treader*, C.S. Lewis provides some insight into the true nature of the unrestrained dreams of man. In this account, a vessel called the *Dawn Treader* encounters a stranger at sea. After the man is taken aboard, he frantically warns its crew of the nightmare that lies ahead:

'Fly! Fly! About with your ship and fly! Row, row, row for your lives away from this accursed shore.'

'Compose yourself,' said Reepicheep, 'and tell us what the danger is. We are not used to flying.'

The stranger started horribly at the voice of the Mouse, which he had not noticed before.

'Nevertheless, you will fly from here,' he gasped. 'This is the Island where Dreams come true.'

'That's the island I've been looking for this long time,' said one of the sailors. 'I reckon I'd find I was married to Nancy if we landed here.'

'And I'd find Tom alive again,' said another.

'Fools!' said the man, stamping his foot with rage. 'That is the sort of talk that brought me here, and I'd better have been drowned or never born. Do you hear what I say? This is where dreams—dreams, do you understand—come to life, come real. Not daydreams: dreams.'

There was about half a minute's silence and then, with a great clatter of armor, the whole crew were tumbling down the main hatch as quick as they could and flinging themselves on the oars to row as they had never rowed before; and Drinian was swinging round the tiller, and the boatswain was giving out the quickest stroke that had ever been heard at sea. For it had taken everyone just that half-minute to remember certain dreams they had had—dreams that make you afraid of going to sleep again—and to realize what it would mean to land on a country where dreams come true.[23]

The unrestrained dreams of the unregenerate man are dark and terrible things. Fallen man is no more aware of his inclination towards sin than a fish is aware of his inclination towards water. Sin and water are all that the two know; all that their natures can comprehend. As such, he believes that the complete removal of God and His imposed limitations will lead to a great and glorious destination.

This is the "secular heaven" that we hear so much about: A place where we have what we want and do what we want whenever we want, all without end. It is Utopia. Every pleasure is ours to experience; every limitation has been lifted. There is no God in this place and to fallen men in open rebellion against Him that is far and away the most appealing part of it all.

After all, only where there is no God can self be fully exalted, and the complete exaltation and indulgence of our precious selves is how we naturally tend to define the state of Heaven. Paul

Washer said it well when he observed, "Everybody wants to go to Heaven. They just don't want God to be there when they get there."

So it is that, in pursuit this secular Heaven where all of the dreams of fallen men come true, we have fled from God. We have put Him away so that "all things might become possible." As we have abandoned life's source, we have abandoned its sanctity.

Enter: The American Holocaust.

America's Holocaust of Convenience

You shall not murder.

EXODUS 20:13

"The Democratic Party strongly and unequivocally supports *Roe v. Wade* and a woman's right to choose a safe and legal abortion, regardless of ability to pay, and we oppose any and all efforts to weaken or undermine that right."

DEMOCRAT PARTY PLATFORM, 2008

Hitler's Holocaust: Roughly 6,000,000

America's Holocaust: Roughly 41,000,000

The sacred 'right' to murder innocent children at any time, in any place, for any reason (or no reason at all), even on the taxpayer's dime: *Priceless.*

By a factor of nearly seven, we have outdone Nazi Germany's most definitive act of evil.

Who said that the spirit of American excellence and accomplishment was dead? With the "progressive" left's embrace and advocacy of this new brand of American exceptionalism, our nation has again found itself on the cutting edge: We are cutting, slicing, sucking, and trashing our way straight to the top.

Hitler never came close to achieving the sort of society-wide autonomic support for the wholesale slaughter of innocents as that which has been attained in the modern United States of America.

Most impressively, we've managed to accomplish this without breaking stride or even a sweat. So in-sync with the holocaust mindset have we become that we are now able to murder or advocate murder on auto-pilot. Death has become our default setting. Allowing for the slaughter of innocents has become as autonomic a course of action as drawing breath and exhaling. The optional nature of innocent life's preservation has become one of our most cherished idols. It empowers us to live "our best life now" as few other idols can.

We literally flush our inconvenient newborns down the drain before prom night, giving more thought to how much better the dress will fit than we ever did to the chi-...*er*..."choice."

We massacre innocents by the millions with a nonchalance that would disturb the average psychopath. (Does that make us something akin to *exceptional* psychopaths? See? The New American Exceptionalism reveals itself once again!)

This is where completely liberated human desire leads. This is the hell at the end of our happy secular rainbow.

When one considers the carnage wrought by our collective decision to treat the preservation of innocent life as a mere *choice*, we are rightly inclined to wonder how many great men and women have been and will continue to be lost as a result of this intense downward shift in human valuation.

How many Einsteins, Edisons, Carvers, and Teslas have been murdered in the womb and lost to the sciences?

How many Tolkiens, Shakespeares, Hugos, and Lewises have been lost to the world of literature?

How many Jeffersons, Lincolns, Churchills, and Reagans have been prevented from ever taking to the political stage?

How many of them have been meticulously dismembered while alive or horribly burned to death in their mother's womb? How many of them have had most of their bodies birthed, only to have their heads intentionally punctured at the last moment so that their brain might be sucked from its skull and their little head imploded, all to technically qualify for disposal as an unborn choice?

Of course, in keeping with the spirit that would allow for innocent (from a human perspective) life's protection to become optional in the first place, we must understand that for every good or great person that has been lost to choice's blade, there have surely been more than a few "less desirables" who have been done in through the same wondrously liberating process.

Many a Michelangelo or Pasteur may indeed have been lost, but, in practice, the option to murder the innocent has surely also spared civilization the ravages of many a Margaret Sanger, Karl Marx, Michael Moore, and Milli Vanilli.

So see? It's not *all* bad.

The math of the matter seems to assure this much. In these instances, so the argument goes, we obviously owe a debt of gratitude to the new god of choice. But even in its use, such a defense only further damns the position promoted by "progressive" advocates of legal infanticide. Arguing over what the net gain or loss might be based upon guesses as to the ratio of Einsteins to Stalins included in the growing mountain of corpses made possible by the golden god of choice misses the point entirely, that point being: Whatever any of those murdered may have one day become had they been allowed to live, there is one thing that we can and do know with absolute certainty: *Each and every one of them was a completely innocent child at the time of their murder.*

And each and every child "chosen" to die today, tomorrow or next week is also, right now, a living, innocent little baby. This is what we know. These are who we *murder*. Thousands by the day...tens of thousands each and every week...hundreds of thousands annually.

The body-count climbs even more surely than the national debt. Murder factories operate near shopping malls and baseball diamonds, interfering with neither our admiration nor use of either one. Bumper stickers and t-shirts are crafted to proclaim fidelity to legalized infanticide, and they are worn with pride by millions.

It's enough to make a Josef Mengele say, "What are you people *thinking*?"

The answer, of course, is as simple as it is clear: We are thinking of **ourselves**.

We Did It Our Way

"The first effect of not believing in God is to believe in anything."

G.K. CHESTERTON

It's almost a sure-fire guarantee that whenever the topic of Nazis or Nazism is inserted into a conversation in contemporary America, those who have been educated by the state will, upon hearing the terms, make three powerful assumptions:

1. Nazism was *uniquely* evil.

2. Those advocating Nazism were *uniquely* evil.
3. As Nazism was a unique, clear and distinct evil, all advanced, enlightened, and civilized cultures are disinclined to its embrace. Neither Nazism nor anything closely related to it is likely to ever again attain prominence in such a culture.

Just like that, with the flick of a mental switch, most who would hear of Nazis and Nazism manage to instantly separate themselves from those systems of thought and the actions that follow. Nazis go straight into the "out there" category, for sure.

Yet when we carefully consider what we actually know of mid-twentieth-century German and contemporary American cultures, we find that there are more than a few intriguing and even disturbing similarities. If we persist in this uncomfortable examination, as truth seekers must, we are confronted by the likelihood that we are, as a whole, perhaps even more hardened and vile than our 1930s German counterparts.

In comparing the philosophies, inclinations, and sentiments of the general populations of Nazi Germany and the modern United States, we are well served to focus on four areas. While none of them will herein receive an exhaustive treatment, a great deal of exceptional academic work has been dedicated to detailed examinations of each issue and the overwhelming consensus in each area seems to strongly support the conclusions presented here. That said, the reader is strongly encouraged to seek out more comprehensive works on these subjects and test any contentions for themself. The four areas in question are:

1. The "death of God" concept as exhibited in each culture.
2. The impact of Darwinian thought on each culture.

3. The general knowledge of the populations with regard to their respective governments' pro-holocaust policies and procedures.
4. The purpose of said policies and procedures.

"God is Dead"

The fool says in his heart, "There is no God." They are corrupt, they do abominable deeds, there is none who does good.

PSALM 14:1

The "death of God" as a concept has already been examined here in some detail. The boisterous rant of Friedrich Nietzsche has echoed right on through the time of the Third Reich and onto the cover of *Time* in the United States. While much in the way of further elaboration on this subject is not necessary, one point worthy of emphasis is the fact that both the German culture of the mid-twentieth-century and the American culture of the early twenty-first each had entered into a post-Christian era.

While this shift was a relatively recent development by the time Hitler emerged from the political storm to claim his leadership role in Germany, the American culture of 2010 is far more advanced in its development of a formally post-Christian identity. America, by the most conservative of estimates, is at least a full generation into its overtly post-Christian era, and as such, we must note that the cultural landscape in the United States of 2010 is far more warm and friendly to the philosophies of Friedrich Nietzsche than was that of 1930s Germany.

The spiritual climate in '30s Germany, while troubled to be sure, was not in the advanced stage of decomposition that we see in the modern United States. Put another way, God is much closer to "dead" in contemporary American culture than He was in that of mid-twentieth-century Germany.

The Darwinian Fuel of Statism

"With savages, the weak in body or mind are soon eliminated; and those that survive commonly exhibit a vigorous state of health. We civilized men, on the other hand, do our utmost to check the process of elimination; we build asylums for the imbecile, the maimed, and the sick; we institute poor-laws; and our medical men exert their utmost skill to save the life of every one to the last moment. There is reason to believe that vaccination has preserved thousands, who from a weak constitution would formerly have succumbed to small-pox. Thus the weak members of civilized societies propagate their kind. No one who has attended to the breeding of domestic animals will doubt that this must be highly injurious to the race of man. It is surprising how soon a want of care, or care wrongly directed, leads to the degeneration of a domestic race; but excepting in the case of man himself, hardly any one is so ignorant as to allow his worst animals to breed."

CHARLES DARWIN, *THE DESCENT OF MAN* [25]

"Man must realize that a fundamental law of necessity reigns throughout the whole realm of Nature and that his existence is subject to the law of eternal struggle and strife...where the strong are always the masters of the weak and where those subject to such laws must obey them or be destroyed, one general law leading to the advancement of all organic beings...let the strongest live and the weakest die."[26]

ADOLF HITLER, *MEIN KAMPF*

Only Charlie Gibson could miss the connection between these two. Darwinian thought gripped and molded Hitler as it has the overwhelming majority of contemporary American culture. As with the "God is dead" phenomena, while both cultures under consideration have suffered mightily under the influence of Darwinism, it is modern day America that is far more advanced in the enshrinement and pursuit of its principles.

For decades, state controlled "education" systems have worked to methodically craft a Darwinian foundation upon which to reconstruct the nation. Such an entrenched, state-sanctioned system of overtly anti-Christian indoctrination simply was not in place for Adolf Hitler as it is for Barack Hussein Obama.

What Did We Know and When Did We Know It?

Do not enter the path of the wicked, and do not walk in the way of the evil.
Avoid it; do not go on it; turn away from it and pass on.

PROVERBS 4:14–15

Consider now a third vital aspect of Germany's and America's respective holocausts: The general knowledge of the population at the time of rampant, state-sanctioned murder. This much is painfully simple and clear: Nearly *every* American is aware of the hundreds of thousands of innocents massacred each year in their "land of the free and home of the brave." Moreover, many celebrate it. In fact, more people defend, advocate, and celebrate this evil in America than existed in the whole of Germany during Hitler's ascent and reign.

Yet how many of these American "progressives" would laugh out loud or roll their eyes at the mere suggestion that they were in any way whatsoever even remotely similar to the Hitlers, Mengeles, and Goebbles of humanity's past?

Those historical figures are relegated to a sort of dark myth status rather than treated as the case study in fallen humanity that they actually represent. They are imagined to be the monsters that enlightened, educated people simply *cannot* become. At least that's the party line of the humanist faithful.

With Nazis safely sequestered in the "out there" section, we've paved the way to ignore the many stunning similarities between the death embracing cultures of 1930s Germany and 2010 America. That's the idea, anyway—an idea that we will dismantle here.

While the overlapping entrenchment of the "God is dead" and social Darwinism philosophies are troubling, and the hyper-awareness of contemporary Americans with regard to their state's sanctioning of mass-murder must surely send a chill, it is our fourth area of consideration that is most disturbing in its revelation.

This final point of contemplation centers on the simplest of questions: *Why?*

Why do we murder?

Why do modern-day Americans so willingly and wantonly target for slaughter the most vulnerable and innocent among them?

Why We Murder

"Those who want to live, let them fight, and those who do not want to fight in this world of eternal struggle do not deserve to live."

ADOLF HITLER

"If we accept that a mother can kill even her own child, how can we tell other people to not kill each other? Any country that accepts abortion is not teaching its people to love, but to use any violence to get what they want."

MOTHER TERESA OF CALCUTTA

For Hitler and what can rightly be referred to as "his Germany," violence was deemed necessary for the survival of the people and their Fatherland. Warped, perverted, and evil though this philosophy certainly was, it was painted in colors of classic Darwinian struggle with nothing less profound than survival itself at stake.

While the Nazi propagandists successfully painted the supremely harsh treatment of "undesirables" as a vital home-front initiative in the battle for German survival, Americans need nothing so lofty or profound to engender support for mass murder of the most defenseless among them.

Where Germans were fueled by fear of encroaching Bolshevism and other perceived external threats to their nation's existence, Americans are inspired to murder by their fear of separation from

BMWs and loss of an easy route to a decent career path. The culture supporting the Third Reich was inspired to murder for a variety of wicked, vile reasons, but none so vulgar as that which motivates the vast majority of the American holocaust.

In America, we murder innocents primarily for *convenience*.

Ours is a most murderous form of narcissism, and this fact alone should inspire shame, horror, repentance, and more than a little hesitation in placing contemporary American culture above that of Hitler's Germany. We have become a vile and wicked people in our rejection of God and subsequent pursuit of unobstructed personal pleasure.

Painful though it will and should be, we must ponder and pray over these things. There is much to be learned by way of honest examination of these truths. In asking difficult questions and diligently seeking their answers, Common Believers will become equipped for the battle they are now called to wage.

So what are the fundamental differences between the cultures responsible for the production of the Third Reich in Germany and the emergence of the YES! WE! CAN! (insert whatever you like here) society in America? Could it be that the differences, while numerous, aren't really fundamental at all? Might we have much more in common than not where the essentials are concerned?

While there are a variety of periphery and even many substantial distinctions to be drawn between the cultures under consideration, it seems more than fair to say, assuming agreement on the four points just covered, that the cores—the philosophical foundations—employed by the two cultures are remarkably similar. This should come as no surprise from a biblical perspective.

Far from being *uniquely* evil, the Nazis of the past were anything but special in their inclinations. They were quite *typically* evil. Scripture provides the Common Believer with a great deal of invaluable insight as to the true nature of fallen man:

The heart is deceitful above all things, and desperately sick; who can understand it?

JEREMIAH 17:9

For out of the heart come evil thoughts, murder, adultery, sexual immorality, theft, false witness, slander.

MATTHEW 15:19

For as were the days of Noah, so will be the coming of the Son of Man.

MATTHEW 24:37

*The LORD saw that the wickedness of man was great in the earth, and that **every** intention of the thoughts of his heart was **only evil continually**.*

GENESIS 6:5 (bold emphasis added)

We see in this sampling of pertinent Scripture that the heart of fallen man is "deceitful above all things," "desperately sick," and the source of "evil thoughts, murder, adultery, sexual immorality, theft, false witness, slander." We are also presented with a description of what mankind was in the days of Noah and what he is to be before Christ's return. In the most damning and vivid terms possible, we learn that "every intention of the thoughts of his heart was only evil continually."

You won't find this stuff in a Joel Osteen "sermon."

Not exactly what you'd call a "pick-me-up" series of passages, is it? Then again, there's nothing pretty about the depraved state of fallen man and God has never demonstrated an interest in "lightening up" the presentation where this vital subject is concerned. No matter how much we like to think of ourselves as "basically good" and God as our hopeful, helpful, non-judgmental wannabe pal, the truth couldn't be farther from these concepts. Our Lord has given us the very dirty details for good reason. His sheep *will* hear and heed His call. In the process, they will be broken and conformed to His clearly expressed will.

This is where the Common Believer can find matchless beauty and hope amidst the storm that rages on the battlefields of the culture war. This is where we can take refuge even as we gain a deeper understanding of just how completely wretched we were before our Lord graciously brought us from spiritual death to life. This is where we can know that even as we fail daily, He is guiding us and we *will* ultimately be completely conformed to His will, however impossible such a goal may seem from our flawed and often struggling perspective.

Of course, if all of these "very dirty details" put you off, or if all of this "being broken" and "conformed to His clearly expressed will" stuff sounds completely unattractive to you, there's always *Blue Like Jazz*.

Or *Your Best Life Now*.

Or *The Shack*.

Or…well, you get the picture.

There are plenty of ego-stroking, self-esteem-building options out there for those of you "basically good" folks just looking for a non-judgmental buddy or "life coach."

For those sticking around and interested in confronting the decidedly uncomfortable yet critically important truth about our fallen nature, let's consider one more challenge as it relates to Nazism and the *typical* rebellious heart.

One of the basic concepts most closely associated with the Third Reich, Hitler, Nazism and Nazis is that of murder. They fit together like a clenched fist in a tight, black leather glove. In this association, we tend to understandably imagine that the heart of a Nazi was, in and of itself, somehow significantly more disposed to murder than that of the average man. And certainly *much* more inclined towards murder than *our own* hearts.

Yet Scripture paints a very different picture:

> *"You have heard that it was said to those of old, 'You shall not murder; and whoever murders will be liable to judgment.' But I say to you that everyone who is angry with his brother will be liable to judgment; whoever insults his brother will be liable to the council; and whoever says, 'You fool!' will be liable to the hell of fire."*

> MATTHEW 5:21–22

As we discussed in the last chapter, Jesus made it plain that one has committed the sin of adultery simply by *thinking* of it. In Matthew 5:21 and 22, He informs us of yet another aspect of the profound ugliness within each of us that we'd much rather pretend doesn't exist. He tells us that we who have been unjustly angry with or insulted a brother are "liable to judgment" as those who have committed the actual, physical act of murder.

You see, it is our *hearts* that murder first. Yours and mine. And often.

Fallen man perpetually seeks to murder truth and in so doing continually violates the laws of God. Accepting and understanding this critical fact of human nature is essential to spiritual and intellectual growth, and is therefore required for those who wish to make an impact for Christ in the culture war.

So it is that things like Nazism, its legendary holocaust or the "progressive" American pro-infanticide movement really must not come as a surprise to the Common Believer. They are each quite natural expressions of a fallen mankind in open rebellion against God.

As the song says, we were each a "wretch" in need of salvation and until that infinitely gracious regenerative act came our way, we were lost as lost could be. Hopefully this truth will take root in each of our minds, so that the next time we're tempted to look down our nose through history at "those evil Nazis," we will remember that every unregenerate heart is completely black and that *our* hearts—each and every one—were once in that state.

When we grasp this truth, we will find ourselves much more inclined toward *sympathetic* dealings with our adversaries when appropriate. We will also naturally have a much easier time seeing connections that we might otherwise have reflexively resisted or ignored.

With the *typical* evil of the individual Nazi heart understood, we will now examine one of the greatest cultural similarities between Nazi Germany and modern day America: Our professed allegiance to the god most responsible for our open, zealous pursuit of self-interest…the god of science.

Science: The Great Enabler

"Christ died so that we might live. Abortion kills so that someone might live differently."

JOHN PIPER

As we have noted, contemporary American culture has followed in the footsteps of 1930s Germany in its flight from (and desired murder of) God as well as in its embrace of Darwinian philosophies. The subsequent release of the human will from any external restraint has been the predictable and, for many, the *desired* result.

As Ivan Karamazov warned in *The Brothers Karamazov*, if God does not exist, then everything is permitted. Once the God of America's founding was left for dead, true liberty and freedom had to go with Him. In their place, we have the new American spirit of "Anything Goes." Where once we sought the will, wisdom, and forgiveness of God, we now seek comfort from a much friendlier and more accommodating source: The almighty scientist.

Science and its practitioners have become the predominant religion and clergy of post-Christian America. En route to achieving their goal of unquestioned religious supremacy, they've relentlessly assailed any and all would-be competitors for the throne of authority.

David Berlinski chronicles some of the more tragically comical aspects of this ongoing antagonism in *The Devil's Delusion*:

In 2007, a number of scientists gathered in a conference entitled 'Beyond Belief: Science, Religion, Reason, and Survival' in order to attack religious thought and congratulate one another on their fearlessness in so doing. The physicist Steven Weinberg delivered an address. As one of the authors of the theory of electroweak unification, the work for which he was awarded the Nobel Prize, he is a figure of great stature. 'Religion,' he affirmed, 'is an insult to human dignity. With or without it you would have good people doing good things and evil people doing evil things. *But for good people to do evil things, that takes religion'* (italics added).

In speaking thus, Weinberg was warmly applauded, not one member of his audience asking the question one might have thought pertinent: Just who has imposed on the suffering human race poison gas, barbed wire, high explosives, experiments in eugenics, the formula for Zyklon B, heavy artillery, pseudo-scientific justifications for mass murder, cluster bombs, attack submarines, napalm, intercontinental ballistic missiles, military space platforms, and nuclear weapons?

If memory serves, it was not the Vatican.[27]

The Science of Secular Sanctification

Every way of a man is right in his own eyes, but the LORD weighs the heart.

PROVERBS 21:2

"Do what thou wilt shall be the whole of the Law."

ALEISTER CROWLEY'S *BOOK OF THE LAW*

Be it stem cell research or cloning of another sort for another need, secular science has given its approval. Genetic manipulation and eugenics experimentation are presented as potential paths to human perfection that would be positively *sinful* to ignore. And that most sacred of rights in "progressive" America, the right to *choose* infanticide, has been pronounced a valid option by the white-coat wearing cultural clergy of our age. They have deemed nearly every available life-destroying option to be good, and we have accepted their proclamation with boundless enthusiasm.

This is the cover that we have long craved. Science and its revered practitioners have provided precisely the consolations and justifications that we covet. With this golden stamp of approval secured, we have been formally freed to pursue every selfish desire and sacrifice anyone or anything that might stand between what we are and what we wish to be.

Through the lens of Darwinian naturalism, the venerated Scientific Class has charted our course away from God and towards self. Sociologists have freed us from the burden of civility, biologists have freed us from the burden of humanity, and ethicists have freed us from the burden of morality.

We are completely free. All things have become possible. We have landed on the island where dreams come true.

Just as the intellectual elite of Nazi Germany so successfully charted a course to that fabled land the better part of a century ago, so too have the scientific saviors of contemporary American culture empowered us to charge toward that same humanistic paradise.

We're almost there. We've made great strides and the island's shores can be seen on the horizon.

At long last, we've finally begun to seriously address the "child problem" and while there's still a long way to go, much progress has been made since 1973. Roughly 41,000,000 dead bodies' worth of progress.

But what to do with the children who've been allowed to live? What's the proper course of action there? How do we assure that *they* will not interfere with *our* pursuit of self-actualization?

Do it for the Children

"Whoever receives one such child in my name receives me, but whoever causes one of these little ones who believe in me to sin, it would be better for him to have a great millstone fastened around his neck and to be drowned in the depth of the sea."

Jesus in Matthew 18:5–6

"I've got two daughters: nine years old and six years old. I am going to teach them first of all about values and morals. But if they make a mistake, I don't want them punished with a baby."

Barack Hussein Obama

With God removed as the first obstacle to our personal fulfillment, all restraint has been removed and the full wrath of selfish desire has been unleashed upon our own children—those that we chose to murder as well as most that we have allowed to live.

The problem is this: Children have for far too long gotten in the way of our hopes, dreams, aspirations, and goals. This is a new problem whose arrival coincides with a shift away from God-inspired, biblical hopes, dreams, aspirations, and goals.

As we have fled the dreams He would have us pursue, the subsequent reorganization of priorities has resulted in scores of shiny new goals and desires being placed between parents and their children.

Where once the thought of having *many* children was a treasured notion and comprised a launching point for countless hopes, dreams, aspirations and goals in the American Christian mind, contemporary Christianity has for the most part followed secular precedent in its embrace of a decidedly child-devaluing worldview and approach to life.

Children in American culture are often viewed as an obstacle to be overcome. They are a burden first and a blessing only if everything else plotted, planned, and hoped for in one's life is all properly arranged and in perfect position.

Lest we begin to feel that familiar urge to look down at the rest of the culture when considering this subject, we must accept that as Christians we have almost totally caved into this secular reprioritization of the child and family. After all, we want nice cars too. All-brick homes in cool subdivisions are a plus. Impressive "educations" are a must. And exotic vacations sure are nice…so we're in!

We've made the same sad trade-off as the rest of the world. We've bought the lie—hook, line and sinker.

Children: Those troublesome, inconvenient little burdens… whatever are we to do with 'em? Well, first off, we need to realize one simple thing: Children are a blessing. A great blessing. One of the greatest that can be known in this life.

Okay, you're probably with me so far, but the true test is yet to come, so brace yourself. Ready?

Try *this* one on: Children are a greater blessing than…nice cars. Even *luxury* cars.

Still there? Well howswabout this: Children are a *far greater* blessing than a high-quality home in a nice neighborhood, they are *much better* than a promising career path, and they are *infinitely more precious and valuable* than *any* formal education.

Have at least most secular standards of valuation been violated here? I sure hope so.

From a biblically submissive perspective, children are simply on a separate plane of valuation when compared with any of these mere *things*. In each and every case, it's not even close. At least it shouldn't be.

Yet nearly all of us have fallen into a secular web of radically distorted priorities and valuations that paints homes, cars, vacations, and digital cable packages as high priority items and things like Christ-centered education and hands-on parenting for children as extravagant options. We rush for the biggest high-def screen we can fit into our living room but balk at the "cost" of arranging for a real live parent to actually stay home and raise their child.

While American Christendom has been lulled into its slow dance with secular standards of success, there are others who have maintained at least *something* of a proper valuation of children and family. And there is one particular child-appreciating group that God may soon employ for the purpose of disciplining His wayward sheep.

As we dialogue, debate, and contemplate the fate of our nation and the proper role of family in our increasingly self-centered lives, we are well served to note one critical fact: Islam doesn't view children this way at all.

Three Converging Evils

Three great evils have converged upon this issue of life's sanctity: The Third Reich of Nazi Germany, the rising tide of Islamic fundamentalism, and contemporary American popular culture.

One is a great evil from the past. Another looms ominously on the horizon. The third is positioned between the other two, having succumbed to virtually every foundational perversion of the first in a sort of suicidal surrender to the second.

Twenty-first century America has embraced virtually every cornerstone concept that fueled the ascent and reign of the Third Reich. Darwinian thought dominates the landscape here as it did there, and the death of God, so loudly proclaimed in earlier times by German philosopher Friedrich Nietzsche, has since echoed and taken root throughout the fruited plain and from sea to shining sea, just as it did in the Fatherland.

As America and the nations of Europe continue on a post-Christian course largely defined by a hyper-relativistic brand of secular humanism, an Islamic tide builds, increasing in mass and vigor. This threat gathers and grows with patient dedication and determination as the God-less West begins to shrivel and fade.

In what may well prove to be one of the greatest of unintended consequences in all of human history, the post-Christian West's culture of death is poised to propel Islam to global domination.

With God dead in our eyes, we've become capable of *anything*.

This is about to cost us *everything*.

Islam's Inheritance of the Earth

The global Muslim population stands at 1.57 billion, meaning that nearly 1 in 4 people in the world practice Islam, according to a report billed as the most comprehensive of its kind.

The Pew Forum on Religion and Public Life report provides a precise number for a population whose size has long has been subject to guesswork, with estimates ranging anywhere from 1 billion to 1.8 billion.

...Germany has more Muslims than Lebanon, China has more Muslims than Syria, Russia has more Muslims than Jordan and Libya combined, and Ethiopia has nearly as many Muslims as Afghanistan.

ASSOCIATED PRESS RELEASE, 2009[28]

As post-Christian European nations suffer from alarming and largely philosophically self-imposed declines in fertility rates, Islamic European populations surge. This is perhaps the most startling example of a global trend that will, barring a dramatic shift in the near future, propel Islam to dominance throughout Western Europe.

No war necessary. Shots need not be fired.

By simply *choosing* the devaluation of children, cultures condemn themselves to death. Other civilizations, in placing a higher value on the child, position themselves well to literally inherit the earth.

Germany, France, and the United Kingdom will simply be inherited by Islam over the next 40–60 years. Apparently, Muslims living in those nations value children more than material possessions or worldly badges of success and honor. They actually seem to appreciate large families as blessings.

Already we see radical transformation sweeping through these lands, and as the population swing intensifies, the changes will naturally magnify at an exponential rate. The Europe that we know today will simply cease to exist. It will be gone forever, lost to the implementation of a suicidal self-centeredness that found its ultimate expression in the shrinking, and eventually dying, "Christian" family. Europe will become, quite naturally, a continent of Islamic states.

We have fallen far. The situation is bleak. Our murderous narcissism has a long list of casualties:

It has first sought the death of God.

It has subsequently attained the death of truth.

It has eviscerated the biblical concept of family.

It has radically perverted the proper valuation of *things*, placing oh-so many of them above the value of a child.

It has inspired the murder of millions upon millions of innocents, mostly in the name of *convenience*.

And now, it is on course to literally take the life of western civilization. Only a miraculous turn can prevent this outcome. Only a return to God's perfect Word can make that miracle possible.

Celebrating Life in a Culture of Death

"The only things we can keep are the things we freely give to God. What we try to keep for ourselves is just what we are sure to lose."

C.S. Lewis

"Whoever finds his life will lose it, and whoever loses his life for my sake will find it."

Matthew 10:39

So here we are, living and participating in a culture that has sought the death of God, murdered truth, waged war on the biblical family, fundamentally perverted the value of *all* things, and consequentially managed to reap scores of apocalyptic consequences, including the murder of tens upon tens of millions of innocent little children for the sake of nothing more than *convenience*. Thus, we have catapulted our "civilization" well beyond that of Nazi Germany on the bad-for-humanity scale.

Even worse, much of professing American Christendom has taken the plunge right along with the rest, far more concerned with attaining relevance in the eyes of God-haters than obedience in the eyes of the God it claims to serve.

Surely all is then lost, no?

No!

While some good old-fashioned shame—*deep shame*—is entirely appropriate here, hopelessness is not. Though we may have done everything within our power to mock God in the process of destroying a once great nation, we may be eternally thankful that He has not chosen to return the favor. Instead, He is preparing His people for a great work.

Fortunately, though not surprisingly, the perfect Word of God has much to say on the subject of narcissism, by way of both description and prescription. Our Lord has given us great clarity as to the nature of narcissism and its antidote. As we *acknowledge* and *apply* His revelation to us in this area, we will witness the very miracle necessary for the restoration of a civilization as vile as that which we have crafted.

To that end, there are three things that we should acknowledge with regard to narcissism:

Narcissism is *pervasive*—it colors every thought and action.
Narcissism is an expression of *pride*.
Narcissism in practice always brings *separation* from God.

These are simple truths. They are also profound in their value as we go about formulating a biblical plan for culture warfare. Let's take a moment to flesh out each of these three points.

The All-Corrupting Power of Self-Adoration

"God made man in his own image and man returned the compliment."

BLAISE PASCAL

Unlike more specified areas of life, such as sexuality covered in the last chapter or economics to come in the next, narcissism is an umbrella under which all areas of human thought and activity fall.

It is a state of mind, a way of thinking, and a state of being. Recognition of this is critical so that we might appropriately apply solutions in as comprehensive a manner as the affliction requires.

We cannot successfully address narcissism by focusing on any single area of life. To solve this problem we must recognize that it permeates all of our being and act accordingly.

Pride: Every Sin's Gateway

"Pride leads to every other vice: it is the complete anti-God state of mind."

C.S. Lewis

Pride goes before destruction, and a haughty spirit before a fall.

Proverbs 16:18

Narcissism is the natural expression of pride. Pride is the gateway through which all other sin enters.

Pride is not imposed from without; it is born from within our naturally rebellious hearts. While the anti-Christian culture in which we live certainly does everything in its power to promote self-absorption and self-glorification, it does so in harmony with our natural inclinations.

So we find two warnings here: First, every sin finds access to our lives through a narcissistic way of life, and second, as it is our fallen nature to embrace such a fundamentally rebellious spirit, we must remain vigilant at all times and in all areas of life.

The Price of Opening the Gateway to Sin is Death

For the wages of sin is death, but the free gift of God is eternal life in Christ Jesus our Lord.

ROMANS 6:23

The goal of a culture at war with Christ is to keep as many as possible from Him and His truth. As one inescapable consequence of narcissism in practice is the separation of the practitioner from God, it is only natural that our culture would encourage and nurture narcissism at every opportunity.

The price of sin separation from God and separation from God brings death. Death as an individual. Death as a community. Death as a culture, a nation, and a civilization. Even death as a church.

So we see that the stakes could not be higher when we speak of narcissism's threat. This we must *never* forget.

With the nature of narcissism better understood, we should now have a much easier time understanding how and why it is that America finds herself in this present cultural darkness. We should also be much better equipped to chart a course from that darkness and back into the light.

There are three things that we can do to apply the truths of Scripture to the problem of narcissism so that we might see the miracle we all long for finally come to the American culture:

We must *distinguish* between God-centered pride and false pride, which inspires narcissism.

We must give thought to and *test all things*, so that we might resist our natural narcissistic inclinations.

We must actively *celebrate life* amidst this culture of death. Every opportunity to do so must be seized.

Perfect Pride

In Christ Jesus, then, I have reason to be proud of my work for God.

ROMANS 15:17

Do all things without grumbling or questioning, that you may be blameless and innocent, children of God without blemish in the midst of a crooked and twisted generation, among whom you shine as lights in the world, holding fast to the word of life, so that in the day of Christ I may be proud that I did not run in vain or labor in vain.

PHILIPPIANS 2:14–16

As with every good thing God provides, it is our nature to screw it up in the most profound manner imaginable. Pride is no exception to this.

So universally condemned has the term become within Christian circles that it may be surprising to some readers that there is even such a thing as good and proper pride. But there is such a thing, nonetheless.

Pride in God and pride in what God has done for and through us as Common Believers is a beautiful thing and must not be allowed to somehow slip from the believer's mind due to our having perverted it so terribly. Just as sex and sexuality are awe-inspiring creations of a perfect, loving God for the benefit of His people, so too is proper pride. The fact of their perversion by many does nothing to minimize the magnificence of what they can be to a

Common Believer when a biblically submissive and life liberating perspective is embraced.

Any pride that exalts man *in even the slightest sense* is vile and leads to destruction.

Any pride that gives *all* glory to God is proper and beautiful.

While we must be vigilant in seeking to identify, separate, and eliminate every perverted expression of pride, we must just as diligently take *perfect* pride in our Lord at every opportunity.

Test All Things

...but test everything; hold fast what is good.

1 THESSALONIANS 5:21

With the pervasiveness of our narcissistic tendency and the price of perverted pride in mind, we face quite a challenge. That challenge, while difficult, is essential, and while it may even seem impossible when we first lay our mind on it, we can know with absolute certainty that the Lord who has called us to this task has just as clearly equipped us for success in its undertaking.

The challenge is: We must test all things. Every thought and every action. Every philosophy and every concept must be filtered. Every joke and habit must be evaluated. Every nook, cranny, corner and cobweb in our life falls under this process of sanctification.

Tall order, I know.

Just typing those words made me cringe a bit at the sheer amount of sanctification left to be done in my life, yet I know that, "He who began a good work will bring it to completion." Sometimes that truth is all that I have to cling to, but it is enough. Every Common Believer can know with absolute certainty that the Lord who has claimed them *will* finish the good work that He has started.

As this process of sanctification progresses, our testing of things will become easier—more natural—and the change in our lives will become apparent. God will be glorified and we will benefit beyond measure.

The closer we grow to Him, the more we will shine in this dark and dying world. The closer we grow to Him, the more we will celebrate life in this culture of death.

Our Celebration of God's Majesty in Creation

"The Gospel is the news that Jesus Christ, the Righteous One, died for our sins and rose again, eternally triumphant over all his enemies, so that there is now no condemnation for those who believe, but only everlasting joy. God is most glorified in us when we are most satisfied in Him. The essence of faith is being satisfied with all that God is for us in Jesus."

JOHN PIPER

With sinful pride identified and tackled, narcissism will fade as our dominant natural way of being and we will finally find ourselves capable of experiencing the matchless beauty of God's blessings. We will celebrate life as never before. And such a celebration is simply beyond the grasp of any non-believer. The fallen, unregenerate man cannot know these joys. The pagan knows *nothing* of the full power and beauty of experience made possible through submission to Christ. We do.

When we submit to Him, we will know peace, joy and fulfillment the likes of which cannot take flight under the impossible weight of narcissistic pride.

In our submission to His truth, we will have more children and murder none. We will adopt, encourage, nurture, and teach in ways and at levels long forgotten in most of this land. We will live, love, and shine as never before. Only then will we have a culture that is vibrant, alive, and able to stand against the coming Islamic tide.

Our Lord specializes in miracles such as these. They are His currency. As for the currency of man, in its perversion we find another series of challenges to God's plan for mankind. This will be our next subject of consideration.

12

On Progressive Marxism
and the Plunge into Socio-Economic

Oblivion

The Common Believer's Defense of Individuality,
Liberty...and Math

*The rich rules over the poor, and the borrower is the slave of
the lender*

PROVERBS 22:7

*Owe no one anything, except to love each other, for the one
who loves another has fulfilled the law.*

ROMANS 13:8

"I know that the status quo is simply not acceptable. It's totally unacceptable and it's completely unsustainable…We're going bankrupt as a nation. Now, people when I say that look at me and say, 'What are you talking about, Joe? You're telling me we have to go spend money to keep from going bankrupt?' The answer is yes, that's what I'm telling you."

These are the words of Joe Biden, Vice President of the United States of America as delivered in July of 2009 to an AARP town hall meeting held to discuss the Democrat Party's plan to nationalize the country's health care system. This was the defense offered on behalf of a radical expansion of government in the midst of an economic meltdown unparalleled in the post-Great Depression history of the nation and on the heels of the passage of an economic stimulus package widely known as "the trillion dollar mulligan."

The formula was simple and clear: Mountainous Debt + "Go Spend Money" = Prevention of Bankruptcy.

Do *not* try this at home.

Then again, this is nothing new. The vast majority of policies and programs advocated by those shaping the modern American government and economy almost never translate into an improved ability to survive, much less thrive. In the words of Joe Biden, we see only the latest installment of open confirmation that the once great American experience has become completely detached from reality.

In recent decades, socialism has surged through the nation's bloodstream in each and every sphere of American life. The political realm has long been conquered territory of Marxist-minded progressives, operating under their imposed rules and principles. Even "conservative" politicians have, more often than not, found the lure of power resulting from the expansion of government to be irresistible. Other conservatives—those who actually manage to remain loyal to their professed values—find some sort of compromise with the overwhelming majority of "progressives" in Washington to be a nearly inescapable requirement of securing even meager conservative successes in any area covered under the political umbrella.

Ronald Reagan is an excellent example of this. While his tax cuts rescued the economy and radically increased the amount of revenue generated for the federal government (yes, that's right: huge tax rate cuts actually inspired a gigantic *increase* in realized income for Washington), the "progressive" dominated congress that the nation had saddled itself with in the 1980s managed to increase spending at an even greater clip.

For well over a generation, ours has been a government increasingly committed to the cause of socialism for the sake of "progress." FDR kicked things into high gear in the '30s and it's been an almost entirely downhill ride since. From that point forward, government became the default first answer to every problem. America has never recovered from this conscious surrender of its founding ideals and principles.

Today, progressives from every sphere often barely seek to conceal their overtly Marxist economic and social philosophies. While most of us are all too familiar with the primarily political advocates of Red power, we do well to acknowledge that Marxism has found formidable, if ironic, representation within the mainstream of American *religious* thought. And this is not a new thing. It's all a part of the ongoing assault upon American culture and biblical truth.

The Rob Baal and Donald Miller socialist gospel types are nothing new to America or the professing church of Christ. They're just the latest retreads to come off the heresy recycling line.

One noteworthy forerunner of brothers Rob and Don was a guy named Jim.

Jonesing for Progress

"Let me present to you what you should see every day when you look in the mirror in the early morning hours...Let me present to you a combination of Martin King, Angela Davis, Albert Einstein...Chairman Mao."

WILLIE BROWN, WELL KNOWN
CONTEMPORARY PROGRESSIVE DEMOCRAT
PARTY POLITICIAN AND ADVOCATE, IN HIS
INTRODUCTION OF THE REVEREND JIM JONES

"I represent divine principles: Total equality, a society where people own all things in common, where there is no rich or poor...wherever there's people struggling for justice and righteousness, there I am, and there I am involved!"

REVEREND JIM JONES

Meet Jim.

Jim Jones.

Reverend Jim Jones.

Famed progressive Democrat activist Reverend Jim Jones, to be painfully precise.

You may remember Reverend Jim from such hits as *I'll Have Sex with Anybody, Methodist? Communist? It's All the Same to Me*, and *Kool-Aid-Kegger at Jonestown* (one night only).

I know, I know, with a resume like that, this guy sure seems well positioned for a successful national run as a modern day Democrat, but that Jonestown kegger masterpiece at the end there mercifully nipped Reverend Jones' political career in the bud back in '78.

While the mass-suicide orchestrated by Reverend Jim may have brought his progressive political career to an abrupt close, his socio-political beliefs continue to impact our world from beyond the grave. Kind of like any Democrat buried near Chicago.

Jim had views on religion, spirituality, social justice, and economics that were strikingly similar to many of those often expressed by the likes of Rob Baal, Donald Miller, Chairman Mao, and Barrack Obama.

In *How the Millennium Comes Violently: From Jonestown to Heaven's Gate*, Catherine Wessinger puts a fine point on Jones' religious cover for his Marxist views and goals: "While Jones always spoke of the social gospel's virtues, before the late 1960s Jones chose to conceal that his gospel was actually communism. By the late 1960s, Jones began at least partially openly revealing in Temple sermons his 'Apostolic Socialism' concept."

"Social gospel"…now there's a term to look for. It tends to be a favored expression of those seeking to advance the gospel *of* socialism through the use of traditional Christian terminology. Social, group and communal fixations are natural markers of this worldview.

Marceline, Jones' wife, described in a *New York Times* interview how Jim had realized that the best way to achieve Marxist social change in America would be to introduce it into the national bloodstream and consciousness through the use of religion. Marceline explained that, "Jim used religion to try to get some people out of the opiate of religion," and had slammed the Bible on the table yelling, "I've got to destroy this paper idol!"

In an ongoing effort to advance the cause of his Apostolic Socialism, the good Reverend Jim would preach the most inspirational of proclamations, including: "If you're born in capitalist America, racist America, fascist America, then you're born in sin. But if you're born in socialism, you're not born in sin."

Seems simple enough. Easy to follow. As the 1970s rolled on, Reverend Jim wasn't exactly hiding his views anymore. At this point, it would be inconceivable for any informed biblical Christian to describe Jones as anything better than an open enemy of Christ; a God-hater.

So we have a pretty good sense of what Reverend Jim is all about, right? Knowing these things, is it really any surprise that this very Reverend was the good Democrat progressive featured at a 1976 gathering of political progressives in California. Willie Brown served as master of ceremonies at the dinner and fawned over Reverend Jim during his introduction of the progressive pastor, describing him as "a combination of Martin [Luther] King, Angela Davis, Albert Einstein. . . Chairman Mao."

The grand event was attended by Governor Jerry Brown, Lieutenant Governor Mervyn Dymally, and other progressive luminaries.

It's important to emphasize that Jones' popularity and celebration within Democrat Party ranks was not in spite of his fundamentally anti-Christian and anti-American views. These views were anything but hidden; they were aired loudly and proudly at almost every opportunity. Reverend Jim's popularity and power within the progressive movement were a *result* of his clearly stated and firmly held beliefs. The good Reverend Jim Jones, with his Christ-hating, Marx-adoring worldview openly on display for the world to see and hear, was a very welcome and important contributor to the California Democrat Party political machine of the 1970s.

In many ways, Reverend Jim Jones was the quintessential progressive.

Suicide by Progress...It's not just for Guyana Anymore

"There's only one hope of glory...That's within you! Nobody's gonna come down out of the sky! There's no heaven up there...we'll have to make heaven down here!"

REVEREND JIM JONES

"During my 2004 presidential campaign, I was fond of saying that it was high time for the Christian right to meet the right Christians."

REVEREND AL SHARPTON

Surely, from the Reverend Al Sharpton's perspective, Rob Baal, Donald Miller, and Brian McLaren are the "right" sorts of Christians, and, as we've already discussed, Rob, Don, Brian & Co. (the "Co." is for "Commune"; *not* "Company") are all about the business of spreading the good word of the "new reformation" throughout the professing church of Christ in America. And, as we've also covered, they've been enthusiastically welcomed to do so. So out went the Gospel of Christ, and in came the gospel of socialism.

In *Blue Like Jazz*, Don tells us how Rick, a friend and mentor of his, "does not have much tolerance for people living alone." (What? A progressive embracing intolerance? Hmmm...) Consequently, Rick wanted Don to live in "community" with others. Miller goes on to flesh this progressive inclination towards the communal ideal out a bit:

He's like Bill Clinton in that he feels everyone's pain. If Rick thinks somebody is lonely, he can't sleep at night. He wants us all to live with each other and play nice so he can get some rest. . . I didn't know what to think about the idea of living in community at first. I had lived on my own for about six years, and the idea of moving in with a bunch of slobs didn't appeal to me. Living in community sounded so, um, odd. Cults do that sort of thing, you know. First you live in community, and then you drink punch and die.[29]

Ah, good ol' progressive Reverend Jim...gone, but not forgotten. Eventually, Don yielded to Rick's promotion of communal living and moved in with a cast of characters that he came to treasure. Among them was "Andrew the Protester," an activist who is "the tall, good-looking one with dark hair and the beard, who looks like a young Fidel Castro." (No, I did not make that last part up.) Andrew was "always talking about how outrageous the Republicans are or how wrong it is to eat beef." Andrew was a communist (kind of an anti-climactic revelation at this point, I know).

Another communal crewmate who made an impression was Simon, the "deeply spiritual" Irish "womanizer." Yes, that was *deeply spiritual* and *womanizer*. Isn't that just precious?

Simon was "always heading down to Kell's for a pint with the lads or to the church to pray and ask God's forgiveness for his detestable sins." Simon was in Portland, site of this six-man commune, "specifically to study our church" so that he might "go back to the homeland" and start a revival.

I have made none of this up. I promise. I really do. These are the folks that Donald Miller lauds in *Blue Like Jazz*. The entire book is sprinkled with overtly anti-Christian and pro-Marxist sentiment. Andrew the Communist would never protest *this* stuff.

Things like communal living, hating Republicans, and exalting Communists are all natural consequences of the progressive religious worldview. This system's counterfeit social gospel centers on the pointedly unbiblical notion of bringing heaven to earth, right here and right now. You might call this heaven a "worker's paradise"…and many have.

Remember the good Reverend Jim? He had a lot to say about this essential component of the progressive religious/political system and its gospel of socialism. One Reverend Jim quote posted earlier bears repeating here: "There's only one hope of glory…That's within you! Nobody's gonna come down out of the sky! There's no heaven up there…*we'll have to make heaven down here!*"

Over thirty years later, the same tired old vulgarity that spewed forth from the mouth of the Guyana Massacre Mastermind is now gurgling from the giggling lips of one Rob Baal. Check this out: "For Jesus, this new kind of life in him is not about escaping this world but about making it a better place, here and now. The goal for Jesus isn't to get into heaven. *The goal is to get heaven here.*"

Can a dead progressive Reverend still sue over plagiarism the way a dead Democrat can still vote in Chicago? Whatever the answer, the above is a representative sample of the painting over of biblical Christianity undertaken in Baal's *Velvet Elvis: Repainting the Christian Faith.*

Three decades after the great Jonestown Kool-Aid Kegger, these predictable tools of ancient delusion are still serving up the same old steaming pile of…*progress.*

And it sells!

Only in Amerika.

The Progressive War on Private Property and Individuality

"You shall not covet your neighbor's house; you shall not covet your neighbor's wife, or his male servant, or his female servant, or his ox, or his donkey, or anything that is your neighbor's."

EXODUS 20:17

"Nevertheless, in the most advanced countries, the following will be pretty generally applicable.
1. **Abolition of property in land** and application of all rents of land to public purposes.
2. A heavy **progressive** or graduated income tax.
3. **Abolition of all rights of inheritance.**
4. **Confiscation of the property** of all emigrants and rebels."

KARL MARX & FRIEDRICH ENGELS,
THE COMMUNIST MANIFESTO (Bold emphasis mine.)

Much of progressive Christianity's energy is spent trying to transform the Jesus of Scripture into something other than a God who authors, defends, and promotes the concepts of individuality and private property all while making it plain that His kingdom "is not of this world" and that Heaven is a place distinct from this fallen earth. With every twist, tweak and spin, they aim to remold the biblical Jesus into a communistically inclined social movement leader who frowns upon the notions of individuality and private property while advancing the cause of a kingdom to be realized right here and right now on this very earth.

This progressive religious movement is a vital cog in the greater machine actively seeking to fundamentally reshape America and destroy biblical Christianity.

Karl Marx, Chairman Mao, Fidel Castro…Jimmy Carter, Barack Obama, Jesse Jackson…Rob Baal, Jim Jones, Don Miller, Jeremiah Wright, Brian McLaren….All of these fine past and present progressives, according to one of their own—a very prominent one of their own—owe a monstrous debt of gratitude to one particular Bible character. According to one Saul Alinsky, the original progressive was none other than Lucifer.

The Devil's Kind of Progress

"Lest we forget at least an over-the-shoulder acknowledgment to the very first radical: from all our legends, mythology, and history…the first radical known to man who rebelled against the establishment and did it so effectively that he at least won his own kingdom—Lucifer."

SAUL ALINSKY'S OPENING PAGE DEDICATION
TO HIS *RULES FOR RADICALS—A PRAGMATIC
PRIMER FOR REALISTIC RADICALS*

Whoever makes a practice of sinning is of the devil, for the devil has been sinning from the beginning. The reason the Son of God appeared was to destroy the works of the devil.

1 JOHN 3:8 (ESV)

Prayerfully consider the following: Saul Alinsky can dedicate his most famous and influential work *to Lucifer by name*, Barack Hussein Obama can openly and actively embrace this man and his satanically inspired vision in innumerable ways and on innumerable occasions, Hillary Rodham Clinton can similarly coddle and adore the ideology and vision of the man, and then, knowing this, millions upon millions of professing Christians can somehow, some way, loudly, proudly and with boundless enthusiasm go to the polls in support of a Democrat Party led by people clearly seeking to lead the United States of America *from* the God of Scripture and *toward* the one to whom Alinsky dedicated his *Rules for Radicals*.

We have definitely arrived at a red alert moment in American history.

Just as we witness the blending of Marxist economic and social concepts into progressive religious presentations, so, too, do we have no trouble finding evidence that Marxism, in practice, actively seeks, by necessity, to radically impact and reshape the constructs of family and religion.

One of the greatest and most destructive myths permeating our age is that the realms of politics and religion are most accurately viewed and treated as separate and distinct entities. Our unconscious acceptance of this lie has rendered us nearly defenseless. With our shields lowered and our eyes averted in denial of the obviously coordinated efforts of political and religious progressive movements working all around us, we are left twiddling our thumbs as the gospel of socialism advances on every front.

Ironically, the same folks who actively seek to obliterate the biblical and American notions of individual liberty are simultaneously scurrying about in a constant effort to convince anyone who will listen that certain vital areas of life can somehow be sequestered and treated individually without fear or concern for how changes to one sphere of life might affect another. It should come as no surprise that this lie has been deliberately perpetuated by the very Marxists who seek to advance a monolithic agenda that covers each and every sphere of human existence.

Lying, after all, is what they do.

(Another) Red Alert

"Political ideology is really an outgrowth of our religious beliefs. You can't separate what a person believes from how a person will govern."

VODDIE BAUCHAM

"A Marxist begins with his prime truth that all evils are caused by the exploitation of the proletariat by the capitalists. From this he logically proceeds to the revolution to end capitalism, then into the third stage of reorganization into a new social order of the dictatorship of the proletariat, and finally the last stage—the political paradise of communism."

SAUL ALINSKY

In *Liberty and Tyranny: A Conservative Manifesto*, Mark Levin puts a fine point on the friction that has always existed between Marxism-inspired progressive Statism and traditional American free-market capitalism:

The Marxist class-struggle formulation, which pits the proletariat ("working class") against the bourgeoisie ("wealthy merchant class"), still serves as the principal theoretical and rhetorical justification for the Statist's assault on the free market. But it is an anathema to the free market in that the individual has unto himself the power to make of himself what he chooses. There is no static class structure layered atop the free market. The free market is a mutable, dynamic, and vibrant system of individual interaction that engages all aspects of the human character. For this reason, the Conservative believes the free market is a vital bulwark against statism. And it would appear the Statist agrees, for he is relentless in his assault on it. Indeed, the Statist's rejection of the Constitution's limits on federal power is justified primarily, albeit not exclusively, on material grounds. In the name of "economic justice" and "equality" the Statist creates the perception of class struggle through a variety of inventions, including the "progressive" income tax."[30]

In order to advance the progressive social and economic agendas, much more than economic and broad, general social programs must be changed. As we will see, the Communist revolution of the "new reformers" aims to fundamentally reshape each and every institution, relationship and concept associated with the human experience.

Beginning, of course, with your family.

It Takes a Village Idiot

Abolition of the family! Even the most radical flare up at this infamous proposal of the Communists. On what foundation is the present family, the bourgeois family, based? On capital, on private gain...

But, you will say, we destroy the most hallowed of relations, when we replace home education by social...

The bourgeois claptrap about the family and education, about the hallowed correlation of parent and child, becomes all the more disgusting, the more, by the action of modern industry, all family ties among the proletarians are torn asunder, and their children transformed into simple articles of commerce and instruments of labour.

> KARL MARX AND FRIEDRICH
> ENGELS, THE COMMUNIST
> MANIFESTO[31]

"With rare exceptions, our activists and radicals are products of and rebels against our middle-class society....Our rebels have contemptuously rejected the values and way of life of the middle class."

> SAUL ALINSKY

A quest for the source material at the root of progressive liberal ideology can lead to many places in many times, but for the purposes of identifying and understanding the formative philosophies that gave birth to the particular ideology driving the progressive movement in modern day America, there is one contributing philosophy that towers above all others. While in the Ten Commandments we find ten problems for the contemporary progressive movement to overcome, we find, at the very least, a much more philosophically sympathetic set of ideals and principles in the Ten Planks of Communism as defined by Marx and Engels in *The Communist Manifesto* and presented here for our consideration:

1. Abolition of private property and the application of all rent to public purpose.
2. A heavy progressive or graduated income tax.
3. Abolition of all rights of inheritance.
4. Confiscation of the property of all emigrants and rebels.
5. Centralization of credit in the hands of the state, by means of a national bank with state capital and an exclusive monopoly.
6. Centralization of the means of communication and transportation in the hands of the State.
7. Extension of factories and instruments of production owned by the State, the bringing into cultivation of waste lands, and the improvement of the soil generally in accordance with a common plan.
8. Equal liability of all to labor. Establishment of Industrial armies, especially for agriculture.
9. Combination of agriculture with manufacturing industries; gradual abolition of the distinction between town and country by a more equable distribution of the population over the country.
10. Free education for all children in government schools. Abolition of children's factory labor in its present form. Combination of education with industrial production.

At the heart of *The Communist Manifesto*, we are offered these ten prescribed steps towards the destruction of a free enterprise system so that it might be replaced by a structure built upon an omnipotent government, thereby bringing about a Communist socialist state. Now before anyone from any place on the political spectrum starts to get all riled up at the mere suggestion of such a thing as this, please just sit back, take a deep breath, simmer down and remember that there really is no need to take any of this too seriously.

Let not your heart be troubled. There's no need to be upset at any of this. There's no good reason for elevated blood pressure, high anxiety, or panic attacks. There's no need to worry at all because, you see...*there are no Communists*.

Werewolves and Vampires and Commies, Oh My!

Be sober-minded; be watchful. Your adversary the devil prowls around like a roaring lion, seeking someone to devour.

1 PETER 5:8

"How do you tell a communist? Well, it's someone who reads Marx and Lenin. And how do you tell an anti-communist? It's someone who understands Marx and Lenin."

RONALD REAGAN

Just as the average leader of the progressive political movement likes to pretend that the devil does not actually exist (unless they're in the process of accurately dedicating their seminal literary work, of course), so, too, does the garden variety progressive activist like to play with the notion that, like werewolves, vampires and middle-class tax cuts from Democrat Presidents, communists simply do not exist. They're a work of fiction.

Use the words "communist," "socialist," or "liberal" in the presence of an American communist, socialist or liberal and you will elicit a response including any or all of the following:

1. A dismissive smirk.
2. An incredulous roll of the eyes.
3. A wonderfully nervous giggle or laugh.
4. An angry demand to "see your papers."

Okay, that last one is at least weeks away from reality, but the first three most definitely apply right now in today's America.

One of the most adorable attributes of the leadership and activist base of the contemporary progressive movement is that they have an awe-inspiringly powerful dedication to the ongoing creation and preservation of their precious land of make-believe. The bubble world pseudo-reality in which they live has become so completely severed from objective truth that they have now convinced themselves that they actually have the power to ignore something—*anything*—out of existence.

Think of this as the Osteen/Hinn/Meyer contribution to progressive political ideology. You simply speak and your words create a brand new reality!

Neato!

Is the whole "Bible thing" impossibly specific and demanding? *Outta here!*

God is getting in the way?

Snap! *poof* *See ya!*

The devil is problematic?

Gone!

Communists and Communism have become rightly attached to Marxism?

No sweat! Consider 'em erased! (And don't worry; Communists, by nature, just *love* erasing history.)

Socialists and Socialism have become rightly attached to Marxism?

What Socialists? *wink*

Liberals and Liberalism have become rightly attached to Marxism?

What's a Liberal? Never heard of 'em…

…I'm a *Progressive.*

And here we are! How cool was that?

What does it say that the biblically submissive Christian core at the base of the political movements *opposed* to the progressive movement never seeks to separate itself from identification with biblically submissive Christianity, while those spearheading the progressive movement seem to blow through intentionally deceptive code names faster than Barack Hussein Obama nationalizes American industries? (Okay, maybe not quite *that* fast, but you get my meaning.)

Issues of basic honesty aside (which is just where the progressives like them), what is the goal of such relentless name-changing? What do we know about those who feel compelled in life to pursue a similar approach on an individual basis? When a person feels the need to constantly change their name, or a product or company is perpetually attempting to "rebrand" itself under an endless parade of new monikers, what does this tell us about their character? What role does this character assessment play in our evaluation of causes, activists, and would-be leaders?

Unfortunately for those who would ignore such matters and seek to impose their land of make-believe ideals upon the rest of us, there are little things that tend to get in the way. Things they haven't been able to 'fix' completely...yet. Things like recorded history, for example.

And books. Books like *The Communist Manifesto* and *Rules for Radicals*.

The Communist Manifesto was the counter-Christian creation of Karl Marx and the open advocacy of Marxism was the stated goal of Saul Alinsky's *Rules for Radicals*, which was enthusiastically digested and implemented by Barack Hussein Obama. See how neatly and completely Karl Marx, Saul Alinsky, Barack Hussein Obama, and the contemporary progressive movement all fit together? When I watch the pieces come together and fit so perfectly—so seamlessly—I cannot help but feel as though, in the best sense, we are witnessing true, good and godly *progress* unfolding right before our eyes.

Communism, socialism, Marxism, Marx, McLaren, Baal, Alinsky, Obama...they're all real, after all. Their deep and profound connections are just as real.

With this truth established and the vampires and werewolves banished to play in Transylvania and *Twilight* flicks, we are liberated to continue our pursuit of truth where the progressive Marxist agenda is concerned.

God Almighty vs. State Almighty

";I will argue that man's hopes lie in the acceptance of the great law of change."

SAUL ALINSKY

"It's not just enough to change the players. We've gotta change the game."

BARACK HUSSEIN OBAMA

A disciple is not above his teacher, but everyone when he is fully trained will be like his teacher.

LUKE 6:40

We see in the Ten Commandments and the Ten Planks of Communism two diametrically opposed worldviews codified into short, approachable, comprehensible, and digestible lists of principles. Whatever one might think of any specific plank or point presented in *The Communist Manifesto*, or however one might view any single one of the Ten Commandments of God to man, it is impossible to credibly maintain that the contemporary progressive movement and its most powerful political tool, the American Democrat Party are not, at the very least, strongly inclined towards one and against the other.

Both Christianity and Marxism speak clearly and forcefully to the subjects of personal property, inheritance, and the nature of a child's education. Both biblical Christianity and the Marxism-fueled progressive movement speak clearly and forcefully to the centrality and significance of the traditional family unit and the sanctity of marriage. Both biblical Christianity and the progressive political movement speak to the nature of man.

The Marxist views man as basically good and infinitely perfectible to the progressive. The biblical Christian identifies man as dead in sin and deserving of destruction. The progressive views the nature of God as malleable, open to interpretation and ultimately optional. The biblical Christian knows and submits to the omnipotent, omniscient, omnipresent "I AM" of Scripture. As for the nature of that Holy Word, it is at best a mix of fact and fiction to the progressive, while to the biblical Christian it is the essential, final, and sufficient authority in all matters.

With two views so clearly positioned in opposition to one another, the time has come for the professing church of Christ to formally and unequivocally stake its claim, state its position, and stand firm in opposition to a *political and religious* movement in open rebellion against the Lord she claims to serve. We are at war. The church must declare its allegiance and fight.

Her enemies have no qualms or reservations concerning their allegiances, intentions and goals; they've been as open as can be. For those with eyes to see, the writing has long been on the wall.

Commandments vs. Communism

"The Revolutionary force today has two targets, moral as well as material. Its young protagonists are one moment reminiscent of the idealistic early Christians, yet they also urge violence and cry, 'Burn the system down!' They have no illusions about the system, but plenty of illusions about the way to change our world. It is to this point that I have written this book."

SAUL ALINSKY, *RULES FOR RADICALS*

Whoever is not with me is against me, and whoever does not gather with me scatters.

MATTHEW 12:30

Those who would distract with Dracula and the Wolf-man are just as prone to pretend that these socialists and communists, if they ever did actually exist, really weren't *really* opposed to biblical Christianity or the Ten Commandments of God to man. Nope, not at all. Nor were they necessarily all that much in favor of the principles found in Marx's *Communist Manifesto*. You see, these kind, gentle folk simply sought to embody an enlightened, open-minded, and tolerant approach to life in all ways without really looking for any kind of trouble or controversy. They're all about peace, love, and happiness, man.

The proponents of the progressive religious and political movements will wiggle and squirm and do their very best to convince you that, just as with all things of great and diametrically opposed significance, the issues so clearly defined in the Ten

Commandments and the Ten Planks of Communism, at the end of the day, simply do not matter enough to divide over. They will say that we must set aside our differences over such things...all for the sake of unity...and, of course, progress.

And who would dare oppose *that*?

Who wants to mess up that whole unity vibe?

Can't we all just get along?

Why would we ever want to actually *engage* an opponent of biblical truth in serious debate or argument?

That sort of thing is awfully uncomfortable and risky, you know.

We might offend someone.

We might look bad to others.

We might have to study and prepare...actually *know* what the Bible says.

We might have to *think*.

God-focused Thought Produces God-glorifying Action

"If I profess with the loudest voice and clearest exposition every portion of the truth of God except precisely that little point which the world and the devil are at the moment attacking, I am not confessing Christ, however boldly I may be professing Christ. Where the battle rages, there the loyalty of the soldier is proved; and to be steady on all the battlefield besides, is mere flight and disgrace if he flinches at that point."

MARTIN LUTHER

"What luck that men do not think."

ADOLF HITLER

In their pursuit of the establishment of an Almighty State, the enemies of liberty have a roadmap. The way has been charted. In the strategically sound spirit of "knowing your enemy," we are well served to make note of a few critical thoughts on strategy and tactics from Barack Hussein Obama mentor Saul Alinsky and the one who so inspired him: Karl Marx.

The first five of Saul Alinsky's thirteen tactics as advanced in *Rules for Radicals* are as follows:

1. Power is not only what you have, but what the enemy thinks you have.

2. Never go outside the expertise of your people. When an action or tactic is outside the experience of the people, the result is confusion, fear and retreat...[and] the collapse of communication.

3. Whenever possible, go outside the expertise of the enemy. Look for ways to increase insecurity, anxiety and uncertainty. (This happens all the time. Watch how many organizations under attack are blind-sided by seemingly irrelevant arguments that they are then forced to address.)

4. Make the enemy live up to its own book of rules. You can kill them with this, for they can no more obey their own rules than the Christian church can live up to Christianity.

5. Ridicule is man's most potent weapon. It is almost impossible to counteract ridicule. Also it infuriates the opposition, which then reacts to your advantage.[32]

In these proposed tactics taken from the mind of Obama's mentor, do we find principles in harmony with or opposition to the clear teachings of Scripture? Is God glorified or angered by the implementation of such ideals as Alinsky's advocacy of the use of ridicule as a weapon to be directed at biblical principles? Is God glorified or grieved by those who embrace Alinsky's desire to employ insecurity and anxiety as the means by which goals can be realized?

For the progressive professing Christian, there are infinite rationalizations and justifications available in the shaping, spinning, and re-casting of these questions into a more favorable light. For the biblically submissive Christian, the answers to each of these questions are clear and utterly formative. They are determining factors in how votes are to be cast.

In *The Communist Manifesto*, Karl Marx closes with the following call to arms:

> The Communists disdain to conceal their views and their aims. They openly declare that their ends can be attained only by the forcible overthrow of all existing social conditions. Let the ruling classes tremble at a communist revolution. The proletarians have nothing to lose but their chains. They have a world to win.
> Working men of all countries, unite![33]

In his philosophical and political pronouncements, Karl Marx was an honest and open man. He knew what he believed and boldly proclaimed it from the rooftops. He sought to inspire and motivate all who could hear with his progressive philosophy of communism. Much the same could be said of Saul Alinsky.

The philosophical and ideological progeny of Marx and Alinsky direct every significant step of the contemporary American progressive movement.

Marx and Alinsky were not vampires. They were not werewolves. They were socialists. Their progeny are socialists.

Communism, socialism, and the desire of both strains of the humanist virus to replace Almighty God with the Almighty State are all very real things.

The American Democrat Party's aversion to God's Ten Commandments to man and sympathy toward Karl Marx's Ten Planks of Communism are very real things.

Every biblically submissive Christian has been given eyes to see and ears to hear. They are without excuse and cannot escape the responsibility to act in accordance with what God has revealed as truth.

As a result of this, are all genuine Christians somehow obligated to vote Republican? That notion is, in a word: Silly. (And more than a little dumb, too.)

While biblically submissive Christians are not compelled to support any particular political party, they are certainly prohibited from supporting any such party that is openly at war with the Christ they claim as Lord.

Can a Democrat Party member who is seeking the power to secure the legalized targeting of innocent children and the legitimization of homosexuality still, in spite of these issues, advocate and do other objectively "good" things.

Of course he can. And Hitler built the autobahn.

So *what?!*

There is simply no credible biblical defense for supporting any party, institution, cause, or candidate what would so openly declare its opposition to Scripture in such a comprehensive manner as has the contemporary American Democrat Party.

This party has, in pursuit of the progressive dream and promotion of the gospel of socialism, willfully charted a course to economic catastrophe. None of this is accidental.

America must be completely broken so that she might be reconstructed in much the same manner as Christ, Christianity, and morality have been obliterated and rebuilt to progressive specifications.

Her people must be stripped of their capacity and will for self-sufficiency and self-government so that the long coveted "worker's paradise" be realized. This is the "heaven here on earth" that so inspires the religious wing of the progressive cause.

The rapid expansion of government and the collapse of our economy are not, as sane people fear, opposing forces destined to collide and ultimately destroy one another. At least not in the happy land of delusion occupied by the ideological decedents of Jim Jones and Saul Alinsky. You see, from the perspective of the enlightened progressive, these forces work in complete harmony. They go hand-in-glove.

The big brother, nanny state, cradle-to-grave, entitlement mentality so carefully propagated and nurtured in America since the time of FDR is about to yield its final product.

Sovereignty is out. Slavery is in. All by design.

And with the new American slave class successfully dominating her culture, the coming economic implosion will serve the greater good's purpose by paving the way for the swift emergence of an Almighty State. The birth of this new state *requires* the complete destruction of the old. This is the conscious goal of the progressive movement in America.

As we continue our survey of the cultural battlefield, culminating in this section with an examination of the progressive goal of establishing an Almighty State, we need only recall and remember the clearly stated views of political and religious leaders throughout the progressive movement in order to confidently confirm their shared Marxist heritage and anti-Christian designs. The progressive movement has, at every turn, made war on the God of Christianity.

With this difficult but undeniable truth in mind, we must acknowledge and declare that it is no more possible for a biblically submissive Christian in contemporary America to credibly support the Democrat Party than it would have been for an intelligent, informed Jew in 1930s Germany to vote Nazi.

13

Aborting the Almighty State

The Common Believer's War Against Statism

*If my people who are called by my name humble
themselves, and pray and seek my face and turn from their
wicked ways, then I will hear from heaven and will forgive
their sin and heal their land.*

2 CHRONICLES 7:14

I can do all things through Christ who strengthens me.

PHILIPPIANS 4:13 (NKJV)

In his Thanksgiving Proclamation of October 3, 1789, in the first
year of the government's formation, our nation's first president,
George Washington, professed, "It is the duty of all Nations to
acknowledge the Providence of Almighty God, to obey His will, to
be grateful for His benefits, and humbly to implore His protection
and favor."

Earlier that year, at his first inauguration on April 30, Washington observed:

"...it would be peculiarly improper to omit in this first official act my fervent supplications to that Almighty Being who rules over the universe, who presides in the councils of nations, and whose providential aids can supply every human defect, that His benediction may consecrate to the liberties and happiness of the people of the United States a Government instituted by themselves for these essential purposes, and may enable every instrument employed in its administration to execute with success the functions allotted to his charge... No people can be bound to acknowledge and adore the Invisible Hand, which conducts the affairs of men more than those of the United States... You will join with me, I trust, in thinking that there are none under the influence of which the proceedings of a new and free government can more auspiciously commence."[34]

The Founding Fathers of the United States of America, as directed by the providential hand of the God that they so frequently and adoringly acknowledged, provided us with a good and God glorifying national foundation and heritage unparalleled in all of human history.

Less than 200 years later, a deep rot had come to the foundation laid by those founders. America—the America they had risked all and labored heavily to birth—had been led astray, far from the principles upon which she was formed. She had been lured away from her God, and found her way into the arms of another lord—one with grand designs for change.

This new spirit moved with lightning speed to swiftly corrupt the culture and reshape American civilization. The God of her foundation was forgotten by America, or so it seemed. She had spurned Him most thoroughly and seemed to be blissfully enjoying the rocket-sled joyride that was plunging her down a steep slope and into an ominously deep, dark valley, when...God found a B-movie actor through whom He decided to work miracles.

One Can Save a Nation

"Ours was the first revolution in the history of mankind that truly reversed the course of government, and with three little words: 'We the people.' 'We the people' tell the government what to do, it doesn't tell us. 'We the people' are the driver, the government is the car. And we decide where it should go, and by what route, and how fast. Almost all the world's constitutions are documents in which governments tell the people what their privileges are. Our Constitution is a document in which 'We the people' tell the government what it is allowed to do. 'We the people' are free."

RONALD REAGAN

In 1961, Operation Coffee Cup reached its zenith.

The campaign was launched by the American Medical Association in the late 1950s in order to oppose Democrat Party plans for socialized medicine. An album was subsequently recorded and distributed to promote public awareness on the issues.

"Back in 1927 an American Socialist, Norman Thomas, six time candidate for President on the Socialist Party ticket, said the

American people would never vote for socialism. But, he said, under the name of liberalism the American people would adopt every fragment of the socialist program....One of the traditional methods of imposing Statism or socialism on a people has been by way of medicine." These words of warning were recorded on the 1961 LP record *Ronald Reagan Speaks Out Against Socialized Medicine*.

Hmmm...God's chosen B-movie actor said *what*? "One of the traditional methods of imposing Statism or socialism on a people has been by way of medicine." Yeah, that's it!

And whaddaya know? Nearly fifty years after those recorded words were spoken, Lady Liberty once again finds herself under assault, with the main charge being made under the banner of *medicine*. Progressive politics are as attached to stale, tired, old and predictable concepts in much the same manner as progressive religion and spirituality. Both are committed to the advancement of very old, anti-Christian ideals, all while relying on historical ignorance and biblical illiteracy so that these very same crusty old concepts can be successfully presented as something shiny and new.

Past as Prologue

"In this present crisis, government is not the solution to our problems; government is the problem."

RONALD REAGAN, FROM HIS
FIRST INAUGURAL ADDRESS

For even when we were with you, we would give you this command: If anyone is not willing to work, let him not eat. For we hear that some among you walk in idleness, not busy at work, but busybodies. Now such persons we command and encourage in the Lord Jesus Christ to do their work quietly and to earn their own living.

2 THESSALONIANS 3:10–12

The goal of the American Statist is and has always been the imposition of an all-powerful government upon the once-free people and culture of our nation. The gradual creation of an entire class of people utterly dependent on government for their very sustenance is an essential component of plan to craft and inaugurate an Almighty American State. This state is the conscious goal of the progressive movement.

And this is why progressives, be they of a primarily religious or political flavor (though if they major in one, they almost always minor in the other), absolutely *despise* Ronald Reagan. They despised him in life and they despise him now. He is their Hitler.

They tend to hate conservatism in a broad, general sense and Republicans in particular, since, sad as it may be, Republicans are the closest thing left to an effective political force for conservatism in America. But God's chosen B-movie actor will always hold a special place in the liberals' blackened collective heart.

And how much did this bother Cowboy Ron? Not a lot, apparently. He laughed, lived, loved, ate jelly beans, and went about the business of destroying the Soviet communist empire without firing a shot; all while being called everything from a trigger-happy lunatic to a narcoleptic moron by the good, happy, tolerant folks on the progressive side of the fence. Even cooler was the manner in which he laughed at their jokes about him while he calmly went about the task of obliterating the very foundations of their warped worldview.

This rare and wonderful combo of Reagan attributes helps to explain why he is still so reviled by the forces of tolerance and progress in America. Even better than *all* of this is the fact that you, too, can be *that* hated.

One of the greatest lessons God has provided through His Reagan example is that one man—one reviled, despised, and ridiculed former B-movie actor of a man—can be enough to change a nation. One man can make waves. World-changing waves.

Any of you reading these words have this potential. No, really. God said so.

Just as the progressive movement is utterly committed to the endless regurgitation of the same, lame old retread arguments for anti-Christian change across the cultural landscape, so, too, is the God of biblical Christianity committed to raising up and using the most feeble of vessels to accomplish the greatest of tasks on His earth.

This is yet another demonstration of God's charity to mankind, all according to His perfect, self-glorifying purpose.

And while we're on the subject of charity, we would be well served to take a good look at the counterfeit version used to support the anti-Christian notion of an Almighty State.

Christian Charity: Target of the Statist

Each one must give as he has decided in his heart, not reluctantly or under compulsion, for God loves a cheerful giver.

2 CORINTHIANS 9:7

When the voluntary aspect of charity is removed, it ceases to be charity, at least from a biblically coherent perspective. Compulsory charity is an oxymoron (as opposed to "Christian worldview," which, we have hopefully established by now, is not).

It should come as no surprise then that the economic systems and policies advanced under the banner of progressivism are founded on a flagrant appeal to covetousness and a fundamental perversion of the Christian concept of charity. In other words, progressive economic principles stand boldly in stark contrast to the clearly expressed will of God.

As mentioned, these shiny, new, "creative," progressive types are nothing if not predictable. When God has a clear standard, they oppose it. It's just what they do.

With this truth established, painful though it may be to acknowledge, we are left without excuse. The enemy has made its views and goals plain. We have been blessed by God with clarity on these matters and we must act accordingly. It's well past time to fight.

With Scripture as our guide, we can always see our enemy in perfect, high-def reality. We can always see the whites of their eyes. And when we see those whites, it's time to bring some fire. One individual shot at a time.

Enemy of the Statist

"General Secretary Gorbachev, if you seek peace, if you seek prosperity for the Soviet Union and Eastern Europe, if you seek liberalization, come here to this gate! Mr. Gorbachev, open this gate! Mr. Gorbachev, tear down this wall!"

PRESIDENT RONALD REAGAN AT THE BERLIN WALL IN 1987, TELLING THE WALL TO FALL AND COMMUNISM TO DIE. (Both obeyed his command.)

If victory will come over the Almighty State, it will come through the individual efforts of individual Christians acting in submission to their Lord. This will be most effectively accomplished through the clear instruction of and submission to Scripture. It is in this perfect sourcebook for cultural battlefield tactics and strategies that we will find our every essential need met. With it in hand, and in mind, we are ready to roll.

In this section we have learned of the progressive Statist's clearly stated views on family, sexuality, individual liberty, the sanctity of innocent life, and the role of government in relation to all of these things. Progressive thought marches in locked-step harmony with the core tenants of the Communist Manifesto. Socialist thought is always Marxist at its core. The gulf between these progressive views and those proclaimed throughout biblical Christianity could not be greater.

In section six we will explore biblical principles for equipping the Common Believer for this war against Statism. Between these two sections, however, we will consider the costs associated with obedience to the Almighty God who is, of necessity, despised by those who advocate an Almighty State.

SECTION FIVE:

On Being Hated

(And Other Not-So-Marketable Benefits of Membership)

14

When Love Picks a Fight

The Common Believer as Branded "Unloving"

Beloved, although I was very eager to write to you about our common salvation, I found it necessary to write appealing to you to contend for the faith that was once for all delivered to the saints. For certain people have crept in unnoticed who long ago were designated for this condemnation, ungodly people, who pervert the grace of our God into sensuality and deny our only Master and Lord, Jesus Christ.

JUDE 1:3–4

"Jude's command "to contend earnestly for the faith" is not merely being neglected in the contemporary church; it is often greeted with outright scorn. These days anyone who calls for biblical discernment or speaks out plainly against a popular perversion of sound doctrine is as likely as the false teachers themselves to incur the disapproval of other Christians."

JOHN MACARTHUR

When I was seventeen, I finished with high school and had no idea what would come next. The college "education" and lifestyle route had little appeal. Yet rural north-central Arkansas, where I lived at the time, had even less and was losing ground by the minute. As the months ticked by without any significant prospects, I was growing anxious. I wanted an adventure. One that didn't involve binge-drinking or being spoon-fed thoughts or being fitted into a lemming-friendly, systemic groove.

Providentially, in the time leading up to this particularly frustrating chapter of my life, one of my closest friends had an older sister who had somehow managed to meet and marry a Norwegian boat captain. In Arkansas. Really.

I have no idea how a girl in that day and age managed to meet a Norwegian boat captain in rural north-central Arkansas, but what do I know about Norwegian boat captains anyway? It is important to note here that Al Gore's invention of the Internet hadn't really taken flight yet. There was no Match.com or eHarmony or *any* dot com, for that matter. At any rate, somehow, some way, Jinger had snagged Olaf the Norwegian Boat Captain, and they seemed quite happy together.

Subsequently, Olaf introduced many in Jinger's family to the Alaskan commercial fishing industry, where he made a very good living. Subsequently, several family members signed contracts and went to work in the high seas, bringing back their own tales of adventure.

It sounded like the Wild West with ice. And water. Big waves of frigid water. I was hooked. I desperately wanted to know more about this exotic world of peril and treasure on the high seas of America's great northern frontier.

Having heard of my interest, Olaf graciously offered to spend some time with me explaining the ins and outs of this very unique industry and the setting in which it operated. He told me about the awful living and working conditions. He emphasized the challenge of it all, how very few people really were cut out for this sort of thing and that not all of this was a matter of personal determination or work ethic. For many, it was even the slightest propensity for motion sickness that would do them in out there amongst the rolling waves of the Bering Sea and North Pacific. Olaf gave me every warning he could and, as he went along, I only became more and more jazzed about the whole idea. I'd already been infected by too many adventure novels, comic books, and action flicks.

I think that when he saw my enthusiasm increase after these warnings—the attraction to adventure aspect of the whole deal went up a notch every time he warned me about something—Olaf decided to get on into some important details about the companies I might work for. He made a list of good companies to work for and named a few that it would be wise to avoid and even gave me tips on the type of contract to aim for and the kind to avoid.

Finally, at the end of this session with Olaf, he emphasized that, for an inexperienced young guy like me to have any real hope of getting hired on with one of the "good companies," I'd have to be there, on hand in Seattle, so that they could meet with me and get a sense of my seriousness and ability.

So off to Seattle I went.

I sold what little I had that wouldn't fit into a duffle bag and took a Greyhound from Springfield, Missouri, to downtown Seattle. Those *days* of Greyhound living hold tales inappropriate for discussion here. Suffice it to say, I will never willfully do that again.

My Great Aunt Lois, Gram's younger sister, and her husband, Don, happened to live in a Seattle suburb at the time and kindly allowed me to come and stay with them during my quest for high seas employment and adventure. Aunt Lois was a good Christian woman. We had overlapping tastes in authors and apologists (she liked Walter Martin, too), so she was cool.

For weeks I went about the business of tracking down Olaf the Norwegian Boat Captain's "good companies" and making my applications. After a month or so of serious effort involving scads of interviews, medical exams, and truckloads of paperwork, I received calls from several on the good list asking me to come in for a final interview. I'd been told that the final interview was something of a formality; a chance for the company to have one last look at a new guy to be sure he wasn't twitching or drooling before they signed him up for an extended tour of duty hundreds of miles off the coast of nowhere.

So it appeared that my moment had arrived. I was in! The mission deemed near-impossible by almost everyone back home in Arkansas who knew what I was trying to do was on the verge of yielding ultimate success. It even looked like I would get to choose from some of the better companies handing out these gigs, so I was psyched. I called Gram, gave her the news, and then sat down at Aunt Lois' dining room table to write my then-girlfriend a note.

I was basking in the warm glow of victory. It was a good moment.

As I was writing, Aunt Lois came up behind me and very calmly let me know that she and Don had made an appointment for me at a local hair salon. (Yes, I had very long hair as a teenager. And yes, you can see where this was going.)

She was very kind in her presentation. Her tone was non-confrontational, but firm. She was, in her mind, simply informing me of something. When I politely declined, the hammer fell.

"If you don't do this you are going to have to find another place to stay." She was not yelling. She was calm. Again, she was simply *informing*. She said that she and Don had discussed this and agreed upon the course of action unfolding there in the dining room.

After soaking it all in for a moment, I rose out of my chair, thanked her for everything she had done, gave a big hug, and went into the guest room, where I packed my duffle bag. To both of our credit, at least as far as the conversation went, it was decent, respectful and sincere—both ways. Lois was never harsh with me and I was sincere with my thanks. I made no protest. It was her and Don's home and they were perfectly able to set the rules by which it would roll along. If I didn't like it, I could leave. And that was the plan.

In hindsight, I'm fairly certain that Lois had assumed, quite reasonably, I might add, that I would relent and get the demanded haircut out of sheer necessity. No doubt about it; that would have been the sane thing to do. I might pout or make a scene about it, but I just *had* to accept that salon appointment. After all, Lois, Don and I were all aware that I knew absolutely nobody northwest of Arizona and, after a month of time job-hunting in Seattle, I was almost totally broke.

Once my single, gigantic bag was packed, I met Lois in the hall, gave another hug-thanks combo, and rolled right out the door and into oblivion. As I walked towards the trusty ol' 307 bus stop near the 7–11 that had become so familiar, I counted my cash so that I could formulate something that might be loosely defined as "a plan." One needs to know one's budgetary limitations when crafting such a thing, after all.

Following my impromptu audit, I clocked in at well under two bucks. Not good.

On the way to the bus stop, I decided that I would purchase an all day pass so that I could at least have the rest of the afternoon, evening, and much of the night to sit someplace warm and dry while I plotted my next step. Warm and dry were important goals here. I did mention I was in Seattle, right?

After buying the pass, I spent the rest of my life's savings on seven pieces of taffy from the 7–11. Not the big flat strips, but the little cube-ish ones. Banana and Sour Apple. Yum.

My taffy and I rode back and forth between the suburbs and Seattle for hours. You will probably not be surprised when I tell you that during this time I was unable to come up with anything particularly brilliant where my master plan for survival was concerned, so when the route was about to shut down for the night, I had to choose a place to exit. I opted for downtown Seattle.

For days after that, I lived on a park bench near the Westlake Center, where I dreamt of french-fries, chocolate chip cookies, and proving the universe wrong by somehow making it to Alaska with my hair intact.

The most enduring image that I have in my head from that episode is one of me reclined and reading a book at my new Westlake residence. Not just any book. Oh no, this was perfect. You see, during my time in the Seattle area, I had hit a few bookstores and picked up a couple of slash-and-burn, fire-sale hardbacks. One of them was Stephen King's *Misery*, and I will never forget reading through that particular book in one setting right there on my bench in downtown Seattle.

Me, *Misery*, and Seattle. It was magic.

Setting *Misery*, park benches, taffy cubes, and Norwegian boat captains aside for a moment, this story seems useful here because, whatever you may think of the actions taken by any of those involved, I believe that we can all see in it with some clarity the lengths to which people—*very good people*, at least in Aunt Lois' case—will go in order to bend another to their will or correct them.

I have no doubt whatsoever that Aunt Lois believed she was doing me a favor by insisting on the haircut. Hers was not an unreasonable position. I am even more certain that she never thought I'd politely skip out the front door to go starve on a park bench rather than cave to her well-intentioned ultimatum. Even as I wandered down the street I am sure that she was confident I would come back.

I knew nobody. I was broke.

What kind of moron would opt for homelessness and starvation over a haircut?

The point is, we all have things that we will fight for and over, and they are usually worth nothing approaching the amount of energy that we are willing to pour into them. Ironically, the things that matter most and are therefore actually worthy of a determined defense…well…*those* things tend to be relegated to low priority status, if not ignored entirely.

We are more than willing to demonstrate fierce tenacity and dogged determination in the defense of things like, well, freedom from haircuts, but when it comes to *actual* essentials—the things that matter most—we more often than not exhibit little if any passion at all.

We can talk up our sports gods, our movie gods, our money gods, and our culture gods. We can debate over favorite teams, musicians, authors, artists, and lifestyles. We can pretty much make a big deal out of any relatively small thing, and we're happy to voice our opinions on all of them. We call this "passion," and passion is good in these carefully defined areas.

But when it comes to the real God, His Gospel, His church, His theology, and His doctrines, sadly, we wouldn't want to say much about those things. To do so would make somebody uncomfortable, after all.

And we call such promotion of discomfort "unloving." We call it intolerant. We call it rigid, harsh, and bad. In these instances and on these subjects, public displays of passion are not welcome. They're just…not…nice.

Nice and Evil

You serpents, you brood of vipers, how are you to escape being sentenced to hell?

JESUS IN MATTHEW 23:3

"This is a battle we cannot wage effectively if we always try to come across to the world as merely nice, nonchalant, docile, agreeable, and fun-loving people. We must not take our cues from people who are perfectly happy to compromise the truth wherever possible "for harmony's sake."...neither Christ nor the apostles ever confronted serious, soul-destroying error by building collegial relationships with false teachers. In fact, we are expressly forbidden to do that (Romans 16:17; 2 Corinthians 6:14-15; 2 Thessalonians 3:6; 2 Timothy 3:5; 2 John 10-11)."

JOHN MACARTHUR

One of the most pervasive forms of persecution that an American Christian will face is that we *will* be branded unloving. This is going to happen to each and every one of us who dares to enter the culture war on the side of biblical Christianity. Think of it as an entry-level, guaranteed taste of persecution that will become a very normal part of our everyday lives on this earth for as long as we are obedient to our God in the proclamation of His undiluted Gospel.

In this culture, even more so than most that have preceded it, any claim to exclusive and essential truth is viewed as inherently unloving. We really do need to understand and accept that fact right out of the gate. The more we understand the necessity of conflict between biblical truth and anti-Christian counterfeits of truth, the more and better we will come to understand the difference between biblical love and anti-Christian perversions of the concept. As we grow in this understanding, we will more easily shrug off the automatic, ever-present attacks of the enemy.

As we progress along this path, we will not only be better equipped to handle the inevitable confrontations that we are called to engage in the secular culture at large, but we will also find ourselves ever more able and willing to enter the fray on a much more treacherous and heated portion of the cultural battlefield.

In this we speak of the battles raging within the contemporary professing Christian church in America. The battle for biblical truth within the professing church has become, in many ways, our greatest challenge. The mere profession of clear biblical truth often inspires at least as much rage from within church walls these days as it does from without.

The progressively reconstructed "love" again comes into play here, this time with even more ferocity. Where any proclamation of exclusive truth is certainly deemed unloving, the correction or rebuke of another's position on the matter is doubly offensive. This counterfeit love has served as the key to countless counter-Christians attaining leadership positions throughout the professing church in America. In the name of love, we have disregarded every one of the scores of distinct warnings and commands given by God where the preservation of doctrinal and theological purity are concerned, and in doing so, we've welcomed wolf after wolf to what they know, and we deny to be, is, in reality, an all-you-can-eat sheep barbeque.

While such demonstrations of biblical love as proclaiming the exclusivity of the Gospel or rebuking a false teacher are now viewed as decidedly *unloving* acts, the use of this new love as a tool to promote all things "progressive"—even, and especially, when they inherently condemn biblical Christian principles as wrong—has been tagged as a most beautiful thing. That's what love is for, after all: The promotion of universal peace, happiness and acceptance. When those are the principles to which the term is attached, then "love" may be used freely and without fear of condemnation.

You know, like the "L" in NAMBLA.

Who can argue with *love*?

Really now, you wouldn't want to judge...would you? Remember: Judging is *bad*. And very *unloving*.

Progressive Love: Nicely Escorting People to Hell

This charge I entrust to you, Timothy, my child, in accordance with the prophecies previously made about you, that by them you may wage the good warfare, holding faith and a good conscience. By rejecting this, some have made shipwreck of their faith, among whom are Hymenaeus and Alexander, whom I have handed over to Satan that they may learn not to blaspheme.

1 TIMOTHY 1:18–20

"The apostle Paul was constantly engaged in battle against the lies of 'false apostles [and] deceitful workers [who transformed] themselves into apostles of Christ' (2 Corinthians 11:13). Paul said that was to be expected. It is, after all, one of the favorite strategies of the evil one: 'No wonder! For Satan himself transforms himself into an angel of light. Therefore it is no great thing if his ministers also transform themselves into ministers of righteousness' (vv. 14-15)."

JOHN MACARTHUR

"We must not suppose that if we succeeded in making everyone nice we should have saved their souls. A world of nice people, content in their own niceness, looking no further, turned away from God, would be just as desperately in need of salvation as a miserable world."

C.S. LEWIS

Remember when phony niceness was a repugnant thing? These days, it's become standard operating procedure in much of the church, and with predictably catastrophic results. In our surrender to the new love and its right-hand hatchet-man, the dreaded "unloving" tag, we have thickly seeded our own lands with mines and built barricades to protect enemy strongholds.

In the coming chapters, we will address several areas in which the new love has been used most hatefully and effectively against the bride of Christ and her Lord. Three general areas to consider as we explore will be:

- Church discipline—This essential component of biblical Christianity has been all but completely abandoned in the name of the new love. If "God is love," so the thought goes, then we can't be having biblical church discipline. That would require judgment, after all, and the one and only concept we are happy to universally judge as evil is the use of biblical judgment itself.
- Defense of the Gospel from external attack—To boldly proclaim the error of religions or worldviews in clear

opposition to Christianity—to openly refer to these anti-Christian systems as *wrong*—is deemed by most professing Christians as a distasteful, unwise act sure to impair the appeal and progress of the church. Those committing this sin against proper secular marketing are almost always labeled *unloving*.

Defense of the Gospel from internal attack—Not content to merely concede the war as waged against the church from without, we have, again in the name of the new love, not only abdicated our responsibility to preserve the purity of the church in its doctrine and leadership, we have also become infinitely more prone to attack those who actually take up the biblical charge to maintain that purity. Incredibly, vocal defenders of biblical truth are more likely to be attacked by professing Christians than those openly acting to undermine the same truth from within the church. Those who dare hold church leadership to a basic standard of biblical fidelity are tagged as, you guessed it, *unloving*.

While enduring this sort of reactive name-calling and character assassination is simply a natural consequence of biblical fidelity in practice, we must take to heart the fact that this is nothing new and it is always a sign of our honoring Christ. Each and every time we get slapped with the unloving tag for these reasons, we should wear it like a badge of honor. Wear it that way because that is exactly how Christ sees it. The "fellowship of persecution" is, as God the Holy Spirit has told us, a beautiful thing.

In the next chapter we will begin a more detailed examination of this "new love" inspired warfare by honing in on what must surely be the most discouraging and disappointing aspect of this battle: The war waged against defenders of biblical standards from within the professing church.

15

No More Reindeer Games

The Common Believer as Shunned by the Professing Church

Do not think that I have come to bring peace to the earth. I have not come to bring peace, but a sword. For I have come to set a man against his father, and a daughter against her mother, and a daughter-in-law against her mother-in-law. And a person's enemies will be those of his own household. Whoever loves father or mother more than me is not worthy of me, and whoever loves son or daughter more than me is not worthy of me. And whoever does not take his cross and follow me is not worthy of me. Whoever finds his life will lose it, and whoever loses his life for my sake will find it.

MATTHEW 10:34–39

"Apostasy poses real and present dangers today as always. Actually, the threat may be more imminent and more dangerous than ever, because most Christians nowadays simply don't care about the prevalence of false doctrine, nor do they take seriously their duty to fight against apostasy. Instead, they want a friendly atmosphere of open acceptance for everyone, tolerance of opposing ideas, and charitable dialogue with the apostates."

JOHN MACARTHUR

Jesus Christ is the greatest divider in all of human history. And the contemporary professing church in America aims to be the greatest unifying force in all of human history.

Houston, we have a problem.

Or maybe we should say *in* Houston we have a great example of the problem—that problem being epitomized by Lakewood Church, the largest professing Christian body of the self-helped in the entire U. S. of A. You see, this enormous operation claiming to represent the Gospel of Christ knows nothing of the Jesus described in the Bible, and, sadly, in this regard, Lakewood is hardly unique.

Joel Osteen, the lead motivational speaker and self-exalter/helper at Lakewood, follows and pitches a Jesus utterly distinct from the God-man who spoke the words recorded in the tenth chapter of Matthew. Where the Christ of biblical Christianity has assured that we will *not* have our best life now so that we will have our perfect life later, The Smiling Osteen preaches precisely the opposite regarding the Christian walk in the here and now. In this, he is as flagrant a heretic as ever there has been.

Let's take a look at precisely the sort of life that the Christ of biblical Christianity has promised His people *now*, as recorded in Matthew 10:34–39:

Do not think that I have come to bring peace to the earth. I have not come to bring peace, but a sword. ~ Jesus

Jesus came to bring into our lives now the very antithesis of peace as this world understands it. Instead, He came bringing a sword and has explicitly warned us against even *thinking* that He has done anything more "peaceful" than that for us here and now.

For I have come to set a man against his father, and a daughter against her mother, and a daughter-in-law against her mother-in-law. And a person's enemies will be those of his own household. ~ Jesus

Jesus came to divide. He came to divide even *families.*

Whoever loves father or mother more than me is not worthy of me, and whoever loves son or daughter more than me is not worthy of me. ~ Jesus

Jesus will not suffer any who value their family members more than they value Him. He hates this. Any who make such a choice are, as He makes plain, simply not worthy of Him.

And whoever does not take his cross and follow me is not worthy of me. ~ Jesus

Crosses are to die on. They epitomize what might be termed "your worst life now." Any seeking to avoid their cross are simply not worthy of Him.

It's certainly true that Helper Joel is one of the more glaring examples of anti-Christian apostasy in the modern professing church, but is he really all that unique? What about Benny Hinn...or Joyce Meyer...or Rob Baal...or Brian McLaren...or Comrade Oxymoron...or any leader in any church *you* attend who publicly opposes core tenants of biblical Christianity?

What do *you* do about them? What are *you* willing to risk?

Weigh these questions carefully as you consider them, my brothers and sisters, because these stands will cost you much. They may, in fact, cost you everything. After all, that's what crosses tend to do.

Christ-less, Cross-less Christianity

"The Church used to be a lifeboat rescuing the perishing. Now she is a cruise ship recruiting the promising."

LEONARD RAVENHILL

"...the evangelical movement isn't really very evangelical anymore. The typical evangelical leader today is far more likely to express indignation at someone who calls for doctrinal clarity and accuracy than to firmly oppose another self-styled evangelical who is actively attacking some vital biblical truth."

JOHN MACARTHUR

While particular approaches to heresy and the promotion of apostasy may vary, they do tend to be, by definition, easily identifiable for the biblically literate and submissive Christian. That's the good news.

We have the perfect tool at our disposal in the revealed Word of God. We are equipped and ready to roll...though getting that roll started can definitely be a challenge. That's the bad news.

We all have inside of us a natural desire to be liked. Stepping out of that comfort zone is a biggie for most of us, yet that's exactly what Christ has called us to do.

That said, we aren't out to offend or assault others for the sake of our desire to look better, brighter, wiser or more loyal to God. Far from it! We of all people know that we are, of our own nature, no better than the lowest of creatures to have ever wandered the charred cultural landscape. We were once God-hating rebels, every bit as much in need of a savior as Marilyn Manson, Barack Obama, Benny Hinn, or the Go-Daddy Girl.

When we do what we must and confront those spreading error in the church, we should earnestly pray for those currently embracing heretical views to renounce them in a spirit of repentant submission to the author and origin of truth. We must desire that all who now oppose biblical Christianity would be moved in such a manner by the Holy Spirit. This is anything but unloving. This is true love, and it always brings glory to God while purifying the bride of Christ.

When a leader persists in proclaiming heresy, we cannot merely ignore every clear command of our Lord to defend His truth and maintain the purity of His bride, preferring instead to "let God handle it" as we avert our eyes and walk along, pretending we've seen nothing and heard nothing. Disobeying God's clear call to action—a call explicitly presented in previous chapters (not that you need *this* book for such clarification)—is akin to spitting on the very Word of the living Lord of creation. This is, to say the least, a most *unloving* thing to do to the God we claim to adore and serve.

In succumbing to this pressure to avoid the dreaded *unloving* tag, we mock God and coddle heretics. See where warped love gets you?

Carrying the Cross of Controversy

But false prophets also arose among the people, just as there will be false teachers among you, who will secretly bring in destructive heresies, even denying the Master who bought them, bringing upon themselves swift destruction.

2 PETER 2:1

A disciple is not above his teacher, but everyone when he is fully trained will be like his teacher.

LUKE 6:40

Of course, those who *do* stand in opposition to apostate teachers, as God has commanded, well...they almost always get precisely the sort of treatment Jesus described. It's as though He knew *exactly* what was going to happen. Weird, huh?

When you stand with and for Christ, you will lose. You will lose friendships, family ties and reputation. You will be branded as troublesome, intolerant and unloving. You will be shunned and abandoned by many, even within the professing church. Yet in losing these and countless other trappings of "your best life now," you will find *true* life in Christ.

Put another way: *Whoever finds his life will lose it, and whoever loses his life for my sake will find it.* ~ *Jesus*

This most precious of promises from our loving, living Lord, is one that we are well served to hold close to our hearts as we obey His command to confront those seeking to spread apostasy within His church and suffer the inevitable personal consequences.

This divine promise will also sustain His obedient soldiers amidst the trials heaped upon them from outside the professing church, which we will examine in the next chapter.

16

The Forces of Tolerance
Are Out to Get You

If There's One Thing They Can't Stand, It's Intolerance!

Behold, I am sending you out as sheep in the midst of wolves, so be wise as serpents and innocent as doves.

MATTHEW 10:16

The Lord knows how to rescue the godly from trials, and to keep the unrighteous under punishment until the day of judgment, and especially those who indulge in the lust of defiling passion and despise authority.

2 PETER 2:9–10

When I was four, I wanted to be either an astronaut or Spider-man.

Gram even made me a very cool, hand-crafted Spidey outfit before I was in kindergarten. I think that, for at least a few months there, I actually believed that I *was* Spider-man.

I'm fairly certain that super hero and space explorer are not uncommon long-term goals to most four-year-old boys. For me, somewhere in the decade that followed my fifth birthday, I lost much of the desire for NASA membership. But I still hold out hope for that radioactive spider bite. A guy's gotta have dreams, you know. Clearly, I have a pretty deep geek streak. And I like it. It does have its limits, but it is pronounced. For example, I've been to many a comic book convention, but never dressed as a super-hero (not that I rule that last part out). I've attended many a sci-fi convention, but I don't know a word of Klingon (I definitely rule *that* last part out). I own practically every video game system known to man, but I'm not very good at playing any of 'em.

Around three decades after Gram crafted that beaut of a Spidey suit, my nerdy inclination led me into a bona-fide, real life adventure. How perfect is that? Even when I was four, God was providentially working through Gram to prep me for hero duty.

An American Baptist at Starfleet

"I condemn false prophets, I condemn the effort to take away the power of rational decision, to drain people of their free will—and a hell of a lot of money in the bargain. Religions vary in their degree of idiocy, but I reject them all. For most people, religion is nothing more than a substitute for a malfunctioning brain."

GENE RODDENBERRY, CREATOR OF *STAR TREK*

The fool says in his heart, "There is no God."

PSALM   53:1

In February of 2006, I decided to check out a local convention dedicated to addressing the interests of my fellow computer-game aficionados and Spidey wannabes. It was called VisionCon. I'd been to one of the VisionCons before moving to Seattle with Kristi in the late '90s. With this being the first winter following my solo return to the southwest Missouri area, it seemed like a happy sort of nostalgic trip down memory lane waiting to happen, so off I went.

While the blessings of fantasy and a capacity for vivid, creative imagination are some of the most wonderful gifts of God to man, the culture in which we live has corrupted them about as thoroughly as it has every other good thing entrusted to our care. That said, one does not attend a sci-fi convention these days for the purpose of basking in the glow of its biblical fidelity.

The typical convention of this sort tends to be tilted a bit further away from Christianity than the general culture at large. New Age ideas permeate the atmosphere and the Forces of Tolerance are generally inclined and encouraged to enforce the party line.

This particular con—the first I'd been to in years—seemed to have ratcheted up the party atmosphere to a level approaching that associated with a sports or rock 'n' roll themed event. As I wandered around the hotel hosting the event, it was pretty clear that this was not your Aunt May's sci-fi convention. The booze was flowing and the music was loud. There were more than a few drunken Klingons and stoned vampires stumbling around the halls.

After taking in the sights and sounds (and nothing else), I was about to head on home when I found myself happily hugging a long lost friend, who we'll identify here as "Vince".

We spotted each other in the hallway at the same time and, before I really knew what was up, Vince was hugging away and I was hugging back. He was thrilled to see me and I was relieved that he was thrilled to see me, which, in an instant, made me thrilled to see him, too.

He and I had known each other a long time ago, and in what seemed to have been a galaxy far, far away. The last time we were what you could call close was well over a decade earlier, when he was still in high school and I was still a teenager, having returned from the Alaskan adventure. He had been raised in a fairly hedonistic atmosphere, and I don't say that meanly. I always liked his mom, but she had embraced, for as long as I'd known her, a flamboyantly counter-Christian lifestyle.

Back in the day, the groups that we ran with in Mountain Home would often gather at his house, in part because it was centrally located in the middle of town and partially because his mom was well-off financially and they had an in-ground swimming pool. We were always welcome there. It was a beautiful thing.

It wasn't uncommon for there to be ten or more of us to be gathered there at once, and what made the whole thing even cooler to me at the time was the fact that these folks—people ranging in age from teenagers to thirty-somethings—were very much open to real conversation. I loved that. They could and would, for the most part, dive deep into *any* subject.

I didn't mind at all that I was usually the token vocal Christian in the bunch. I liked it, actually. It was everything a wannabe super-hero Christian kid could hope for.

We really did tear up the subject matter back in those impromptu discussion sessions at Vince's house. Most would participate, though there were many who mainly just looked on and laughed as we let our passions for the issues of the day run completely wild. Generally, I tended to be the squeaky wheel of opposition to the prevailing views in the room, but I didn't mind. It was fun. It wasn't uncommon for these poolside chats to center around the divergent opinions of me and one particular friend who was a cherished part of the group, a man we'll call "Rob".

Rob was a very bright and articulate guy. He was five or six years older than me and he absolutely loved a good debate. And if there was one thing he lived to oppose, it was biblical Christianity. I loved the fact that he was bold, open, and eager to advance his views almost as much as I enjoyed making every attempt to mercilessly pummel those views into oblivion. Rob was a blast!

He and I would tend to go at it and, maybe more than we should have, dominate these debates the longer that they went on. But it was all in good fun and, as intense as these things would get (and I'm talkin' very intense here, folks), we rarely, if ever, wrapped up one of these sessions personally angry with each other. That, in my opinion, qualifies these little get-togethers as nothing short of miraculous. Providentially so, you might even say. And apparently, I wasn't alone in this assessment.

As Vince and I stood there happily smiling and reminiscing, and probably making fools of ourselves with the strange display we must have presented to the stormtroopers and werewolves passing by, he relayed to me how he had often looked back at those glory days of Mountain Home debate events hosted in his home, and how they had impacted him. The impact that he described to me centered on how, as a teenager, he had basically embraced every major expression that Rob had made in his presence during those formative years. Subsequently, he'd taken some incredibly destructive trails in his young life. As if that wasn't intense enough, Vince followed these remarkable revelations up with what was, for me, both a welcome and terrifying observation. He expressed to me there in the VisionCon hallway that, as he had in recent years frequently recalled and rethought those raging arguments between Rob and me, and all that had come his way in their wake, he had come to view Rob as the devil on his left shoulder, and me as the angel on the right.

I hoped that he was making some kind of joke. Spider-man I could cope with. But an angel? No way.

A Personal Invitation to the League of Spirituality

Now who is there to harm you if you are zealous for what is good? But even if you should suffer for righteousness' sake, you will be blessed. Have no fear of them, nor be troubled, but in your hearts honor Christ the Lord as holy, always being prepared to make a defense to anyone who asks you for a reason for the hope that is in you

1 PETER 3:13–15

And you will be hated by all for my name's sake.

MARK 13:13

After hanging out for a while longer, Vince insisted that I attend a get-together he was having at his place in Mountain Home the following month. I was instantly flattered, honored and intrigued. His place was the same home that was the scene of all of those pitched philosophical battles of yesteryear, so I was not only honored that he would invite me, but excited by the nostalgic appeal of it all.

Apparently, this was a gathering that he hosted annually, bringing in friends from throughout the region for a whole weekend of socializing, sharing ideas, and playing games. The more I heard, the more serious—and seriously fun—the whole thing sounded. This was a pretty big deal, and I became anxious for April to roll around.

In the weeks leading up to the grand gathering, Vince sent out some emails to the group list, which he'd added me to. He graciously introduced me to the guys and gals in the group, and the more I pondered the situation, the more apparent it became that I was not only a long-lost, treasured blast from the past being happily introduced into a new circle of close friends, but I was also enthusiastically welcomed in that I would be filling a specific role in this group.

The informal club already had a wide variety of worldviews and religions represented through its membership, but doggonit if they just didn't seem to have an actual, real, live Bible-believing Christian on the roster. So it was most fortuitous that I had re-emerged. (You might even say providential.) Finally, the collection could be complete, with me filling the Christian chair at the annual spring gathering of this League of Spirituality.

Vince was happy. Everyone else was warm and welcoming. I could hardly wait. I only wished Rob could've been there.

An American Baptist in the Happy Land of Tolerance

"Pluralists can only tolerate other pluralists."

RAVI ZACHARIAS

It was a very cool thing to see Vince's home again. There were a lot of good memories in that place. I had met Kristi right there in the driveway.

My introduction to the rest of the weekend's participants went well. They were all very nice, welcoming, and warm to me. Everyone was aware of where I was on the belief spectrum, for the most part, and they really were wonderful in their accommodation.

They never asked me if I wanted a sip of this or a drag of that. They knew better and they were respectful. I appreciate that even more as I tell this story now.

The afternoon was a hoot and the evening started well. We talked and played games, mostly. There was one huge table that we all gathered and sat around. Everyone seemed to be having a good time and, every now and again, there'd be some kind of heavier subject matter thrown around for consideration. It was only a tiny taste of what I'd remembered from so long ago at that same place, but I liked it.

The others seemed to as well. There were three other guys who did most of the chiming in on religious or spiritual or political things, and I was happy to jump in when the way was made open and the path was clear.

Yet as the conversations progressed, it became obvious that there was an increasing discomfort building after one person in particular would speak; that person being me.

Was I loud? Nope. I didn't yell at anyone.

I joked around and laughed at the jokes told by others. I was a generally happy, smiley guy. The trouble was that if someone asked a question, I would answer it honestly and, to the best of my ability, accurately. Talk about a buzz kill.

The whole deal came to a head when one of the League members treated me to the whole "God on the mountaintop" illustration. You see, he said, we may all be on different paths up the mountainside, but they all lead up to the same summit at the end of the day. He smiled as he said it. I smiled too. Then I responded. And then he wasn't smiling anymore.

When I said that all non-Christian paths do indeed lead to the same place, and that biblical Christianity alone led to another, the rest of the League of Spirituality seemed to immediately regret the notion of having a Christian chair on the panel.

All of a sudden, there was only one happy person in the room where just a moment before there had been many.

Their postmodern views simply could not tolerate anything about the core of my worldview. Any claim to exclusive, objective truth simply could not be accommodated by their peculiar brand of selective openness. Once my mouth was opened, however warmly or kindly my words may have been packaged, their presence alone made the uncomfortable truth of the League's rank hypocrisy unavoidably clear. These folks weren't tolerant at all.

But then, by definition, they never could be. You see, pluralists can only tolerate other pluralists. They can and do talk a good game about all of that peace, love and happiness stuff, but they absolutely, positively cannot suffer any of the core claims of biblical Christianity. They simply *hate* the stuff....as they must.

Jesus can be God *for me*. The Bible can be truth *for me*. Christianity can be the way *for me*. That much is fine. Moreover, it'll qualify you for a prime position on the League of Spirituality discussion panel. All you have to do is change "Jesus is *the* truth" into "Jesus is *a* truth" and you're in. It'll be peachy keen. But should you insist that this Jesus, Bible, and Christianity are the objective truths by which to judge *all* people in *all* places at *all* times...well...the happy land of liberal tolerance will plant its collective boot up against your backside and dropkick you straight out of their hypocritically intolerant little bubbleworld fantasyland. And pronto!

It matters not how nice you are; coddling 'em will never make enough of a difference. It matters not how respectful you are; there's no compensating for the offense of an *objective* truth with teeth.

At the end of the day, if you clearly express fidelity to the universally applicable truth of Jesus Christ as the one and only Savior and Lord described in Scripture, you are outta there!

I knew all of this going in, so when Vince emailed me after the magical gathering of the tolerant to inform me that I made many of his other guests so uncomfortable that they'd not be attending next year if I was still in "the Christian chair," I let him know that I understood completely, thanked him for the original invite and a wonderful, enlightening time. I told him that he didn't have to worry or stress about any of it. I wished him well and happily moved along.

After all, that's what tolerant guys do, right?

Let's Get Ready to Rumble!

The way of the Lord is a stronghold to those with integrity, but it destroys the wicked.

PROVERBS 10:29 (NLT)

These are encounters for which all Common Believers should be prepared. They're going to come our way, and with increasing frequency as the culture continues its descent into open warfare against the Lord we serve and with whom we are identified. When we understand this and prepare accordingly, we are equipped to glorify God in even these challenging circumstances and situations.

It all begins with recognition. We must have no illusion that biblical Christianity can or ever will be tolerated by any opposing perspective or system of belief. And remember: *All* non-Christian views are anti-Christian by definition. There is no middle ground. The starkness of this truth is a blessing in that it allows us great clarity as to who is "on our side" and who is an active opponent. The answer is and always has been that only biblical Christians are allies and all others are opponents. The current climate of increasing hostility to truth makes this all the easier to recognize.

This is certainly a hard truth, but it is truth nonetheless. Embracing it is an essential first step in our preparation for the battles that we absolutely, positively *will* face so often in this life.

As we saw in the previous chapter, even many *within* the professing church will come to hate us as we clearly proclaim and exalt the undiluted truth of biblical Christianity. It should come as little surprise then that we would meet equally intense opposition from those more openly opposed to biblical Christianity from outside the church.

We will lose friendships.

We will be excluded.

We will be isolated.

We will even lose that beautiful, comfortable, ornate "Christian chair" at the League of Spirituality, wherever and whenever it meets.

We will be hated by the world. That's a promise. It's not a maybe, could be, or possibly kind of thing; it's a locked-in, absolute, incontrovertible fact of Christian life in this world.

And, as we will see in the next chapter, this is a beautiful thing.

17

Hated...Yet Happy
How Does That Work?

Welcome to the Family

And you will be hated by all for my name's sake. But the one who endures to the end will be saved.

MARK 13:13

Indeed, all who desire to live a godly life in Christ Jesus will be persecuted,

2 TIMOTHY 3:12

So yeah, we're hated. A lot.

But by whom? Enemies of Christ.

And why? Because we are His.

They *must* hate us because He is in us, and the more they see Him in us the more they will hate us for it. Unless and until He regenerates them, raising them from spiritual death to life, they really have no option in the matter. They must hate Him and therefore they must hate us.

This is emphasized so that we might never be surprised by what should be the most obvious of truths concerning the nature of every fallen man. We are easily tempted to assume neutrality in the nonbeliever, but this assumption sets us up for fall after fall, failure after failure, and disappointment after disappointment. There is no middle ground. There is no neutral state.

You might say that while there are Swiss people, there are no Switzerland people.

Our great and unwavering comfort even in the face of such hostility and hatred is that before this world hated us, it first hated Him.

Happily Hated

"If the world hates you, know that it has hated me before it hated you. If you were of the world, the world would love you as its own; but because you are not of the world, but I chose you out of the world, therefore the world hates you. Remember the word that I said to you: 'A servant is not greater than his master.' If they persecuted me, they will also persecute you. If they kept my word, they will also keep yours. But all these things they will do to you on account of my name, because they do not know him who sent me."

JOHN 15:18–21

"You speak the name Jesus Christ...and all hell breaks loose....It is explosive!"

BRIT HUME

As we continue our study of The Jesus Not Preached at Lakewood, we are likely to be comforted and amazed by the words of our Lord as recorded in the fifteenth chapter of the Gospel of John: "*If the world hates you, know that it has hated me before it hated you.*"

This world crucified Him for what it considered to be *very good* reasons. It hated Him that much. As He now dwells in us and we are each being conformed into His image, we will quite naturally be hated in like manner and crucified in every manner, including, sometimes, the literal.

> *If you were of the world, the world would love you as its own; but because you are not of the world, but I chose you out of the world, therefore the world hates you.* (Jesus in John 15:19)

Pay attention the next time you are given the opportunity to express that you are saved because Jesus chose you and not the other way around. The fact of Christ doing the choosing in this equation will not only net you some serious grief from the garden variety pagan, it'll also send many a professing Christian into an apoplectic fit.

> *Remember the word that I said to you: 'A servant is not greater than his master.' If they persecuted me, they will also persecute you. If they kept my word, they will also keep yours. But all these things they will do to you on account of*

my name, because they do not know him who sent me. (Jesus in John 15:20–21)

How is it that we could have ever imagined that this world would not hate us, much less *like* us?

Our desire for affirmation can blind us, our yearning for peace can betray us, and our longing for approval can destroy us, so long as the affirmation, peace, and approval in question is being sought from the world that hates our Jesus.

Perfect Peace through the Hated Christ

I am not praying for the world but for those whom you have given me, for they are yours. All mine are yours, and yours are mine, and I am glorified in them. And I am no longer in the world, but they are in the world, and I am coming to you. Holy Father, keep them in your name, which you have given me, that they may be one, even as we are one. While I was with them, I kept them in your name, which you have given me. I have guarded them, and not one of them has been lost except the son of destruction, that the Scripture might be fulfilled. But now I am coming to you, and these things I speak in the world, that they may have my joy fulfilled in themselves. I have given them your word, and the world has hated them because they are not of the world, just as I am not of the world. I do not ask that you take them out of the world, but that you keep them from the evil one.

They are not of the world, just as I am not of the world.

JOHN 17:9–16

Later in John's account, we are treated to even more wondrous comfort and peace as conveyed in our Lord's prayer to His Father on our behalf. He prays not for the world, but for *us*. This is a precious revelation that we must not overlook.

Here we find the certitude, peace, and joy that must surely have captivated Blaise Pascal those many years ago. On the eve of our Lord's crucifixion, He made these pleas for *us*:

> *But now I am coming to you, and these things I speak in the world, that they may have my joy fulfilled in themselves.* ~ *Jesus*

Joy. We are to have Christ's joy fulfilled within us. Amazing!

> *I have given them your word, and the world has hated them because they are not of the world, just as I am not of the world.* ~ *Jesus*

With the Word of God as our guide, this world will hate us just as it hated and continues to hate Him.

> *I do not ask that you take them out of the world, but that you keep them from the evil one.* ~ *Jesus*

We remain here on the field of battle according to His purpose and for His glory. He has equipped us with perfect protection from our adversary. With these truths embraced, why would we take to this field with anything less than the joy He has secured for us? Our Jesus has prepared us perfectly for the victory He has ordained.

While there will be trials, losses, and sadness at points along the path to that coming victory, the fact of His perfect intercession onour behalf should inspire in us matchless peace, joy, and a burning passion for His warfare.

A Passion for Warfare

"I hope you get a black eye fighting for something you believe in."

PAUL HARVEY

This charge I entrust to you, Timothy, my child, in accordance with the prophecies previously made about you, that by them you may wage the good warfare.

1 TIMOTHY 1:18

No matter how big the smiles from a Lakewood or Crystal Cathedral pulpit, we must oppose their message. No matter how sweet sounding or self-affirming the words of a Don Miller or Rob Baal, we must oppose their message. No matter how warm the greeting from an apostate teacher in a tiny, friendly, backwoods church, we must oppose their message. And we *will* be hated for this opposition.

Being hated by this world is one of the most clearly stated "benefits" of biblical Christianity in all of Scripture. Peace with Christ is enmity with the world...and we shouldn't want it any other way.

The Common Believer's Blueprint for Victory

18

The Beginning of Wisdom

The Common Believer's Call to Christ-centered Knowledge

The fear of the LORD is the beginning of wisdom; all those who practice it have a good understanding. His praise endures forever!

PSALM 111:10

The fear of the LORD is the beginning of knowledge; fools despise wisdom and instruction.

PROVERBS 1:7

"In the state of California, if I had a child there, I wouldn't put the youngster in a public school.... I think it's time to get our kids out. And I'm going to get hit for [saying] that." These words were spoken by Dr. James Dobson during the March 28, 2002 broadcast of his *Focus on the Family* radio show. This statement, coming from one of the nation's most influential evangelical Christians, served to up the ante in a long-simmering dispute within American Christendom.

Marshall Fritz, President of the Alliance for the Separation of School & State, subsequently expressed support: "For years, Dr. Dobson has supported three options for Christians: Public schools, Christian schools, and home schooling. With today's courageous and insightful statement, Dr. Dobson joins the millions of Americans who have already discovered that the public schools have become government indoctrination centers which are no place to train new generations of freedom loving Americans."

Our Embrace of Christ-less Education

"By law, you are no more allowed to teach religious values and religious views in our public schools than you are in the schools of Russia tonight...as far as all religious teaching (except the religion of Humanism, which is a different kind of a thing) it is just as banned by law from our schools, and our schools are just as secular as the schools in Soviet Russia—just exactly! Not ten years from now. Tonight!"

FRANCIS A. SCHAEFFER (FROM A 1982 SPEECH
AT CORAL RIDGE PRESBYTERIAN CHURCH)

"...the American school system is inferior in terms of academics, bankrupt in terms of morality, and corrosive in terms of spirituality and religion. In short, the government education system is no place for the children of people who claim allegiance to the King of Kings."

VODDIE BAUCHAM

We love a good lie. This is our nature.

Just ask Bernie Madoff. Or Joe Isuzu. Or Barry Obama. Or...well...you get the picture.

One of the greatest of delusions willfully pursued, captured, and cherished by the vast majority of professing Christians in recent American history is the notion that Christ can be removed as the clear, ever-present center of education in all areas, and that anything better than an unending series of completely catastrophic consequences will emerge as a result.

Before we dive into any detail, just think of it. It's such a simple thing. This question, as all others of significance, finds its every good and true answer in one place: Christ.

The Jesus Christ of biblical Christianity is either the *required* centerpiece of a Christian understanding where education is concerned or He is *nothing at all*. He is God over all or He is a relatively trivial accessory. In biblical Christianity, there is never, in *any* area of life, an optional Jesus. If there is a single place where a Christian would consider his Christ as optional, then he is not dealing rightly with the Lord of Scripture.

Jesus defines and claims ownership over everything in the life of the Common Believer. And "everything" certainly must include education, every bit as much as it covers sexuality, spirituality, sobriety, entertainment, and business practices. Therefore, education, once separated from Christ at any time and for any reason, inherently and automatically pollutes any subject under its influence or authority. It accomplishes this inevitable result by transferring its own Christ-less nature to anything with which it comes in contact. Once Jesus was nudged oh-so-politely to the side where education was concerned, everything covered under its umbrella of authority was shifted into the very same "Christ optional" category.

This seems like such a stark, obvious sort of thing, yet I have no trouble recalling how I, as a teenager at Mountain Home High School, in a small, rural Arkansan Bible Belt setting, was convinced that my being in the public school system was no problem at all. I was a professing Christian and my presence there was completely *natural*.

As I said, the comfortable fit of a good lie does come quite naturally.

It was so easy to go there. And I'm sure that it was easy to be sent. I certainly hold no animosity towards Gram, the angel God used to save me from so much and for so long, for shipping me off to school. She had little idea as to what was going on there and, as many a professing American Christian in those days as well as our own, she simply didn't know what the Bible had to say about education. She was going along with a crowd that had long abandoned the virtues it frequently professed with its lips. In a secular cultural context, my going to public school was the *natural* thing to do.

Even Gram was not familiar with the serious Christianity that accompanied the birth of this nation. She was drifting along with the cultural tide along with most everybody else. Again, this was natural. Most of her spiritual growth and biblical knowledge came long after I had finished doing my time at MHHS. Fortunately for Gram, for you, and for me, we are not doomed to the future prepared by the mistakes of our past.

You see, God has a perfect plan. And He simply will not let us wreck it.

Removal of the Lord is the End of Wisdom

"...the government school system is a foe to be defeated, not a friend to be reformed. Government education is one of the most corrosive influences in the history of the United States. It has served as an incubator for ideologies like Darwinian evolution, Gramscian Marxism, feminism, progressivism, and the radical homosexual agenda (to name just a few)."

VODDIE BAUCHAM

The fear of the LORD is hatred of evil.

PROVERBS 8:13

The point here is not to rail against those who might have been even more "in the know" than Gram as they sent their little treasures off to Caesar for Christ-less programming. We have all played a role in propping up this God-hating system—even those of us with no children at all. We are so completely on board with the Christ-less education program that its support has become our default setting; it is automatic...we automatically finance it through our taxes, we automatically advocate it through our votes and we even automatically *defend* it, as if, by sheer volume or raw numbers of forced participation, we might somehow validate our open rebellion against God through blind fidelity en masse to this Christ-less system of indoctrination.

My hope would be that we would set aside our pride and ego long enough to repent, submit to Christ's expressed will in this, as all other areas of our lives, and begin to seriously approach the challenging and difficult path that we face where the reclamation of education is concerned. We've dug a deep hole, indeed. Yet He is faithful. He has provided us with every answer and every tool that we need to effectively apply that answer in each of our lives.

While there are many wonderful works dedicated to exploring the subject of Christ-centered education in detail, my aim here is much more humble and simple. What I hope to formalize here is an agreed upon starting point—a necessary centerpiece—for *all* of education.

The Word of God is not vague or hazy on this subject.

If genuine knowledge and wisdom have no beginning outside of Christ, why would we send our impressionable children to a Christ-less system for the purpose of acquiring its version of knowledge and wisdom as their own?

If the fear of the LORD really *is the beginning* of wisdom...if it *is the beginning* of knowledge...if we actually *believe* these things, then how is it possible that we would even entertain for an instant the thought of sending any child of ours to an overtly Christ-less institution for the purpose of receiving formative instruction in life?

Is this tricky? Of course it's not.

Am I annoying? Surely.

But trickiness or nuisances are not vital concerns here. All that matters is: Is what I am saying *true*?

Removal of the Lord is the End of Knowledge

"There is no doubt that we are in the midst of a great battle and the government schools in many ways represent the front lines. As such, it is important that we have well-trained, well-equipped men and women (not children) engaging in warfare there when possible. Unfortunately, few Christian teachers understand this. As a result, the vast majority of Christian teachers (ignorant of the battle raging all around them) are merely serving as willing accomplices. Of course, they will argue that the mere fact that they are Christians makes all the difference, but this is a farce. Other Christian teachers see themselves as 'missionaries' working to save souls on a sinking ship. This, while admirable, is ultimately a band-aid on a cancer. This is the equivalent of teaching slaves 'inner freedom' without rejecting or opposing slavery."

VODDIE BAUCHAM[35]

It has been said that were an identifiable foreign power have done to our children what the modern public education system has "accomplished" in America over recent years, we would certainly consider it to be an act of war. And this view comes from a secular perspective.

We, as Common Believers, should know all too well that there *is* a well-defined opposing power that has indeed committed an act of war upon our children. This has been done deliberately and as a part of a meticulously planned and ongoing assault upon biblical Christianity in an effort to transform and conform our civilization to a progressive mold. We must also confront the painful reality that we have been willing allies in the very same atrocity committed against the little boys and little girls entrusted to our care. While we may be tempted to look backwards in unproductive ways, the path to restoration not only lies ahead, but it is well lit.

The good part is that this well lit path has been made so clear by the Lord we serve. The bad part is that this well lit path has been made so clear by the Lord we serve. As I mentioned...be careful what you wish (and pray) for.

Embracing Christ-Centered Education as Essential

For I rejoiced greatly when the brothers came and testified to your truth, as indeed you are walking in truth. I have no greater joy than to hear that my children are walking in truth.

3 JOHN 3–4

A disciple is not above his teacher, but everyone when he is fully trained will be like his teacher.

LUKE 6:40

How far do you think "progressive Christianity" would have ever advanced in America if every professing Christian in the land embraced the biblically mandated, Christ-centered approach to education?

Do you think that "progressive morality" would have ever had a chance of gaining traction in such an environment? Without the success of counterfeit of religion and morality, the progressive political movement would exist as an utterly impotent, extreme fringe movement, if at all.

Every progressive triumph of the past sixty years has been aided more by the Christian abandonment of Christ-centered education than by any other single decision or force in American culture. It is therefore impossible for any true, God-honoring, and lasting recovery to be found without this most fortified and critical of enemy strongholds being stormed, razed, and burnt to the ground.

Sound a little too dramatic? Well, it *is* dramatic. But, in light of Scripture, is it not true? And isn't that what matters?

I know that, while once I thought very differently on this subject, and I do not even have a wife or children at this time, I cannot help but have radically changed in my views in light of the revealed truth of God's perfect Word. What reconciliation can there be between Christ-less systems of education (or Christ-less systems of *anything*, for that matter) and Christ-centered biblical Christianity? None that I can see.

That kind of revelation can be painful, and much more so in this instance for those of you who have already sent your children down a path founded upon Christ-less education. Please know that God has purpose for you in precisely the position in which you and your children find yourselves. Remember: He *loves* to work through desperate situations, so take heart. That said, this will be anything but easy.

We have to ask ourselves questions, but much more than this, we have to want to find the answers. And whatever The Artists Formerly Known as The Emergent Church might have to say, God's perfect Word *does* have the answers. All of 'em. I see this as both a blessing and a warning.

God's revealed truth in this context makes for what we might call the quintessential "be careful what you wish for" proposition.

Do you want a Christ-centered life?

Do you pray for a Christ-centered home and family?

Do you desire a Christ-centered community, culture, and nation?

Do you dream of a Christ-centered restoration of that shining city on a hill that once was the United States of America?

Do you seek a reformation of the professing church of Christ in that same America?

I believe that, as a Common Believer, you do. You must.

With that in mind, I ask: Can you imagine *any* of the lofty goals listed above being even remotely possible without our *personal insistence upon* the Christ-centered education of children?

In the final three chapters, we will take a solid look at the three core essential components of any grand strategy that might bring about these most dramatic of personal, communal, and national improvements: The centering of life on God's Word, God's Gospel and, ultimately, God Himself.

19

Sharpening the Sword of Truth (For Use)

Preparing the Perfect Weapon for Battle

Do not think that I have come to bring peace to the earth. I have not come to bring peace, but a sword.

MATTHEW 10:34

In all circumstances take up the shield of faith, with which you can extinguish all the flaming darts of the evil one; and take the helmet of salvation, and the sword of the Spirit, which is the word of God.

EPHESIANS 6:16–17

THE COMMON BELIEVER'S BLUEPRINT FOR VICTORY

I always assumed that the first time I went to Florida, it would be for the expressed purpose of visiting Disney World. This was just a given.

As a life-long amusement park lover and fan of most things fantasy, the Magic Kingdom was high on my list of things to check out. Sure, the Disney Company had plummeted into a rather pathetic state during my lifetime, but I was willing to set that sad reality aside long enough to squeeze in at least one tour of that iconic fantasyland. I'd dreamt of it since I was a kid. If I ever got near Orlando, I'd be there...but a funny thing happened on the way to 2009.

In the spring of that year, my friend Jerry and I took a trip to Orlando. We got a hotel room right up the street from the castle that Mickey Mouse built. (Now there's a funny picture.)

I was jazzed. But not for the reason you might think, or for the one that I would have assumed just months earlier.

We were in town for the 2009 Ligonier Ministries National Conference. The theme of that year's conference was the holiness of God. Incredibly, it had absolutely nothing to do with Mickey Mouse, Peter Pan, or EPCOT Center.

And despite this, I had to pinch myself at the prospect of being there, in that place, about to meet those people: Sinclair Ferguson... DA Carson... Albert Mohler... Steven Lawson... Thabiti Anyabwile... Alistair Begg... R.C. Sproul, Jr.... Derek Thomas... Ligon Duncan... Robert Godfrey...and... *R...C... Sproul!*

Woohoo! Shazam! Man, I was psyched! And so was Jerry. We were like a couple of kids heading to the Magic Kingdom. Only much, much better in every meaningful way.

Iron Sharpens Iron

This is the message we have heard from him and proclaim to you, that God is light, and in him is no darkness at all. If we say we have fellowship with him while we walk in darkness, we lie and do not practice the truth. But if we walk in the light, as he is in the light, we have fellowship with one another, and the blood of Jesus his Son cleanses us from all sin.

1 JOHN 1:5–7

Iron sharpens iron, and one man sharpens another.

PROVERBS 27:17

I met Jerry and his wife Jill at the First Baptist Church of Ozark, Missouri. From the very start, there was something really weird about these people. My kind of weird.

Jerry was serious—the kind of serious about the pursuit and apprehension of deep biblical truth that makes a person seriously happy. He taught a Sunday School class at the church and after a while I gave it a whirl. Once in the door, I remained in that class for the duration of my time at FBCO.

We ended up hanging out quite a lot. We had been led to many of the same conclusions to many of the same questions. We had many of the same concerns about many of the same problems. The ideas we shared were relatively controversial in this day and age of candy Christianity, and the issues we contemplated were often heavy and demanding, but we could always joke, laugh, and bask in the glow of that certain, particular sort of peace that can only come through complete reliance upon the sovereign God of Scripture.

For a time there was a third musketeer in the club, a guy named Mike. Mike, Jerry, and I would get together and just talk theology. And doctrine. And dogma.

You know, the things deemed most boring and unnecessary by the vast majority of professing Christians these days. I suppose it was that sad reality that made Jerry and Mike so very cool and valuable to me. That sounds selfish—"valuable to me"—but I think it was only so in at least a mostly good way. Their scarcity made them valuable. There's no denying that. And my access to them was a treasure.

They were challenging. Jerry was so challenging, in fact, that without saying a word he managed to make me do a little self-evaluation on more than one occasion. One such instance came on our fabled trip to Orlando.

I Won't Drive 55

Then he said to them, "Therefore render to Caesar the things that are Caesar's, and to God the things that are God's."

MATTHEW 22:21

Just when I had become accustomed to and appreciative of Jerry's dedication to the pursuit of scriptural truth and ability to communicate the truth he'd come to know and love so effectively, he managed to find a new way of tweaking me towards thought. By driving. Well, sort of driving.

When we picked up the rental car that Jerry had reserved at the Orlando airport, we were treated to the revelation that, if *I* wanted to drive the car, there would be a neat little mountain of extra fees to be paid for the privilege. That tweaked us, so we declined. The down side was that Jerry had to do all of the driving. The other down side was that Jerry had this thing about "obeying the law." As in: the speed limit.

From the moment we rolled out of the parking lot, his seriousness on the matter was inescapable, undeniable, and more than a little jarring to little old me. I could hardly believe it. I stretched my ability to covertly employ peripheral vision to its limits as I strained to confirm that we were, in fact, going as slow as I had feared.

I felt a building temptation to pull the lid lower on my Marvin the Martian ball-cap and slink down in the seat as to avoid being too easily identified as a passenger of Grandma Jerry's.

Things got worse as I became acutely aware that he was stopping for yellow lights. I was mortified. What horror would come next? Respecting pedestrians?

And how could this be Jerry's doing? He was a *man*. He liked HEMIs. He loved guns. He grew a full beard every winter. He was a fan of Stonewall Jackson, for crying out loud! What...went...*wrong?!* How could this have happened to Jerry? How did such a tough guy go so soft? Where was the seedpod?

Finally, somewhere in the embarrassingly underused recesses of my puny little brain, something clicked. Where once I was confused, I was then convicted. Jerry was doing these things simply because *they were the law*. Ouch!

See? I told you Christianity was hard.

The Christian's Call to Ever Increasing Depth

I myself am satisfied about you, my brothers, that you yourselves are full of goodness, filled with all knowledge and able to instruct one another.

ROMANS 15:14

To know God is to know truth. He is the author and origin of truth, and He has made known every essential thing through His perfect Word. The pursuit of ever deepening understanding of biblical truth is, to the Common Believer, a non-negotiable. It's not an option. It is a required component of a fulfilling life.

As our knowledge of Him increases, we will progress. We will grow.

As we neglect His revealed truth, we will grow stagnant. We will become weak.

Fortunately, all biblical Christians are, by the fact of the Holy Spirit's presence within them, imbued with an inherent appetite for this truth. Beyond this, every Common Believer is also equipped with a desire to submit to this revealed truth.

Remember: knowledge of truth without submission to it is of little value. All biblical Christians are compelled by the indwelling Holy Spirit not only to acquire knowledge, but apply it. This is another essential component in the Common Believer's lifelong process of sanctification.

The absence of either the desire to acquire or submit to God's revealed truth is also one of a handful of clear biblical identifiers of a false Christian conversion. The phony convert will have no such thirst for studying the Word of God, and certainly won't be into the whole submission deal.

While true biblical Christians will struggle, slip and waver from time to time, never will one be comfortable in such a state. The Holy Spirit simply will not allow it. He will always inspire us to thirst for His truth. He will always inspire us to submit to His truth.

He will always inspire us in both of these ways, and one of the greatest blessings that He bestows in this context is that embodied by God-fearing, Scripture-honoring brothers and sisters through whom we can learn and test ourselves in knowledge and ability. As His proverb says, iron sharpens iron.

It is a particular wonder from above for one to be allowed fellowship with true believers. Through these unique relationships with our brothers and sisters in Christ, we are graciously given the opportunity to learn, grow, struggle, and laugh together.

Through these relationships, we will hone our skills with the Sword of Truth. Through our ever-increasing knowledge of His Word, we will grow in understanding of our God. Through this increasing appreciation of and submission to our sovereign Lord and His revealed truth, we will minimize and eventually overcome completely many of our self-serving, sin-worshiping impulses. In doing so, we will find the life that He has promised.

Who knows what might then become possible? We may even learn to obey the laws of traffic. And like it.

Paper Cuts

"Wherever the natural will of man is spoken of in the Bible it is always spoken of as being a depraved will; a degenerate will; an evil, sinful will."

JIM McCLARTY

"The only answer to Hell fire is Holy Ghost fire."

LEONARD RAVENHILL

Rarely are we able to learn a thing about God's character without finding ourselves cut by the revelation. All of Scripture, as all of creation, is about God's self-revelation for the purpose of self-glorification. The more we learn of truth, the more we will learn of His holiness. With His holiness defining His every other attribute and His character demonstrated so clearly and beautifully through every teaching of Scripture, we cannot help but, with each new insight given us, realize all the more how great He is and how utterly insignificant we are in and of ourselves.

This is the ultimate example "no pain, no gain" where the acquisition of true and accurate knowledge is concerned. With every step taken towards a right understanding of God, our egos will suffer agony after agony as we axiomatically acquire added insight into our own self-insufficiency.

We'll learn all sorts of terrible things about ourselves. Really. Sounds like fun, huh?

Actually, it *is*.

Every added bit of clarity regarding our true nature, when taken in under the light of God's grace shown towards us by His choice, cannot help but inspire the sort of warmth, smiles, happiness, and laughter that could not come any other way. This realization of one's total lack of inherent goodness as a *positive* thing is simply beyond the comprehension of the philosophers, teachers and self-helpers of the world. It rubs them the wrong way, and totally so. It makes them crazy (or crazier). They hate it.

The depravity of man—that being a total depravity that applies perfectly to each and every one of us before God regenerates us—is one of the most repugnant of Christian essentials from the progressive perspective. Deepak Chopra and Dr. Phil have built careers dedicated to its opposition. Joel Osteen and Rob Baal have built "ministries" around its repudiation.

Yet, not-so-surprisingly in conflict with the likes of Deepak, Osteen, and Baal, we are called by our God to pursue an ever-increasing depth of understanding where our former depravity and His eternal holiness are concerned, all through relentless exploration of and submission to His Word.

Ditching Kiddie-Pool Christianity

The proverbs of Solomon, son of David, king of Israel: To know wisdom and instruction, to understand words of insight, to receive instruction in wise dealing, in righteousness, justice, and equity; to give prudence to the simple, knowledge and discretion to the youth—Let the wise hear and increase in learning, and the one who understands obtain guidance, to understand a proverb and a saying, the words of the wise and their riddles. The fear of the LORD is the beginning of knowledge; fools despise wisdom and instruction.

PROVERBS 1:1–7

"What about the jackass in the church? The jackass in the church is the person that always screams, 'I want to go deeper!'"

PERRY NOBLE

Meet Perry.

He's what qualifies in much of professing American Christendom these days as a pastor.

Perry thinks I'm a jackass.

Before you go getting all superior on me, know this: he almost surely thinks that *you're* a jackass too.

You see, Perry likes to keep things shallow. He insists. He cares, um, very *deeply* about this. Shallow teaching is better teaching, because shallow is better than deep, at least where your biblical knowledge and understanding are concerned. It's just better for you that way, and by "better for you," Perry means "better for him."

Perry may be annoying, arrogant, and destructive, but he's no fool. Well, he's something of a fool, as scripturally defined, but he definitely knows where his bread is buttered and from where his influence and power is derived.

Like most garden-variety truth abusers, he has a vested interest in keeping Christians from the depths of Scripture. Keeping folks in the theological kiddie-pool is important to the likes of Perry. The less that you know about the deeper truths that the God of biblical Christianity has called you to learn and inscribe on your heart, the easier it is for those of his ilk to distort those truths and manipulate you with impunity.

Perry is a predator. One of many. And he needs your help.

In seeking this help, he frequently rails against those who would seek depth in their understanding of Scripture. In a recent blog post titled *Seven Thoughts I'm Wrestling With*[36], he elaborates as follows:

1. Why is the church so content with being normal when God has promised the supernatural?
2. Why are some in the church obsessed with obtaining information but have no desire to live out the transformation that Jesus brings?

3. Why do some in the church excuse non-excellent standards by saying phrases such as, "well, after all…it's just church?" Our standards of doing things should not be lower than the worlds…they should be higher; after all, what the church does matters!
4. Why do we claim to follow a God who changes things…and yet often times we refuse to change things?
5. Why do we set our expectations on the lives that Jesus wants us to live so low when Scripture sets them so high?
6. Why does the church always try to control people when Jesus died so that we could be unleashed?
7. Why is it that so many church leaders would rather lead through imitation (becoming just like someone else) rather than revelation (listening to God and then doing what He says?)

I included all seven "thoughts" to maintain context, but it is points two, five, six and seven that seem to speak clearly to the often Perry-promoted theme of perpetual spiritual shallowness.

"Pastor" Perry often uses a line of argument represented in point two in order to justify the suppression of depth in his congregants' scriptural understanding. He is fond of expressing this idea again and again and in a variety of ways, but it generally follows a "why bother learning deeper truths when you haven't come close to perfectly applying the simpler ones yet?" line. This is the point from which he launches into calling out the "jackasses" who express a desire for depth in their biblical understanding.

About this we have much to say, and it is hard to explain, since you have become dull of hearing. For though by this time you ought to be teachers, you need someone to teach you again the basic principles of the oracles of God. You

need milk, not solid food, for everyone who lives on milk is
unskilled in the word of righteousness, since he is a child.
But solid food is for the mature, for those who have their
powers of discernment trained by constant practice to
distinguish good from evil.

HEBREWS 5:11–14

So it is that those depth-desiring Christian folk really do annoy Perry. A *lot.*

In Pastor Perry Land, only a jackass would want to "go deeper" into God's perfect written revelation of truth before they have managed to perfectly apply—by Perry standards—any bits of information that they've already gleaned. When these troublesome folks are led to a greater depth through a Spirit-fueled pursuit of deeper biblical knowledge, they are to be mocked, ridiculed, and dismissed as confused, insincere, and problematic. Or, in a word, as "jackasses."

In Biblical Christian Land, things work quite differently. Here the pursuit of scriptural understanding and depth is encouraged from the get-go. Here a God-fearing and obedient shepherd will feed and nurture their Lord's flock, always with depth of understanding as a primary goal.

Theology is vital. Doctrine is critical.

These things, derided though they may be within the walls of many a church building these days, are vital elements to the Christian walk. Sound theology and doctrine are essential. They are the gateway through which the Christian life is lived in practice.

And His sheep will crave sound teaching. His Spirit within them will never be content with less. With God the Holy Spirit as our indwelling guide, an ever-present appetite for an ever-deepening understanding of His truth is *guaranteed.*

What kind of jackass would dare attempt to stifle or suppress this appetite? Well, in a word: Perry.

Pastor Jackass goes on in his fifth point to wonder why, oh why, do "we set our expectations on the lives that Jesus wants us to live so low when Scripture sets them so high?" One can only wonder how we are to know of the "high scriptural standards" in question if we are discouraged from learning them in the first place, but such incoherence barely phases the likes of Perry. He's a man-child on a mission, and pesky things like intellectual consistency and fidelity to biblical truth aren't about to get in his way.

His sixth point speculates as to why the church seeks to "control people" when Jesus died to "unleash" them. Yet Scripture, should one be encouraged to actually *read* it, sure does seem to describe the relationship between Christ and His sheep as one of owner and property. This biblical Jesus fellow seems to be all about the control and conformity...and in a big, all-encompassing kind of way. Biblical Christians are presented as nothing more or less than Christ's *slaves*. They are His possessions; His children. They are utterly dependent upon Him and are drawn to an ever-deepening relationship with and understanding of Him, because it is *His* will that they do so.

In point seven, Perry does a fine job of finishing things off with a flurry of irony-laced self-contradiction. Here we learn that church leaders have stooped so low as to actually advocate that church members become "just like someone else." But isn't becoming "just like" Jesus the point and goal of biblical Christianity from the perspective of a Spirit-filled believer?

And once again we are treated to a rebuke for not "listening to God and then doing what He says" when our expression of a desire to know what He says is just what got us branded as jackasses by the good "pastor" Perry in the first place.

So what's a jackass to do, anyway? How do we deal with the likes of "Pastor" Perry?

Well, I am happy to report that we deal with him by doing just the very thing that he seems to hate so very much: We study, learn, and submit to Scripture.

We pursue depth. Daily. Hourly, even. We read, pray, grow and become just the sort of Christian that cannot be had by the likes of Pastor Jackass. We develop discernment. We "test all things." We "hold fast to that which is true." All by the perfect light of Scripture.

As we do this, amazing things will happen. They are as guaranteed as the appetite for truth that brought us down this path in the first place. We will see lives transformed. We will see families and communities restored. We will see the church reformed and maybe, just maybe, we will see a nation saved. We will swim deep, make waves and change the world.

20

The Matchless and Essential
Whole Gospel of Christ

The Power and Obligation of a Fire Breathing Christian

So Jesus said to the Jews who had believed in him, "If you abide in my word, you are truly my disciples, and you will know the truth, and the truth will set you free."

JOHN 8:31–32

"Can we have that power again in our day? We can. But only if we hold to the full-orbed Reformation gospel and do not compromise with the culture around us....How does it happen? It happens by the renewing of our minds...by study of the life-giving and renewing Word of God...empowered by the Holy Spirit [so that] we will begin to take on something of the glorious luster of the Lord Jesus Christ and will become increasingly like him."

JAMES MONTGOMERY BOICE

There were tables full of pictures and books at Kristi's funeral. The books were things she'd loved while she was here and the pictures were of the one we'd all loved and lost, at least for a little while.

I have never before or since that day been so aware of being in a fog, if that makes any sense. It was an impossible sort of simultaneous hypersensitivity and numbness. As if this wasn't strange enough, I also felt both intensely alone and completely covered by another all at once.

I know that the loneliness and the numbness were there because, at the moment Kristi went on ahead of me to paradise, I lost my purpose. Or so I thought and felt. I had no idea what my practical meaning was anymore. It had been so clear just days earlier, but now, at my wife's funeral, it was gone.

I think that the clarity and focus paradoxically present with me on that day came because I knew that I wanted and needed to soak up every possible detail. Every moment was precious. Every face was precious. Every thought was precious. I had to savor every bit of it now, because once this ceremony was done, Scott and Kristi would be nothing but history to this world.

It was this strange awareness that helped me to dwell in the memories inspired by every one of the hundreds of pictures placed on the tables and in the pages of every one of the treasured books stacked and opened amongst those pictures. It encouraged and equipped me to make some kind of connection with every person in the room. These moments of clarity, recall, and contact made me warm. They were wonderful.

I remember looking at one of the pictures from our wedding day just over ten years earlier and wondering how Rustin was going to handle this day. Rus was my best friend and, back on that happy summer day more than a decade earlier, he had been the best man at Scott and Kristi's wedding. Now he would be preaching at Kristi's funeral.

Rustin and I had come a long way and seen many things. We'd traded comic books in junior high and gone treasure hunting in the frigid extremes of the wintertime Bering Sea. We'd made liquor store runs when Clinton won Michigan in '92 and struggled through poverty and comedy through our adventures in Seattle. We'd endured, experienced, and conquered much. But for all of those past trials, I knew that this would be the hardest test I'd ever seen him face.

Before the ceremony, Rus and I got together to plan things. He wanted to know what I wanted and expected in this; if I had any specific ideas as to how it should all be done. Not only did I have such notions, but I knew he would be completely on the same page before I even opened my mouth, which made the whole thing even more of a weird and wonderful thing.

The plan was this: Preach the Gospel. The Gospel that saved Kristi. The simple, undiluted Gospel. Then preach it again. And after that, give it one more shot.

We both instantly knew that this was as magnificent a plan as ever there could be, and I think that for a moment there, in the midst of this realization, there was actual unrestrained happiness in sight. A ray of sunshine had broken through the darkness. There was warmth and hope. It was real.

Then it was up to Rustin to *do* the good thing that we had planned. And that was very hard. He was shaky and he started to cry more than once. And it was one of the most beautiful things I have ever seen or heard.

A perfect, holy God…a fallen, spiritually dead little girl destined for His wrath…an infinite gap between her and this perfect God as a result of her sinful state…and then Her redeemer came. He came for *her*.

He lived the perfect life that she never could…He suffered the wrath of God on her behalf…and now she was with Him in His paradise.

And all of those for whom He died, those who were given to Him by the Father before the foundation of the world, would one day be with Him, too. And they'd meet Kristi there. They'd get to know her. In that place with her Jesus, they would all grow and laugh and love forever.

And *there* was power. Nothing was added because nothing comparatively good *could* be added. It was perfect. This perfection was not a result of smooth production or carefully crafted appeal to the felt needs of a crowd. Anything but. Rus and I tended to think lowly of those sorts of things even then.

It was a simple display of, and appeal to, the greatest force in all of God's creation: The Gospel of Jesus Christ.

Undiluted Perfection Cannot Be Improved

"Christ needs no new inventions to glorify Him. 'We have invented a new line of things,' says one. Have you? 'We have discovered something very wonderful.' I daresay you have, but Christ, 'the same yesterday, today, and forever' (Heb. 13:8 NKJV), needs none of your inventions, discoveries or additions to His truth. A plain Christ is the forever the loveliest Christ. Dress Him up, and you have deformed Him and defamed Him. Bring Him out just as He is...."

CHARLES SPURGEON

"A man can no more diminish God's glory by refusing to worship Him than a lunatic can put out the sun by scribbling the word, 'darkness' on the walls of his cell."

C.S. LEWIS

The Gospel of Jesus Christ is perfect.

It will always appeal to His sheep and it will always repel goats. It is perfectly effectual in both regards, each and every time it is preached in its undiluted form.

It *will* save all of His sheep. It *will* inspire conviction, repentance, and then joy in them. It will always generate discomfort, rejection and hatred in goats. It will *never* elicit a neutral response.

It *never fails*. It cannot be successfully subdued or resisted by the will of any man, woman, angel, or demon.

It is not the tiniest bit dependent upon our personal persuasiveness or charisma. It is not the least bit interested in our opinions. It cares not a whit for the preferences or desires of our precious wills and egos. It is not assisted by sports programs or seminars on practical living techniques. It is not amplified by clever little witticisms or compelling intellectual argumentation. It is not aided by philosophical constructs or Madison Avenue marketing. It cannot be improved upon in any way at any time in any place. It…is…*perfect.*

And we would be wise not to play with perfect. Each time that we do, we mock God and the Christ at the very center of His Gospel. There is but one seeker where salvation is concerned, and He is God.

We cannot help the Gospel. We can only proclaim it.

Death and Life

"For God so loved the world, that he gave his only Son, that whoever believes in him should not perish but have eternal life. For God did not send his Son into the world to condemn the world, but in order that the world might be saved through him. Whoever believes in him is not condemned, but whoever does not believe is condemned already, because he has not believed in the name of the only Son of God. And this is the judgment: the light has come into the world, and people loved the darkness rather than the light because their works were evil.

JOHN 3:16–19

"How can men sit and hear the Word of the living God and not catch fire?"

LEONARD RAVENHILL

Here is power: God is holy. We were all born children of wrath, God-haters by nature, in open rebellion against Him, and deserving of death and eternal punishment. This was our nature as a result of Adam's fall. The sin that he brought into the world through his willful act of disobedience toward God has infected all of creation. As a result, everything, including our very ability to see or do anything genuinely good, was terminally corrupted.

Subsequently, we were incapable of honoring God's law. We violated it constantly by nature, and we liked doing it. A lot.

We were each proud law-breakers to and through our rotten, fallen little core. The fact of God's law written on our hearts was a constant reminder to us that we were broken, rebellious creatures separated from this holy God by our all-encompassing sin nature.

When left there, we are helpless in this state. We are spiritually dead; incapable of even recognizing, much less reaching out for or positively responding to the holy God of creation.

Yet even while we were in this vulgar and pathetic condition, burdened by a debt that we could not possibly (and would not even *desire* to) pay, God arranged for the redemption of His people. He did this by sending His Son as the perfect sacrifice on their behalf.

Jesus the Messiah came and lived among men, living the sinless life required by His character and for His purpose. God then poured out His holy wrath on Jesus so that the debt produced through our natural wickedness might be satisfied.

In His death on the cross, Jesus accomplished the salvation of all who the Father had given Him before the dawn of creation. He came to save each of them individually, specifically, and by name, and He is literally incapable of losing even a single one of them. This Jesus never fails. By this sacrifice, all of His people were freed of their sin debt vicariously through the atonement of the crucified Christ.

With their debt paid completely and forever, each and every one of His own was eternally secured by His hand, and will glorify and enjoy Him forevermore as they spend an eternity of eternities with Him in His restored creation.

This is our great weapon. This message never fails.

The Narrow Way

"But, of course, being a Christian does mean that where Christianity differs from other religions, Christianity is right and they are wrong."

C.S. LEWIS

"That we enjoy relative safety from violent attacks against us may indicate a maturing of modern civilization with respect to religious toleration. Or it may indicate that we have so compromised the gospel that we no longer provoke the conflict that true faith engenders."

R.C. SPROUL

For all of the incomparable beauty and grace that we as Common Believers see in this life-sustaining and defining Gospel, the world will never cease or slow in reminding us that it hates the message every bit as much as we adore it. This hatred for the undiluted Gospel springs from its exclusivity.

The Gospel of Christ is unambiguous and uncompromising. Wherever anyone dissents from it on any matter, they are wrong. It will always be so. And we must not shrink from acknowledgment and even proclamation of this essential truth.

There is not a force in this universe more politically incorrect than the whole Gospel of Jesus Christ. There is not a force more repulsive to unregenerate, sinful man than the exclusive Gospel of Jesus Christ.

This very Gospel is the only power by which a person can be saved from the righteous wrath of a holy, sovereign God. In this, we each find our purpose in a dark and fallen world: To proclaim His perfect Gospel without qualification, hesitation, apology…or editorial license. We are to go boldly in His name, according to His purpose and for His glory.

As with everything else in His creation, God's Gospel of Jesus Christ is all about *Him*. It's not about us, as much as we may wish it were so. We are not the lead characters. We are not the center. We are not the main attraction. *He* is.

Even things like funerals for Common Believers, just as the lives lived before them, really are not about the people in question. Not mainly, anyway. No, these lives and events are all about their God. The God by whom and *for* whom all things were made. The God who *always* does whatever He wants, whenever He wants, and however He wants, all the while defining truth and goodness by those very actions and bringing glory to Himself in the process.

The God who owes nothing.

The God who *struts*.

The Meaning of Life and Everything Else

21

The God Who Struts

It's all about Him

"God is the only comfort, He is also the supreme terror: the thing we most need and the thing we most want to hide from."

C.S. Lewis

"If you find God with great ease, perhaps it is not God that you have found."

Thomas Merton

Before my parents divorced, we lived in an old farmhouse. I was four. I remember sitting out on the porch one day with my dad. We were sitting side-by-side, looking up at the sky and talking about God.

He said he could see His footprints up there in the clouds. His eyes were locked in a fixed gaze upwards. He was definitely focused on *something* up there as he spoke and I was convinced that God must right at that particular moment be walking amongst those particular clouds. What a privilege to have Him so close, I thought. I only wished that I could see Him, too.

When I was a little boy, I thought that people naturally wanted to find God. Now I know better.

Holy Terror

And the four living creatures, each of them with six wings, are full of eyes all around and within, and day and night they never cease to say, **"Holy, holy, holy, is the Lord God Almighty, who was and is and is to come!"**

REVELATION 4:8 (bold emphasis mine)

And I said: "Woe is me! For I am lost; for I am a man of unclean lips, and I dwell in the midst of a people of unclean lips; for my eyes have seen the King, the LORD of hosts!"

ISAIAH 6:5

There are, at this very moment, the most peculiar and magnificent of angelic creatures circling the throne of God. They sing without end or interruption of our Lord's defining attribute: His perfect holiness.

They do not tire. They neither relent nor regret.

They somehow even manage to resist the most terrible scourge of our age: boredom. Where we cannot imagine tolerating, much less desiring, such an existence, they yearn for nothing else. Nothing less than audibly proclaiming the holiness of God even appeals to them.

This is the task for which they were made: To endlessly announce God's perfect holiness. He made them for this purpose, and that truth alone tells us much about Him, if we'll let it.

Hundreds of years before John the Revelator was granted a vision of these amazing six-winged heralds of God's majesty, the prophet Isaiah had a momentous encounter with one of them.

The creature approached Isaiah just after he had beheld the holiness of God. In that instant, having been confronted with his own complete depravity in light of the Lord's perfect holiness, Isaiah utterly unraveled and collapsed, proclaiming, "Woe is me! For I am lost; for I am a man of unclean lips, and I dwell in the midst of a people of unclean lips; for my eyes have seen the King, the LORD of hosts!"

R.C. Sproul described the encounter this way:

"We are fortunate in one respect: God does not appear to us in the way He appeared to Isaiah. Who could stand it? God normally reveals our sinfulness to us a bit at a time. We experience a gradual recognition of our own corruption. God showed Isaiah his corruption all at once. No wonder he was ruined.

Isaiah explained it this way: "My eyes have seen the King, the LORD Almighty" (Isa. 6:5). He saw the holiness of God. For the first time in his life Isaiah really understood who God was. At the same instant, for the first time Isaiah really understood who Isaiah was.

Then one of the seraphs flew to me with a live coal in his hand, which he had taken with tongs from the altar. With it he touched my mouth and said, "See, this has touched your lips; your guilt is taken away and your sin atoned for." (Isaiah 6:6–7)

Isaiah was groveling on the floor. . . The seraph pressed the white-hot coal to the lips of the prophet and seared him. . . He was refined by holy fire.

In this divine act of cleansing, Isaiah experienced a forgiveness that went beyond the purification of his lips. He was cleansed throughout, forgiven to the core, but not without the awful pain of repentance. He went beyond the cheap grace and the easy utterance "I'm sorry." He was in mourning for his sin, overcome with moral grief, and God sent an angel to heal him. His sin was taken away. His dignity remained intact. His guilt was removed, but his humanity was not insulted. The conviction that he felt was constructive. His was no cruel and unusual punishment. A second of burning flesh on the lips brought a healing that would extend to eternity. In a moment, the disintegrated prophet was whole again. His mouth was purged. He was clean."[37]

Once Isaiah had an accurate understanding of his own wretched nature and his Lord's perfect holiness *imposed* upon him, and the infinite gap between God and the "holiest" of men was made plain, he was fully prepared for service. Then God used him.

Holy, Holy, Holy

And I heard the voice of the Lord saying, "Whom shall I send, and who will go for us?" Then I said, "Here am I! Send me."

ISAIAH 6:8

"God saved you for Himself; God saved you by Himself; God saved you from Himself."

PAUL WASHER

"God doesn't choose those who would choose Him. He chooses those who would never choose Him."

MARK DRISCOLL

Our God is holy. We are on the opposite end of the spectrum…in every way and without exception. When Isaiah was made to understand these things, he was transformed.

In all of Scripture, there is not an attribute of the Lord more emphasized or highlighted than that of His holiness. When we view His every other identifiable attribute with this over-arching holiness as a guiding light, we better understand any characteristic under consideration and, as a result, increase in right knowledge of Him.

The seraphim do not sing *Love, love, love!* They sing *Holy, holy, holy!* This is not accidental.

God *is* love, insofar as we understand this as *holy* love. Of course, the love of God tends to bear little resemblance to this fallen world's numerous redefinitions, reincarnations, and repudiations of the biblical concept. It is important to note that the same world that has so radically redefined the notion of love would very much like to have us focus on any of the resultant soft counterfeits as our guiding principle when we seek to gain a better understanding of God and His truth. This is a temptation that we must not only resist, but refute whenever and wherever we find it lurking about.

How many times have you heard God's *holy* wrath questioned, disputed, or openly refuted because "God is love" and that such a thing as this "holy wrath" deal is simply incompatible with love? The same is often said of God's *holy* justice, His *holy* vengeance, His *holy* discipline, and His *holy* jealousy.

These perversions and slight-of-mind tricks aside, God's perfect love is and must always be understood as holy love, just as his wrath is always holy wrath, his jealousy is always holy jealousy, and his judgment is always holy judgment. God is not held to man's standards on any subject at any time. God is the author, origin, and continually sustaining source of all of these things. God owes man no explanation. God, in short, is God.

God *defines* what is good and true simply by His actions, which are the demonstration of His will.

God's love is *not* soft. It is not easy. It is perfect. It is *holy*.

Once we rightly understand this, we will not merely accept it. We will celebrate it as nothing else. When we celebrate the fact that God, and *only* God, is capable of this perfectly holy love, wrath, jealousy, and justice, we are then made able, willing, and even eager to fully and completely trust in the sheer perfection of His nature as our very sustenance. Only then can we accept and ultimately celebrate what is, to this fallen world, the most terrifying attribute of our holy God: His complete sovereignty.

The God Who Struts Through Scripture

"O the depths of the riches both of the wisdom and knowledge of God! how unsearchable are His judgments, and His ways past finding out"

ROMANS 11:33

Imagine, if you will, the following game-show scenario: The production features ten intelligent, honest, and sincere adults. These people, though they are very well educated in every other area of inquiry, have absolutely no knowledge of the Bible or Christianity whatsoever. One last bit of info on our ten hypothetical folks: They have a perfect understanding of language. They are literally unencumbered by any weakness in this area.

Now, let's imagine these ten intellectual and linguistic freaks of nature are summoned to appear on our game show. Or maybe it's more like a "challenge show" in that there is a prize offered for doing an immense amount of detailed research in solitude and then correctly answering simple, clear questions pertaining to the subject under consideration.

No tricks or trick questions. No gimmicks. No wacky, out-of-the blue surprises or peculiar angles to be played. Just simple, clear answers to equally simple, unambiguous questions.

Now, imagine that these lucky boys and girls are each individually sequestered for as long as it takes them to thoroughly read through the Bible. Then, having just methodically read through it for the very first time, and without exposure to outside sources or contaminants of any sort, they are asked to answer four simple questions about Christianity based exclusively on what they had just read:

1. How did our world come into being?
2. What was "the fall"?
3. Who is Jesus?
4. Who determines salvation for each individual member of fallen mankind?

Our ten participants are not required to agree with or evaluate the concepts under consideration. They are merely asked to explain what this religion's sacred book has to say on the matters. Nothing more; nothing less.

If the potential of a ginormous cash payout would help to emphasize the point here, feel free to imagine a multi-million dollar windfall promised to any of the ten who are able to give simple, clear, and accurate responses to each of these four questions.

As Christians, we expect clear and unified responses to these questions. At least the middle two, anyway.

"The Fall" was the fall of mankind through the original sin of Adam's disobedience of God. This transgression plunged the human race and all of creation into its current darkened state. This basic description would surely be the unanimous position taken by our ten participants, and on that point we'd all agree, too. Similarly, Jesus would be rightly identified as God—the Word made flesh; the exclusive Savior, come into the world so that He might bear the price of sin that had submerged humanity into its depraved state. Unanimous harmony on this answer as well would be the clear expectation of every Christian viewer of this particular game-show.

But when it comes to those bookend questions, we run into some trouble. Not trouble with the ten participants. Nope, they will each still provide completely harmonious and unanimous answers where the first and fourth questions are concerned. The problem is with the Christian audience.

You see, the Christian audience would *not* agree on the answers to those two questions at all, no matter how complete the harmony was amongst the game-show participants.

The God Who Struts Unencumbered

And we know that for those who love God all things work together for good, for those who are called according to his purpose. For those whom he foreknew he also predestined to be conformed to the image of his Son, in order that he might be the firstborn among many brothers. And those whom he predestined he also called, and those whom he called he also justified, and those whom he justified he also glorified.

ROMANS 8:28–30

Having read through the Bible and emerged unencumbered by any personal tradition, habit or outside interference, these ten would each answer questions one and four as follows:

Q1. How did our world come into being?
A1. God made it in six literal days.
Q4. Who determines salvation for each member of fallen mankind?
A4. God does, and He does so alone.

Having read the Bible, and only the Bible, and with millions of bucks on the line, I might add, these ten people would be thankful for the clarity in those pages on even these two subjects. They would have no trouble at all providing these answers, and with total confidence in their accuracy.

Money in the bank, they would think. And they'd be right.

With no pet tradition to steer them and no outside whispers in their ear to explain why the book they just read doesn't actually mean what it so clearly said (there's that "did God *really* say?"

deal again), these good people would consider their multi-million dollar paydays in the bag, so to speak. Especially since, as we've already covered, they are not being asked to affirm or agree with these sentiments at all. All they have to do is accurately express what the written word says. That's all.

Of course, were they required to express only interpretations of this new-to-them Scripture that they *agreed* with, well, that's a whole 'nother story. With that significant change of rules in place, we could expect significant divergence between the ten answers provided. Kind of like the division we find in the Christian audience.

While some would maintain the same positions expressed in Scenario #1, there would be many—almost certainly a majority—who would not. They would feel compelled to mold the creation account in Genesis 1 to conform with contemporary scientific postulates and theories. The Genesis record would be dismissed as a mere "story."

Similarly, many of these folks would have no interest whatsoever in acknowledging, much less claiming, a God who owned them so completely. They'd want nothing to do with a God so total in His sovereignty ("total sovereignty" being redundant, of course), that *He* would be the determiner of *their* fates. Thus, Romans 9, John 6, and countless other crystal clear proclamations of God's uncompromised sovereignty over *all* things would be radically modified in their minds, or jettisoned altogether.

It's important to note that, in all likelihood, question one, on the matter of creation, would inspire less controversy than question four. The reason for this is that question four completely impacts each and every person considering it in a manner that is comprehensive. It hits the macro and it hits the micro...and completely on both counts. It is both worldview and personal identity defining in its nature. Being told that one is not the center of the universe—or even the central figure in determining their own fate—is not something that one will, of his own volition or nature, *ever* embrace.

Which is precisely why God has to impose upon us even the ability to do *that*. Remember: Before He did that very thing for each of us on an individual basis at a specific moment in time, each and every Common Believer was in that sovereignty-rejecting boat. That was our nature. It was who we were.

During the answer section for question four—the portion of our show where contestants give voice to their answers to the questions put to them—we'd witness the full fury of indignant human opposition to the very notion of a sovereign God. We'd be treated to rants about "robots," "puppets," "free will," and the ultimate expression of outrage regarding the clear pronouncement of Scripture on the matter of predestination: "But that's...*not*...*fair!*"

God's response to this? Boo. And Hoo.

I am, of course, paraphrasing. His actual Word on the subject are much more abrasive and challenging.

The God Who Owns Your Will

But the LORD hardened the heart of Pharaoh, and he did not listen to them, as the LORD had spoken to Moses.

Then the LORD said to Moses, "Rise up early in the morning and present yourself before Pharaoh and say to him, 'Thus says the LORD, the God of the Hebrews, "Let my people go, that they may serve me. For this time I will send all my plagues on you yourself,—and on your servants and your people, so that you may know that there is none like me in all the earth. For by now I could have put out my hand and struck you and your people with pestilence, and you would have been cut off from the earth. But for this purpose I have raised you up, to show you my power, so that my name may be proclaimed in all the earth.

EXODUS 9:12–16

Our God is sovereign. Completely sovereign.

As He is the only being capable of holy perfection in all things at all times, we must celebrate the notion that He is also *complete* in His sovereignty over all things at all times. Any lesser view of God's sovereign control always has catastrophic results. This was, it should be noted, the prevailing view of Christians who founded the first colonies in the now-United States of America as well as most of those who actualized the American Revolution.

This is no small thing. It is not coincidental.

The fact that the Reformation, the Pilgrims, and the American Revolution are so closely linked by this very *specific* Christianity is one great key to our understanding how and why we have fallen as a nation, as well as how we might be revived. History declares that this high view of God and low view of man was an essential component to both the Reformation and Revolution. It is therefore only reasonable to expect that this view is an essential ingredient for any genuine, lasting American renewal.

This God saves. He saves completely and without fail. He never "tries" to do anything.

This God is sovereign over every action befalling or taken by any creature that He has made:

Are not two sparrows sold for a penny? And not one of them will fall to the ground apart from your Father. (MATTHEW 10:29)

This God is sovereign over every roll of the dice:

The lot is cast into the lap, but its every decision is from the LORD. (PROVERBS 16:33)

There is no randomness in this God's cosmos. Nothing is left to chance. Nothing happens outside of His purpose. This God even uses *apparently* random devices to secure significant decisions as a part of His perfect plan:

And they cast lots for them, and the lot fell on Matthias, and he was numbered with the eleven apostles. (ACTS 1:26)

This God is sovereign over the hearts of men:

The king's heart is a stream of water in the hand of the LORD; he turns it wherever he will. (PROVERBS 21:1)

This God has crafted everything and everyone, including the wicked, for a specific purpose:

The LORD has made everything for its purpose, even the wicked for the day of trouble. (PROVERBS 16:4)

This God is sovereign over every step that every man takes in life:

A man's steps are from the LORD; how then can man understand his way? (PROVERBS 20:24)

This God is sovereign over every human will, even regarding that man's salvation:

So then it depends not on human will or exertion, but on God, who has mercy. (ROMANS 9:16)

This God is sovereign over every ruler or person of power, be they evil or good. He makes them and uses them for His purposes. They are His tools; His property. Yes, even Michael Moore. He lifts them up and brings them down all according to His will in pursuit of His perfect, self-glorifying plan:

For the Scripture says to Pharaoh, "For this very purpose I have raised you up, that I might show my power in you, and that my name might be proclaimed in all the earth." (ROMANS 9:17)

This God is sovereign over who will receive His mercy and who will not:

So then he has mercy on whomever he wills, and he hardens whomever he wills. (ROMANS 9:18)

This God commands dead men to rise from their graves, and they always obey:

[Jesus] cried with a loud voice, Lazarus, come forth. And he that was dead came forth... (JOHN 11:43–44)

This God slays those who steal His glory:

"Immediately an angel of the Lord struck him down, because he did not give God the glory, and he was eaten by worms and breathed his last." (ACTS 12:23)

This God sends delusions to men, so that they will not believe what is true and be condemned:

> *Therefore God sends them a strong delusion, so that they may believe what is false, in order that all may be condemned who did not believe the truth but had pleasure in unrighteousness.* (2 THESSALONIANS 2:11–12)

This God is the sovereign determiner over *all* things, including the eternal state of every individual:

> *But it is not as though the word of God has failed. For not all who are descended from Israel belong to Israel, and not all are children of Abraham because they are his offspring, but "Through Isaac shall your offspring be named." This means that it is not the children of the flesh who are the children of God, but the children of the promise are counted as offspring. For this is what the promise said: "About this time next year I will return, and Sarah shall have a son." And not only so, but also when Rebekah had conceived children by one man, our forefather Isaac, though they were not yet born and had done nothing either good or bad—in order that God's purpose of election might continue, not because of works but because of him who calls—she was told, "The older will serve the younger." As it is written, "Jacob I loved, but Esau I hated."* (ROMANS 9:6–13)

And right on cue, this God demonstrates His sovereignty even over our own silly questions, as He anticipates our favorite ("But that's not fair!") right here:

What shall we say then? Is there injustice on God's part? By no means! For he says to Moses, "I will have mercy on whom I have mercy, and I will have compassion on whom I have compassion." (ROMANS 9:14–15)

We really hate that part. Until He chooses to regenerate us, that is. It's bad enough that He's sovereign, but He comes across as such a smart-alecky sovereign when He answers our questions before we even ask them. How rude!

But then again, as I paraphrased earlier: Boo and Hoo.

Sovereigns do what they want to do. They *always* get their way. That's what sovereign means. Before one is regenerated, they hate even the thought of this. Afterward...they adore it. Now, back to this (hopefully less) uncomfortable sovereignty thing.

Another annoyingly anticipated question answered in advance by God the Holy Spirit in the book of Romans comes when Paul records the following:

You will say to me then, "Why does he still find fault? For who can resist his will?" But who are you, O man, to answer back to God? Will what is molded say to its molder, "Why have you made me like this?" Has the potter no right over the clay, to make out of the same lump one vessel for honorable use and another for dishonorable use? What if God, desiring to show his wrath and to make known his power, has endured with much patience vessels of wrath prepared for destruction, in order to make known the riches of his glory for vessels of mercy, which he has prepared beforehand for glory—even us whom he has called, not from the Jews only but also from the Gentiles? As indeed he says in Hosea, "Those who were not my people I will call 'my people,' and her who was not beloved I will call 'beloved.'" "And in the very place where it was said to them, 'You are not my people,' there they will be called 'sons of the living God.'" (ROMANS 9:19–26)

Barrack Hussein Obama has his "obscure passages from Romans," and, sadly, the professing church in America has hers. Both sets find themselves dismissed by willful men. Sometimes with a disdainful chuckle or diligently crafted philosophical work-arounds, but dismissed nonetheless.

It really isn't very hard to understand why this particular God is so intensely unpopular, is it? After all, who naturally tolerates, much less aspires to, the notion of being the wholly owned property and tool of another from even before their conception?

Nobody I know.

Yet that is what each and every one of us are: God's tools to be used for His purpose on His schedule in pursuit of His self-glorification. Put another way: It's all about Him. And the "it" in question is *everything*, including us.

Talk about *this* God even in the presence of many sincere professing Christians and you are almost sure to get a particular response: "I could never worship *that* kind of God!"

And, left to our own devices, none of us could. That's the point.

None of us could worship that God...unless He made us able to do so, against our natural, fallen will, by imposing upon us a *new* nature—a nature that *wanted* Him as opposed to hating Him; a nature that could not live without Him. Of our own accord, we are utterly repulsed by such a God as He. Only when He regenerates our fallen nature, bringing it from death to life, can we then recognize and instinctively desire the God of biblical Christianity.

This is the God who, when He is described accurately, will always inspire one of two things in a man: Peace or terror.

For the Common Believer, this God *is* peace.

The God Who Struts Through Prophecy

And when they heard it, they lifted their voices together to God and said, "Sovereign Lord, who made the heaven and the earth and the sea and everything in them, who through the mouth of our father David, your servant, said by the Holy Spirit, "'Why did the Gentiles rage, and the peoples plot in vain? The kings of the earth set themselves, and the rulers were gathered together, against the Lord and against his Anointed'—for truly in this city there were gathered together against your holy servant Jesus, whom you anointed, both Herod and Pontius Pilate, along with the Gentiles and the peoples of Israel, to do whatever your hand and your plan had predestined to take place."

ACTS 4:24–28

Ever since I was a little kid, I've been fascinated by Bible prophecy. I think that this is a fairly typical, and a very good, thing. For me, early thoughts on the subject were greatly colored by Hollywood lunacy (thank you, Damien) and Christian quackery (hello, Hal Lindsey).

From *Rosemary's Baby* to *Left Behind*, there has been a wide range of material produced in recent decades where the subject of eschatology is concerned. While the spectrum of opinions on the subjects of Christ's return or "the end times" is large, and the products produced by the minds subscribing to any of them range from the sublime to the ridiculous, there does seem to be one essential component in any right understanding of biblical prophecy.

Perhaps the one and only thing that *is* crystal clear where Bible prophecy is concerned is this: God must be sovereign over everything, including, obviously, the will of every man, woman and child, in order for these detailed prophecies to be 100% fulfilled 100% of the time. Otherwise, with a less impactful God, and more impactful men, the whole thing just wouldn't fly. How could it?

The Sovereign Sustainer of Israel

"I will make a covenant of peace with them. It shall be an everlasting covenant with them. And I will set them in their land and multiply them, and will set my sanctuary in their midst forevermore. My dwelling place shall be with them, and I will be their God, and they shall be my people. Then the nations will know that I am the LORD who sanctifies Israel, when my sanctuary is in their midst forevermore."

EZEKIEL 37:26–28

But it is not as though the word of God has failed. For not all who are descended from Israel belong to Israel, and not all are children of Abraham because they are his offspring, but "Through Isaac shall your offspring be named." This means that it is not the children of the flesh who are the children of God, but the children of the promise are counted as offspring.

ROMANS 9:6-8

For neither circumcision counts for anything, nor uncircumcision, but a new creation. And as for all who walk by this rule, peace and mercy be upon them, and upon the Israel of God.

GALATIANS 6:15-16

God the Son has *one* Bride.

He has always and will eternally have but *one* "apple of His eye". That eternal object of His undying affection is His chosen people – the true Church.

While the complete dispersal and subsequent reconstitution of a national culture is quite remarkable and rare in human history, the emergence of the modern secular nation state named Israel is not to be confused with the "Israel of God" described in Galatians 6:15-16 or the "children of the promise" and "offspring" described in Romans 9:6-8.

Whatever God's purposes with the modern secular nation of Israel may be, and however much they may be misunderstood and misapplied, this "resurrection" of a nation can be rightly noted as a type that points to the perfect preservation of His chosen people, the Bride of Christ, the Church.

As our Sustainer makes plain in His perfect Word, ". . . For not all who are descended from Israel belong to Israel, and not all are children of Abraham because they are his offspring, but 'Through Isaac shall your offspring be named.' This means that it is not the children of the flesh who are the children of God, but the children of the promise are counted as offspring." (Romans 9:6-8)

By God's sustaining grace and according to His perfect purposes, here we stand as God's chosen nation, Israel.[1]

We are the people of the promise and He will never fail us. He will sustain us here and forever more, all by His grace and to the glory of His name. How awesome is our God!

Omnipotence + Omniscience + Omnipresence = Unqualified Sovereignty

"Providence is a soft pillow."

OLD PURITAN SAYING

---

[1] This section has been rewritten to correct confusion in the original edition of *Fire Breathing Christians*. Modern Israel as a nation state demonstrates the sovereignty of God in many ways, but it is not the author's intention to paint the modern secular political state of Israel as "God's chosen people" above or alongside His *only* chosen people, the Church. We are all works in progress and learning as we grow, by His grace. Your patience with this clarifying correction is much appreciated.

Among the first things I remember learning about God were "the three omnis." God is, we are rightly told, omnipotent, omniscient, and omnipresent. These three attributes are typically summarized as:

1. His omnipotence—God controls all things directly; He is all-powerful. There is nothing that derives its power at any time from any source apart from God.
2. His omnipresence—All of creation exists in the direct presence of God. He is always active over all things in every location and in every moment of time.
3. His omniscience—God knows all things, and He knows them completely. As He has brought them into being by His power (a power they are constantly dependent upon), they must completely serve His purpose and are therefore completely known to Him.

God transcends time. This is important. It's an easy thing for us puny little time-based creatures to forget, but it is critical that we keep this concept front and center as we consider the three omnis.

God's omnipresence obviously includes all of time. As He transcends any limitations of time, He can be rightly described as, from our perspective, equally present in all times at the same time. And now my head hurts. I'm sorry if yours does too, but that's just a natural consequence of this sort of subject matter. Yet, on we must trudge.

God's omnipotence also transcends time. He therefore has complete power over every past, present, and future thing. His power—the only self-sufficient power—sustains them all.

God's omniscience then is a natural function of His omnipotence and omnipresence. All things are created by a God equally present in all times, equally defined and sustained by His power, all exclusively for His purpose and glory. This is how we get perfect Bible prophecy, among other things.

The convergence of the three omnis can produce nothing less than a completely sovereign God. For the Common Believer, this is news wonderful beyond description. For the non-believer, it is a most terrible truth.

The God Who Struts Through American History

"If the average American citizen were asked, who was the founder of America, the true author of our great Republic, he might be puzzled to answer. We can imagine his amazement at hearing the answer given to this question by the famous German historian, Ranke, one of the profoundest scholars of modern times. Says Ranke, 'John Calvin was the virtual founder of America.'"

Dr. E.W. Smith

"The Pilgrims who left their country in the reign of James 1, and landing on the barren soil of New England, founded populous and mighty colonies, were his sons, his direct and legitimate sons; and that American nation which we have seen growing so rapidly boasts as its father the humble Reformer on the shore of Lake Leman."

Jean-Henri d'Aubigné

God's sovereign hand guides all of human history. It often makes itself so plain that one must look away and close his eyes in order to miss it. Which is precisely what fallen men are prone to do. Our own nation's history is uniquely intertwined with the biblical belief in and reliance upon a completely sovereign God.

Nearly 500 years ago, the bride of Christ was rescued through the Protestant Reformation. Shortly thereafter, the Reformation-minded Pilgrims came to America.

Nearly 250 years ago, the American Revolution changed the course of world history. Again, this was a movement spearheaded and supported first and foremost by those who openly embraced the biblically submissive spirit of the Reformation and confessed open allegiance to a completely sovereign God.

In between these two grand events came the establishment of various Christian denominations. The Westminster Confession of Faith (1646) and London Baptist Confession (1689) defined the religion that would seed and then give birth to the United States of America.

What do you see here? Purpose or coincidence? Providence or chance?

What if there is a connection between a faith obsessed with the proclamation of a sovereign God and the greatest moments and triumphs of Western Civilization?

What if there are no accidents?

What if God doesn't play dice? At all.

And what if He doesn't *really* let anyone else play either?

What if God is *that* sovereign. You know, like the Bible says.

Would you feel cheated or comforted? Insulted or inspired?

Could knowing and embracing this *particular* God be the key to everything from your own personal peace to a new American Revolution or cultural reformation?

If not, then I suppose that the man-obeying god of our age is the best shot we have, which is another way of saying, "no shot at all."

If so, then He is the *only* key to *any* good thing, be it personal, national, or global.

The Undeniable, Irresistible I AM

Let all the earth fear the LORD; let all the inhabitants of the world stand in awe of him!

PSALM 33:8

When Jesus walked the planet, He exercised authority over every facet of His creation:

He changed the nature of animals when He rode on a donkey that had never been sat on, making it gentle and subservient (Luke 19:30-35).

He changed the nature of fish when He caused them to jump into the nets (John 21:6).

He changed the nature of water when He caused it to become wine (John 2).

He changed the nature of storms when He caused them to cease with just a word (Matthew 8:25-26).

He changed the nature of a budding fig tree when He caused it to wither and die by His word (Matthew 21:18-20).

He would have changed the nature of stones and caused them to cry out, had the people been silenced (Luke 19:40).

There is no difference when Christ works in the hearts of men. When the Sovereign Lord speaks, His creation obeys Him.

JIM MCCLARTY[38]

Only when we cry "woe" as Isaiah did will we be empowered to accept and adore the truth about the story in which we live: That it is not about us. This amazing tale—the story of creation and all therein—has been written for the purpose of God making each of His holy attributes known. It is a story of His self-expression for the purpose of His self-glorification. It is all about *Him.*

Only when we embrace our true place in His creation and celebrate *His* free will over it will we finally find ourselves able to fully join in Job's proclamation: "The Lord gives and the Lord takes away. Blessed be the name of the Lord!"

Only when we bask unrestrained in the magnificence of His sovereignty will we come to find the "abundant life" promised to His own. With egos completely surrendered, our once precious desire for some measure of power over God—even if only for an instant or only over one decision—will simply fade away. We will celebrate what we once abhorred. All by His decree. All to our benefit.

We are all His tools; His wholly owned property. For the Common Believer, this is bliss. For the non-believer, it is an affront to their self-perceived dignity—an offensive and horrible proposition of the highest (or lowest) order.

No man "makes Jesus Lord" of anything. Christ is, has always been, and ever shall be the Lord over *every* man.

He requests nothing from man, as He owns all.

He learns nothing from man, as He knows all.

He doesn't need any man's validation or permission to do anything at any time.

He benefits nothing from man; He is completely self-sustaining and self-fulfilling. His state cannot know improvement; it is perfect.

His call is completely effectual; it *always* succeeds in summoning His sheep while repelling goats.

He is not merely the *most* powerful, He is the *All* Powerful.

There are none who have the power to oppose His will because He has *all* of the power. The math of it isn't tricky at all: None have the power to effectively oppose Him precisely because He holds *all* power in His hand and will use every bit of it for His self-glorifying purposes.

This power concept is critical, and it really is a 100% God, 0% everybody else proposition. Grasping that fact alone will go a long way towards guiding us to a right understanding of the God we serve.

He is *All* Mighty. This God *is* God.

What could be more relevant than that? And what could possibly be more comforting to the Common Believer?

When we struggle, flounder and fall, *He is sovereign.*

When we doubt, *He is sovereign.*

When we weep, *He is sovereign.*

When we lose our every possession, *He is sovereign.*

When we are maligned, mocked and persecuted, *He is sovereign.*

When we wage His war and suffer every consequence, *He is sovereign.*

When we see our cherished loved ones snatched away in the prime of their lives, *He is sovereign.*

And because He is sovereign, *all* things—every item and event—in His creation are purposeful by *His* design. There are no accidents. There is no coincidence. There is no chance and nothing is random. Every single solitary thing, thought, and action is gloriously purposeful. Every tear that we shed; every pain that we endure; every tragedy that befalls us; every great and small mistake that we make—each of these things are *completely* purposeful. They have meaning and it is an *intended* meaning; a perfect, purposeful place in the eternal plan of God.

He said so. That's enough to make it so, since, as you might have picked up by now, *He is sovereign.*

And He is a consuming fire... *"FIRE...God of Abraham, the God of Isaac, the God of Jacob, and not of the philosophers and savants. Certitude. Feeling. Joy. Peace."*

He is certitude. He is Joy. And He is peace to the Common Believer. All by way of His undeniable, incontrovertible, unquestionable, and complete *sovereignty*.

He is why our security is certain.

He is why our victory is assured and was *never* in question.

He is the God who struts and flaunts and perfectly displays His majesty through every inclination and move of every part and particle of His creation. And we, of all people, wouldn't want it any other way.

According to His purpose, *He* chose *us*.

Why? That's *His* business.

Who are *you*? Besides the former God-hating reprobate who *He* chose to raise from spiritual death to life, I mean? Whatever your answer, I invite you, one former God-hating reprobate to another, to simply join me in surrendering any pretense of cooperative contribution to our salvation and praise Him for doing it *all*.

Why did He choose me? I have no idea. I'm just glad to be here.

This God inspires each of His own in different ways, but always for the same purpose: His. It is *this* God who gives hope; a hope sustained not by our will or ability, but a hope defined by His will and made alive by His almighty power. This God was once the focus of our hearts, our families, our churches, and yes, even our nation. And it can be so again.

If you have read these words and He has used them in their weakness to move or inspire you towards Him, then you probably feel, as I do, that He is even now raising up vessels throughout our land for the purpose of reformation, revival, and restoration. Change is indeed coming to America.

All by His purpose. All for His glory. All as He ordained from the foundation of the world.

This is the God we serve, and His is the Gospel we are called to proclaim—the Gospel for which the martyrs gave their lives and the Gospel that may soon require the same of us.

His is the Gospel for which we will be hated and by which we will know eternal life. His is the Gospel for which we cannot suffer compromise.

This is the time for which we were made.

Confessions of a Fire Starter

One Pathetic Vessel's Proclamation of Truth

For consider your calling, brothers: not many of you were wise according to worldly standards, not many were powerful, not many were of noble birth. But God chose what is foolish in the world to shame the wise; God chose what is weak in the world to shame the strong; God chose what is low and despised in the world, even things that are not, to bring to nothing things that are, so that no human being might boast in the presence of God. And because of him you are in Christ Jesus, who became to us wisdom from God, righteousness and sanctification and redemption, so that, as it is written, "Let the one who boasts, boast in the Lord."

1 CORINTHIANS 1:26–31

God *loves* working through inferior talent. In fact, it would seem that the more inferior the talent, the more inclined He is to make use of it. How convenient for me!

And, I suspect, convenient for you as well. Okay, I more than "suspect" this, but even I can err on the side of politeness every once in a while.

The twin truths that each of us are, of our own accord, incapable of even the slightest little bit of non-evil, and that, once chosen and regenerated by God, we—these most flawed, pathetic little vessels—are then commanded to boldly proclaim the full, undiluted Gospel of Christ—the most beautiful, powerful force in the universe—is a paradox worthy of wrestling during our short time here. So it is that with *Fire Breathing Christians* safely completed and behind us, I feel awkward and squeamish, yet am compelled to briefly address the subject of its author.

If anything is more repulsive than personal, prideful arrogance, it is false modesty or humility. Throughout the writing of this book, I have operated under the assumption that, in giving voice to the often harsh and challenging propositions expressed in its pages, I will surely be accused of both. Much as I wish it were not so, to some extent, these accusations will be founded in truth. I wish that I could argue; I really do. But I can't.

I believe that my pride, personal prejudices, and intellectual weakness are sure to have introduced many an imperfection into this work. It is my hope that God will, in spite of these many flaws, use this book to bring readers closer to Him through the pursuit and embrace of His truth, and, in doing so, bring glory to Himself. Only God can accomplish this, of course, and I find great comfort in the fact that He so often chooses to accomplish that very thing through the weakest of tools. Working through pathetic vessels is His M.O., so to speak.

Reminded of that, I suddenly feel quite qualified, as "pathetic" is one attribute that I seem to have nailed down quite well throughout my life.

For all of the open enemies of biblical Christianity identified here—the Bells, McLarens, Obamas, Osteens, Millers, and Clintons of the world—there is one heart whose darkness I know far better than any of theirs, and it is *mine*. For all of the counter-Christian plagues that I've described as crippling and undermining the church, I know that I have personally contributed to most, if not all of them. For all of the bold and challenging calls made in these pages to all biblical Christians so that they might submit to God's clearly expressed will, take action, and win the victory that He has ordained, I am often inclined to fearfully crawl into a fetal position in the corner of the room and do *nothing* myself. I know all too well that, of myself, I am incapable of doing any good and God-glorifying thing. Worse yet, and every bit as true, is that not only can I not of my own accord do any good thing, but I can only do evil.

That is my reality, or, perhaps better expressed: That is the reality of me.

Be Careful What You Pray For

My son, if you receive my words and treasure up my commandments with you, making your ear attentive to wisdom and inclining your heart to understanding; yes, if you call out for insight and raise your voice for understanding, if you seek it like silver and search for it as for hidden treasures, then you will understand the fear of the LORD and find the knowledge of God. For the LORD gives wisdom; from his mouth come knowledge and understanding.

PROVERBS 2:1–6

One year ago, I was struck by a bolt of inspiration the likes of which I've not known before or since, and, just as soon as it hit me, I knew it was His. I think it came in part as a delayed reaction to something I'd heard from a preacher only hours earlier.

I had just attended a Wednesday evening service at a Texas church in January of 2009, when, on the heels of one of the pastor's comments, I thought, *"That's just about the most idiotic thing I've ever heard from a pulpit."*

This mental outburst was accompanied by a roll of the eyes and probably even an audible sigh. I'm proud of none of these reactions. I was just so tired.

The park and pray, do nothing, sacrifice nothing, obey nothing, and wait for God to fix everything brand of Christianity was making me a little more sick every time I heard it pitched and, with this latest installment, brief though it was, I felt a deeper chill than I had endured on any of the other million or so occasions I'd heard a similar spin offered up. The twinge left as quickly as it had come, but it left a scar.

Three minutes earlier, the sermon had been solid and inspiring in nearly every healthy sense. It really was good. Three minutes later, it was back on that track. The pastor delivering the message was pleasant, articulate, and passionate. I met with him briefly later in the evening and found him to be warm, sincere, and personally engaging. By the time I left the church, I had managed to suppress my critical inclination and stow the troublesome thoughts into a back corner of my mind. There they were locked safely away, or so I believed at the time.

Hours later I was making the long drive from the Houston area to my home in southwest Missouri. I had no more than reached the south Dallas suburbs when the thoughts I'd quarantined made a jailbreak and stormed center stage. The frustrated, sometimes even hostile ideas that had been percolating inside my head for so long in sequestered silence made their jump back into prime time with new found converts and urgency. These newly enlisted allies were other suspicions, concerns, fears, and hopes that I'd pondered on and off again over many years' time: Memories of a childhood filled with peace and joy despite the fact of divorce and near ever-presence of dysfunction. Recollections of my earliest adventures in the Bering Sea. Warmth at the thought of my marriage and awe at the four-year struggle with cancer that ultimately saw my young wife pass from this life and into the next. The ever-increasing hopes, dreams, and goals that I cherish in excited anticipation of the days to come. These chapters and thoughts on my little slice of history and the long life to come seemed to take on a new coherence as I rode the wave of energy that began somewhere in the heart of the Lone Star State on I-45.

The surge of thought that overtook me on the Texas Interstate carried on through Oklahoma and into Missouri. Over the ensuing 48 hours, I recorded most of the thoughts that comprise this book.

As the words poured out, I realized that all of the anger that I was feeling—well, most of it, anyway—was *good*. It was *right*. I may have been neither good nor right, but my reaction had been because it was not of me.

The disgust was proper. The revulsion was entirely appropriate; beautiful even.

Every time that I hear Rick Warren give a detailed description of his man-centered, purpose-driven model for religion, I…want…to…*vomit!*

What I understood on that snowy January day is that I *should* want to vomit. I *should* be angry. And I *should* act on that anger and disgust. I *must* act, just as my Christ has commanded.

I don't want a purpose-driven life. I want a Christ-centered life.

I don't want a purpose-driven church. I want a Gospel-driven church.

I neither want nor need from my church another seminar, workout regimen, twelve-step program, basketball league, movie night, or puppet show.

I want and need from my church the undiluted, uncompromising, unwavering, and incomparable whole Gospel of Jesus Christ.

I *want* to be offended when the Holy Spirit is offended, even when I am the one who caused the offense.

I *want* to be corrected when I am in error, even if it crushes me for a season.

I *want* to be drawn to depth in Him, even if it costs me everything, and I *need* to have that depth in Him because it is only there that I will be empowered to handle the loss of every lesser thing weighing me down.

I *want* to do and become everything that He has called me to do and become, all for *His* glory.

He matters. He not only matters; He is *everything!*

That is why I am sick and tired of what the Rick Warrens, Joel Osteens, and Rob Bells are doing to the Gospel of my Jesus, and I think that's a good kind of sick and tired to be.

If I had a girlfriend or a wife and I knew of a man treating them the way that the Osteens and the Warrens are treating my Lord and His Gospel, whatever limited ability I had at my disposal would be spent in action. I may be beaten black and blue or worse in the process, but certain things would be made clear. Honor would be defended. A stand would be taken. There would be a price to be paid in this by both sides.

Now, here's where I might cross over from merely flaky to acutely annoying in the eyes of many, but I respectfully ask that you consider the following: If you professed to be a dear friend of mine, and it came to my attention that you had witnessed my girlfriend or my wife being abused in such a manner and had done nothing to assist or defend her, what might you expect from me? A warm hello? A great big hug?

This is a crude example, I know, but I trust that the point is still made clear. I also pray, hope, and trust that you will understand what I mean by these words, and what I do not.

I believe that we should not only exalt and proclaim Christ, but we must cherish Him. We must value His Gospel as the matchless treasure that it is.

Sunrise, Snow, and Fire

For the LORD your God is a consuming fire, a jealous God.

DEUTERONOMY 4:24

In that moment of intense revelation under the Texas sunrise, my Lord had revealed His decision to do something good with the most flawed person that I know. Now that you've read through the result, I pray that you will be graciously led past the flaws of the author and towards the perfect light of the God whom I am blaming for everything (the good parts, anyway; the bad ones are all mine).

The *bad* fires of controversy fanned by this work are all mine. I hate even the thought that any such things may have made it through the prayerful, thoughtful process of crafting this book, but they may indeed be there. Had I recognized any of them beforehand, I assure you that they would have been snuffed out immediately. That said, any God-glorifying controversy inspired by this work is something that I cherish and for which I will be eternally thankful.

It's not hard to see great irony in that the very same Holy Spirit whose first personal lesson to me was the unflinching and relentless revelation of my own fallen, naturally vile, God-hating nature would eventually lead me to realize, contemplate, and ultimately record whatever good things are found here in these pages.

From this world's perspective, I'm an unknown, un-credentialed nobody from nowhere. I'm just a guy in a pew who reads his Bible and wonders. In the midst of that wondering, I've been led to write a book. And I am most appreciative that you have been led to read it.

I want to thank you for your kind patience with me and for any time that you may spend prayerfully considering this work.

In closing, I hope for three things:

- **That all contentions made in this book will, whenever possible, be measured in the perfect light of the whole counsel of God's Word.** This book is of positive value only insofar as it is in direct harmony with the revealed truth contained in God's perfect Word. Please never forget or minimize this. Always pray for and apply this standard.

- **That every person and institution described herein will benefit from the prayers of every Common Believer reading this book.** I can think of nothing more personally appealing than God sovereignly choosing to regenerate Barack Obama or Donald Miller or any other individual mentioned in these pages. Please pray for this.

- **That every reader will know that I am not *Fire Breathing Christians*.** I am the guy, the *very* pathetic vessel, used to write *Fire Breathing Christians*. This is a vital distinction.

I am more thankful for your consideration than you can possibly know, though I do intend to do my best to convey this gratitude. For those fellow Common Believers who I am privileged to connect with here in this life, I look forward to sharing stories and encouraging one another as we march together in the war we've been called to wage. For those whom I will not see or know here on this side of paradise, I intend to find you there, in that perfect land to come, so that we might share stories and bask together in the glow of the victory that our Lord has secured.

Even the thought of spending an eternity developing the deepest possible personal relationship with Christ and each and every individual Christian is awe-inspiring beyond description. And I mean that literally. We are incapable of fathoming even this one mammoth beauty of what's to come.

Just think of it: Each and every one of us will come to know each and every other with a depth of relationship and understanding not currently possible for even the closest two people on this earth. This is one of the majestic results of placing a perfect, sinless, restored creation in a setting unbound by the negative constraints of time...but it is only one such result...and we will experience them all.

That is the world for which we should live. That is the world in which we should store up our treasures. And that is the world for which we should now fight.

Like you, I cannot wait to be in that promised, perfect place. Also like you, I am not yet there. I am here. At war.

The Next Best Thing to Rapture

"There's a war going on now...I'm in my eighty-third year now and I have a bigger fire burning in my heart than ever in my life, and I'm determined, by the grace of God, to wage war...I don't have any doctorates...I have no degrees—you can have thirty-two and still be frozen. There is only one thing I covet: I want to be one of the ten most wanted men in hell."

LEONARD RAVENHILL

Sometimes I like to imagine what I might be like when I am very old. It's a weird quality, I know, but by now this sort of revelation should come as no surprise.

I've always had this image in my head of an ideal future built around a huge family. I imagine myself reading books to mountains of grandchildren. Smiles, laughter, warmth, and happiness, all with Christ as both source and goal. It's that sort of family that comes closest to emulating the family life to come, I think, and it's that sort of family most likely to produce children who will follow us there to that perfect place, where we can share, explore, smile, laugh and grow together with the Christ who is source and goal...forever.

I very much look forward to that place, as I am sure that you do. Not so long from now, we will be there together with Him. In the meantime, there is much work to do.

There are stands to be taken and enemy strongholds to be destroyed. There are truths to be defended and enemies to be annoyed. There are many prices to be paid and sacrifices to be made.

Yet, in all of these things, there is matchless life, joy, certitude and peace to be found.

I pray that you will experience and cherish each of these treasures as He guides you to the fulfillment of your commission.

Soli Deo gloria...*and let's roll!*

Scott Alan Buss, January 2010

Acknowledgments

I would first like to express unending gratitude to my loving, living Lord Jesus, the risen Messiah and sovereign ruler over all that is. I thank Him for the adversity, strength, trials, perseverance, and sense of humor (both His and mine) necessary to the completion of *Fire Breathing Christians*.

I thank Him also for my Grandmother, Ruth (aka Gram), who endured much of the prolific, self-centered stupidity that was ultimately used by our Lord to produce prolific, God-centered writing. Her patience, tenacity, intelligence, humor, and boundless (some would say irrational) confidence have made impressions that I will never fully appreciate on this side of eternity. Oh, and the cooking...the gloriously high-fat, high-octane, often fried, and butter-fueled cooking. That deserves more than just a mention here as well, since it was clearly of the Lord and has brought so much joy to so many people.

I also wish to thank my Savior for providing John and Anita Pennell, who have been like two angels on earth to me. None know more of the challenges faced during the completion of this work, and I am constantly amazed by the grace, kindness, and support that you both offered in what were some very dark times before the sunrise. I also apologize in advance for any subsequent hassle involved in being affiliated with me or my work. At the end of the day, both the hassle and the credit are unavoidable. *Fire Breathing Christians* simply would not have happened without you and I will never be able to thank you enough (though I fully intend to keep right on trying).

I am also eternally thankful to my loving Lord for Jerry and Jill Perryman. Jerry, my good man, you are one fire breathing inspiration! (Hey, I think there's an idea for a book in there.) Your Sunday School teaching is a rare and substantive treasure to His hungry sheep, your commitment to and appreciation of our sovereign King is amazing to behold, and your rapidly growing family is a wonder beyond description. Keep your Bible open and your powder dry, my man…not that you need me to remind you.

I must thank our sovereign God for four particular previously unknown-to-me teachers whom I discovered while I was writing. They didn't know I was listening, yet made a profound impact on my frazzled little mind from afar. Paul Washer, Voddie Baucham, James White, and Jim McClarty have taught and inspired as few can or will in this day of American candy Christianity, and I am deeply indebted to the teachings that they've made available online. (I am also compelled at this point to thank Al Gore for inventing the Internet. Nice job, Al!)

Speaking of pastors, friends, inspirational Christians, and all of the above, I am way beyond happy to thank the living Lord for my best and Swiss Army friend, Rustin Cunningham, and his godsend of a wife, the lovely Carol. You are both dearer to me than you will ever know. Even when I disappear for a year (or two) to write books. Among the impossibly long list of timely contributions that Rus has made to my life since our junior high school days is his unwavering belief that I have the potential to annoy people on a global scale. Thanks, man! I could never have become this much trouble without you. Thanks also goes to God for the gracious and supercool Mr. and Mrs. Roger Cunningham, without whom there would literally be no Rus and figuratively be no Scott.

I must also thank my loving God for the most wonderful cousin a man could ever have. Princess Michelle, you are a wonder (just ask anyone in the family, if you dare). You never cease to amaze. Ever since demanding that the three-year-old me stop chewing with his mouth open, you've played a pivotal role in pointing me towards a better, brighter, and infinitely more civilized future. That husband of yours, Ron, is pretty cool too, but I'm not going into detail here since we both know that'd do more harm than good where your ability to endure daily coexistence is concerned. The less Ron inflating, the better, so I will simply say that the Ron and Michelle Shong household has been about as inspirational to me as a Christian home can be. Your commitment to honoring our Lord's will in *all* things is, for me, extra-biblical Exhibit A where Christ-centered home building is concerned.

With regard to the beautiful fruits of Exhibit A, I am ever-increasingly thankful to our Lord for Major and Faith Shong, the son and daughter of Ron and Michelle, who are both blessed and blessings beyond compare.

Speaking of siblings, I thank my perfect God for Dale, the coolest and most talented brother a guy could have. Oh, the stories he can tell...and they're all true! (Except for some of the ones about me, of course.)

Family, for the Common Believer, means all fellow Common Believers under Christ. Nothing more; nothing less. With this truth in mind I am particularly thankful to God for the Hill clan in Texas. You, along with the Shong family (see: Exhibit A above), are an inspiration for which I am eternally thankful. Your trials, adversities, encouragement and tolerance of yours truly are treasures that I will forever cherish. I look forward to sharing eternity with you in the presence of our perfect Savior.

Another supernatural addition to my family in recent months has been the Holmbergs. I thank God daily for bringing Eric, Ronda, Laura, Jake, Ryan, Jael, and Volleyball Queen/Les Mis Megafan Regan into my life. The intersection of our very strange paths is one miracle that still has me awestruck and smiling every time I take a moment to give it a second, third, and fourth thought.

To my fellow conspirators, pirates, and counterrevolutionaries on board The Apologetics Team warship, I say, *Soli Deo Gloria*...and *Let's Roll!* And *Woohoo!* I thank God for each of you and the unique beauty of your contributions to the advance of His Kingdom. Erik Hollander, you are an artistic genius and, more importantly, theologically sound (meaning, of course: you agree with me completely).

Mark and Mita Pogue, you are two true gems! It's through the formation of friendships like ours that I come to have an even greater appreciation and anticipation of the eternal Kingdom to come (were all will finally agree with Erik and me theologically, obviously).

To my fellows at the Ozarks Chapter of American Christian Writers, both those who loved and those who hated what I was coming up with (everybody did seem to file neatly into one camp or the other), I thank God for your incalculably valuable patience and support or antagonism and dissent. I hope, pray, and know that God will use each of your unique talents to His glory.

I will always be thankful to God for Miss Ami Naramor, whom He providentially used to provide the one special bit of critical input that just sort of clicked all things *Fire Breathing* right into place. You are a wonder, Ami!

To WND Books, who gave an unpublished nobody a contract and, in doing so, made plain to him that there was "something real here", I am eternally thankful. I love what you do and look forward to fighting alongside you on the cultural battlefield.

I thank God for the encouragement of John Watson, Jedidiah Moss, Pam and Gene Trotter, and the many First Baptist Church of Ozark members who were supportive in so many ways.

I thank my HEMI-ordaining Lord for General Motors, Chrysler, Ford, and their production of Challengers, Camaros, and Mustangs, respectively. In an age of emasculated and emasculating econoboxes and battery powered Begleymobiles, these magnificent and quintessentially American creations powerfully demonstrate that there still is a United States worth saving. Now if y'all could just do it without government funding... [Insert bonus points to Ford here.]

On a much more serious note, I cannot begin to convey the gratitude to God that I feel for all of those who are and have been out there in this fallen world, fighting the good fight, and boldly proclaiming the whole Gospel of Jesus Christ. The Augustines, Luthers, Calvins, and Spurgeons of the past, as well as the MacArthurs, Pipers, Sprouls, and Packers of the present...you are a constant source of God-centered amazement and inspiration.

To every Common Believer, I close with an expression of gratitude to our perfect Savior for you, your trials, your prayers, your hopes, and your roles in our sovereign God's perfect plan for the ultimate restoration of all things.

2nd Edition Acknowledgments

When the first edition of *Fire Breathing Christians* was crafted, I had zero experience in book production and found myself flying solo with the responsibility of tackling everything from writing and editing to graphical layout and cover design. In many ways, it was like an Our Gang production, and I thank God for making good use of such feeble skills. I also wish to thank readers of the first edition for their patience and incredibly encouraging support.

Since then, He has seen fit to send two particular Fire Breathers my way, without whom this polished, revised edition would not have been possible. My eternal thanks and love go to Trina and Jan.

I am also happily compelled to give a shout out (aka "Amen, hallelujah, and woohoo!") to the cast and crew of *The Ladies of Dotson Manor*. What an inspiration!

ABOUT THE AUTHOR

Photograph Copyright 2012 Cali Ashton Photography, Nashville, TN

Scott Alan Buss is a wretch saved by grace, a husband to Holly, and father to Rosie and Wolfgang. He and his family make their home in Middle Tennessee, where he is a thankful member of Christ the King Church.

Scott is a writer, speaker, and the founder of R3V Press, where he has published several books. He regularly blogs and podcasts at *Fire Breathing Christian.*

www.FireBreathingChristian.com

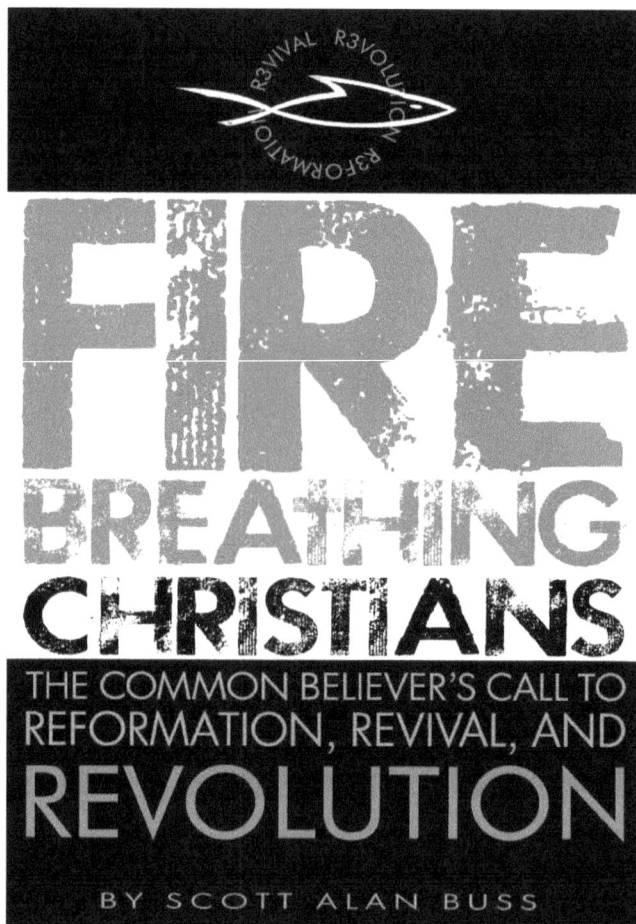

Same book – different look. This alternate aesthetic treatment for *Fire Breathing Christians* includes a vibrant multi-color cover and an interior layout featuring bold graphic designs.

www.FireBreathingChristian.com

ALSO FROM SCOTT ALAN BUSS AND R3VOLUTION PRESS:

Apathetic Christianity: The Zombie Religion of American Churchianity

Satan's Jackass – The Progressive Party's War on Christianity

Stupid Elephant Tricks – The Other Progressive Party's War on Christianity

the beginning of knowledge: Christ as truth in apologetics

On Education - Thoughts on Christ as the Essential Core of Children's Education

Gender Chaos, America Worship, and the Redefinition of Everything - Fire Breathing Christian, Volume 1

the
FIRE-BREATHING CHRISTIAN

PODCAST

HELL RAZING RADIO
www.FireBreathingChristian.com

STiCK PEOPLE FOR JESUS A Tale of Two Churches

See: Matthew 28:18-20; Matthew 6:9-13; 2 Cor 10:5   See: Matthew 7:13-23; Jude 1:4

For more *Stick People for Jesus* comics, visit
www.FireBreathingChristian.com.

Check out the latest Fire Breathing Tees designs
at www.FireBreathingChristian.com

HOME SCHOOL DESIGNS

ALL KNOW GOD DESIGNS

RAZE HELL DESIGNS

BE DANGEROUS DESIGNS

Endnotes

[1] Hank Hanegraaff, *Christianity in Crisis* (Eugene, OR: Harvest House Publishers, 1993), p.12

[2] C.S. Lewis, *Mere Christianity* (New York, NY: Harper Collins, 2001) p. 196-197

[5] Jeffrey Bell, *Why They Hate Her* – an article published in 2008 by *The Weekly Standard* and recorded online at:
http://www.weeklystandard.com/Content/Public/Articles/000/000/015/534rly sq.asp?pg=1

[6] *The End of Religious Liberty in Canada* posted at Crosswalk.com
http://www.crosswalk.com/1264412/page0/

[7] *The End of Religious Liberty in Canad*a posted at Crosswalk.com http://www.crosswalk.com/1264412/page0/

[8] Obama speech to Call to Renewal organization as recorded by Media Matters for America at mediamatters.org on June 24, 2008 (http://mediamatters.org/print/research/200806240007).

[9] Rob Bell's *Dust* video. http://nooma.com/nooma_dust_008_rob_bell.php

[10] Rob Bell, *Velvet Elvis: Repainting the Christian Faith* (Grand Rapids: Zondervan, 2001), p. 26-27

[11] Brian McLaren, *A Generous Orthodoxy* (Grand Rapids: Zondervan, 2004), p. 264

[12] Joel Osteen Easter service at Lakewood Church, sermon #CS_002 – 4-23-00, 23 April 2000, transcript formerly online at http://www.lakewood.cc/sermons/cs_002.htm; transcript archived online at http://web.archive.org/web/20040408215244/http://www.lakewood.cc/serm ons/cs_002.htm, retrieved 15 April 2009.

[13] Joyce Meyer, *The Most Important Decision You Will Ever Make: A Complete and Thorough Understanding of What It Means to Be Born Again* (Fenton, MO: Life in the Word, 1991), 37.

[14] Donald Grey Barnhouse, The Invisible War (Grand Rapids: Zondervan, 1965), p. 119

[16] A.W. Tozer, *Knowledge Of The Holy*, as posted at http://www.heavendwellers.com/hdt_preface_koh.htm

[17] John MacArthur, The Truth War (Nashville, Tennessee: Thomas Nelson, 2007), p. 171-172

[19] CNN.com/entertainment, *Hollywood embraces Roman Polanski*, as posted at http://www.cnn.com/2009/SHOWBIZ/09/29/hollywood.embraces.polanski/ind ex.html?iref=newssearch

[20] James White, in an audio broadcast titled *Barack Obama's Dream for a Secular, Non-Christian Nation*, posted at http://www.youtube.com/watch?v=6Azd9DByT5w&feature=player_embedded

[21] Albert Mohler, *"Simply Unprecedented" – President Obama and the Gay Rights Movement*, as posted at Crosswalk.com (http://www.crosswalk.com/news/commentary/11609651/)

[22] Friedrich Nietzsche, *The Parable of the Madman*, as published http://oldpoetry.com/opoem/30001-Friedrich-Nietzsche-Parable-Of-The-Madman

[23] C.S. Lewis, *The Voyage of the Dawn Treader* (New York, NY: HARPER Collins – First Harper Trophy edition, 2000), p. 183-184

[25] Charles Darwin, *The Descent of Man* (1871-1896), p. 133-134

[26] Adolf Hitler, *Mein Kampf*, Chapter 10

[27] David Berlinski, *The Devil's Delusion* (New York, NY: Basic Books, 2009), p. 20-21

[28] http://www.foxnews.com/world/2009/10/08/report-nearly-people-worldwide-muslim/

[29] Donald Miller, *Blue Like Jazz* (Nashville, Tennessee: Thomas Nelson, 2003), p. 175-176

[30] Mark R. Levin, *Liberty and Tyranny* (New York, NY: Threshold Editions, 2009), p. 63

[31] Karl Marx and Friedrich Engels, *The Communist Manifesto* (New York, NY: Signet Classic published by New American Library, 1998), p. 71-72

[32] Saul D. Alinsky, Rules for Radicals – A Pragmatic Primer for Realistic Radicals (New York, NY: Random House, 1989), p. 127-128

[33] Karl Marx and Friedrich Engels, *The Communist Manifesto* (New York, NY: Signet Classic published by New American Library, 1998), p. 91

[34] Washington's Inaugural Address of 1789, as recorded at:
http://www.archives.gov/exhibits/american_originals/inaugtxt.html

[35] Voddie Baucham, Question of the Month, as posted on January 11, 2010 at
the Voddie Baucham Ministries website in his blog at:
http://www.voddiebaucham.org/vbm/Blog/Entries/2010/1/11_January_Questi
on_of_the_Month.html

[36] Perry Noble, as posted at his blog
(http://www.perrynoble.com/2010/02/03/seven-thoughts-im-wrestling-with/)

[37] R.C. Sproul, *The Holiness of God* (Tyndale, 1998), p. 30-31

[38] Jim McClarty, *By Grace Alone*
(http://www.salvationbygrace.org/uc/sub/docs/bygracealone.pdf)

www.ingramcontent.com/pod-product-compliance
Lightning Source LLC
Chambersburg PA
CBHW072106270326
41931CB00010B/1469